Chantal Akerman

MANCHESTER
1824

Manchester University Press

FRENCH FILM DIRECTORS

DIANA HOLMES and ROBERT INGRAM *series editors*
DUDLEY ANDREW *series consultant*

FRENCH FILM DIRECTORS

Chantal Akerman

MARION SCHMID

Manchester University Press

The right of Marion Schmid to be identified as the author of this work has been asserted by her in accordance with the Copyright, Designs and Patents Act 1988.

Published by Manchester University Press
Altrincham Street, Manchester M1 7JA
www.manchesteruniversitypress.co.uk

British Library Cataloguing-in-Publication Data
A catalogue record for this book is available from the British Library

First published in paperback 2017

ISBN 978 0 7190 7716 6 *hardback*
ISBN 978 1 5261 1686 4 *paperback*

The publisher has no responsibility for the persistence or accuracy of URLs for any external or third-party internet websites referred to in this book, and does not guarantee that any content on such websites is, or will remain, accurate or appropriate.

Pour Hugo

Contents

List of plates

All plates except plate 7 courtesy of Paradise Films. Plate 7 courtesy of Gemini Films.

Series editors' foreword

To an anglophone audience, the combination of the words 'French' and 'cinema' evokes a particular kind of film: elegant and wordy, sexy but serious – an image as dependent upon national stereotypes as is that of the crudely commercial Hollywood blockbuster, which is not to say that either image is without foundation. Over the past two decades, this generalised sense of a significant relationship between French identity and film has been explored in scholarly books and articles, and has entered the curriculum at university level and, in Britain, at A-level. The study of film as art-form, and (to a lesser extent) as industry, has become a popular and widespread element of French Studies, and French cinema has acquired an important place within Film Studies. Meanwhile, the growth in multi-screen and 'art-house' cinemas, together with the development of the video industry, has led to the greater availability of foreign-language films to an English-speaking audience. Responding to these developments, this series is designed for students and teachers seeking information and accessible but rigorous critical study of French cinema, and for the enthusiastic filmgoer who wants to know more.

The adoption of a director-based approach raises questions about auteurism. A series that categorises films not according to period or to genre (for example), but to the person who directed them, runs the risk of espousing a romantic view of film as the product of solitary inspiration. On this model, the critic's role might seem to be that of discovering continuities, revealing a necessarily coherent set of themes and motifs which correspond to the particular genius of the individual. This is not our aim: the auteur perspective on film, itself most clearly articulated in France in the early 1950s, will be interrogated in certain volumes of the series, and, throughout, the director will be treated as one highly significant element in a complex process of film production and reception which includes socio-economic and political determinants, the work of a large and highly skilled team of artists and technicians, the mechanisms of production and distribution, and the complex and multiply determined responses of spectators.

The work of some of the directors in the series is already well known outside France, that of others is less so – the aim is both to provide informative and original English-language studies of established figures, and to extend the range of French directors known to anglophone students of cinema. We intend the series to contribute to the promotion of the formal and informal study of French films, and to the pleasure of those who watch them.

DIANA HOLMES
ROBERT INGRAM

Acknowledgements

This book began life during a semester's research leave for which I would like to thank the University of Edinburgh and my colleagues in the French Section. My warm thanks also go to my students at Edinburgh on whom many ideas in this book were first tested and who have inspired me with their unwavering enthusiasm for Chantal Akerman's work and their keen interest in her multifaceted film language. I am hugely grateful to my friend Kim Knowles for commenting on drafts of the book and sharing her knowledge of experimental film with me and to Martine Beugnet and Loreta Gandolfi for their stimulating suggestions on particular sections of the manuscript. Thank you also to Marie Campbell whose expert proof-reading and good humour were greatly appreciated in the work's final stages. It has been a delight to work with the team at Manchester University Press who have offered guidance and support throughout the project. I wish to express my particular gratitude to Diana Holmes and Robert Ingram, who have been wonderful editors. I am also indebted to Leslie Vandermeulen for her kind assistance with finding film stills and to Paradise Films for graciously providing the illustrations for the book.

My most heartfelt thanks, however, go to my husband Hugues Azérad, with whom I have had the immense joy of sharing and discussing Akerman's cinema and whose intelligence, warmth and passion for film have accompanied and inspired every step of this project. The book is dedicated to him, with love.

Introduction: the multiple faces of Chantal Akerman

One of Europe's most acclaimed and prolific contemporary directors – critic J. Hoberman calls her 'comparable in force and originality to Godard or Fassbinder ... arguably the most important European director of her generation' (Hoberman 1991: 148) –, Chantal Akerman is also one notoriously difficult to classify. The director came to prominence with *Jeanne Dielman, 23, quai du Commerce, 1080 Bruxelles* (1975), her minimalist portrait of a Belgian housewife and daytime prostitute which, overnight, brought the twenty-four-year-old international recognition and placed her at the centre of debates surrounding women's cinema and feminist film-making. At its commercial release in 1976, the French daily *Le Monde* hailed the movie, which runs to a demanding 3 hours and 20 minutes in length, 'le premier chef d'œuvre au féminin de l'histoire du cinéma'[1] (Marcorelles 1976); the influential New York newspaper *Village Voice* has since rated it among the one hundred best films of the twentieth century.

More than thirty years on, Akerman has authored over forty films, straddling a wide range of genres – burlesque and romantic comedy, epistolary film, musical, experimental documentary, video installation – and embracing such diverse thematic concerns as coming of age and adolescent crisis, the construction of gender and sexual identities, wandering and exile, Jewish culture and memory. Strongly indebted to 1970s experimental film-making, she has gradually ventured into more commercial cinema, but remains true to the detached, anti-illusionist style that has become her signature, even in more mainstream works. Labelled a feminist and a queer

1 'the first masterpiece in the feminine in the history of cinema.'

director, an experimental ethnographer and a conceptualist, a hyper-realist and a minimalist, a diasporic film-maker and a great European *auteur*, she, to a greater or lesser degree, at different stages of her career, has been (and continues to be) all of these, but cannot – and refuses to be – pinned down to any one denomination. Expounding a dazzling diversity, her work resists easy appropriation into theoretical debates, artistic movements or national schools or traditions. Intensely personal but always distanced, blurring the boundaries between fiction and autobiography, obsessed with borders and liminal spaces, her cinema is characteristically *entre deux* (in-between). Her self-portrait *Autoportrait en cinéaste* (2004), an invaluable source for understanding the ideas and aesthetic principles that have shaped her films, in its meandering style and multilayered narrative, testifies to her resistance to conventional forms of (self-)representation and to her profound distrust of simple binaries and rigid categories.

Akerman was born in Brussels on 6 June 1950, the first child of Jewish Polish immigrants who settled in Belgium in the late 1930s. Her family history is intimately bound up with the horrors of the Holocaust. Both her maternal grandparents were murdered in Auschwitz. Her mother survived deportation and internment, her father hid in a small apartment in Brussels. In both interviews and *Autoportrait*, Akerman has repeatedly commented on the decisive influence her parents' – especially her mother's – silence about their experience has exercised on her work. The incomplete passing-down of stories from one generation to the next, she explains, prompted her to invent false memories – alternative fictions, indeed an alternative autobiography – that were to act as a substitute for the blanks in her family history: 'Un enfant avec une histoire pleine de trous, ne peut que se réinventer une mémoire ... Alors l'autobiographie dans tout ça ne peut être que réinventée'[2] (Akerman 2004: 30). Film-making, for her, was an imaginative and creative engagement with the silence that weighed heavily on her childhood: 'J'ai voulu remplir ce silence bruyant de bruyant silence, dans un espace-temps. J'ai voulu faire du cinéma'[3] (ibid.: 56). In a process she calls 'ressassement' (turning-over), and which she explicitly associates with a return of

---

2 'A child with a history full of blanks has no option but to reinvent her memories ... So, autobiography, given all of this, can only be reinvented.'

3 'I wanted to fill this noisy silence with silent noise, in a space-time. I wanted to make films.'

the repressed that haunts second-generation Holocaust survivors,[4] many of her films relentlessly revisit the traumatic experience of her parents' generation whilst working through her own feelings of loss and uprootedness.

Akerman's relationship with her Jewish heritage is ambiguous. She received a religious education in her early childhood, but was moved to a non-confessional school after the death of her grandfather. In recent years, in line with a more open engagement with her Jewish roots, she has revealed her continuing attachment to Jewish ritual despite the fact that, as she states, she is not a religious person, and has stressed her indebtedness to Jewish prayer and litany in the scripting of her chant-like film dialogues. Her marginal status as a Jew in a predominantly Christian society and her belonging to a minority group of immigrants with distinct cultural customs and traditions fostered in her, from an early age, a sense of alterity and non-belonging, which has crystallised as a major theme in her work. The economically modest environment in which she grew up (her parents owned a leather goods shop in a Brussels shopping arcade, but, in the immediate post-war, struggled to make ends meet) and the middle-class culture which was imposed on her at school alerted her to class and cultural difference and to the realities of social division, another dominant concern of her oeuvre.

Considering cinema an 'impure' art form, an inhibition she attributes to the Jewish prohibition against visual representation in the Second Commandment – 'Thou shalt not make graven images' –, Akerman was initially more inclined towards writing rather than directing. Although she happily defies this injunction in her work, nonetheless, as she states in an interview with Jean-Luc Godard, it profoundly influenced her attitude to visual representation, making her prefer indirect, 'distilled' images over more direct representational strategies (cf. Bergstrom 2003: 94). Literature and other forms of writing remain an important reference point for her as is evinced in her frequent mention of works of fiction and philosophy – in *Autoportrait*, she cites Kafka, Proust, Faulkner and Baldwin alongside Lacan, Deleuze, Didi-Huberman, Benjamin and Levinas – as well as in her own activities as a writer. She is responsible for most of her film

4 'Je pense que nous représentons la génération où il y a un retour du refoulé' (I think we are the generation where the repressed comes back) (cit. in Bergstrom 2003: 98).

scripts and has also authored a play, *Hall de nuit* (1992), in addition to an autobiographically inspired prose work, *Une famille à Bruxelles* (1998). The written, especially in the form of letters, is present in many of her films and the figure of the writer, an autofictional[5] incarnation of the director, is central to her latest feature film, *Demain on déménage* (2004).

According to her own testimony, it was the discovery, at the age of fifteen, of Godard's *Pierrot le fou* (1965), one of the most emblematic works of the French New Wave, that incited her to become a director, having revealed to her the experimental and intensely personal quality of a certain type of independent cinema. Thanks to Godard, who remains a constant reference point in her work, Akerman realised that the cinema could vie with the most original of creative writing. In interviews, she deliberately avoids aligning herself with any cinematic tradition or movement, but has nonetheless given some clues to her preferences in terms of film style. As we will see, she is deeply indebted to the American avant-garde of the 1970s, but she also mentions fellow European directors Eric Rohmer, Jean Eustache and Rainer Werner Fassbinder alongside Godard as directors with whom she shares thematic and aesthetic concerns, and stresses her affinity with the cinema of the silent era, whose anti-naturalism and anti-mimetic approach converges with her own film aesthetic (Philippon 1982: 22). It seems more than mere coincidence that the films to which her style is often likened are those she herself remembers having seen in her youth: Robert Bresson's *Pickpocket* (1959), Alain Resnais's *L'Année dernière à Marienbad* (1961) and Michelangelo Antonioni's *Le Désert rouge* (1964) (Akerman 2004: 125).

In professional terms, Akerman is an autodidact. She has followed none of the official circuits of film school and assistantships with prestigious directors that helped to establish other film-makers of her generation like, for instance, Claire Denis. Having dropped out of high school aged seventeen, she enrolled at the INSAS, the Belgian academy of the performing arts and broadcasting, in 1967, but left after a mere three months, disappointed by the Academy's stifling theoretical approach and eager to make her own films. The following year, she briefly studied at the Université internationale du théâtre in Paris. Her first short, *Saute ma ville*, made in revolutionary 1968,

---

5 The term 'autofiction' designates a blending between autobiography and fiction. It was coined by the French critic and writer Serge Doubrovsky.

is self-taught, self-financed and features Akerman as a teenager who blows up herself, and her eponymous town, during a performance of domestic routine which escalates into self-destruction. Lacking the necessary funding to have it developed, this audacious first film was left gathering dust in a lab for two years until Akerman showed it to the director who was to give her contacts in Flemish television. It was broadcast in Eric de Kuyper's *Alternative Cinema* series, where it received a rave review from Belgium's best-known film-maker, André Delvaux, and was screened at the prestigious Oberhausen Short Film Festival.

After a second short made in Belgium, *L'Enfant aimé ou je joue à être une femme mariée* (1971), which shows a similar preoccupation with women's everyday life, and exhibits Akerman's predilection for long takes, she left first for Israel, where she briefly worked in a kibbutz, and, then, in November 1971, for New York, which became her adoptive home during two extended stays in the course of the 1970s. Much more than the French post-New Wave where she is sometimes classified, it was her discovery of the American avant-garde that was to have a determining influence on her work. Akerman, critics agree, is part of the adventure of American modernity, of the predominantly underground culture animated by a few hundred artists, many exiles like her, who, in a variety of media, challenged conventional forms of artistic expression and representation and opened up exciting new avenues for artistic production. Under the wing of Babette Mangolte, a friend closely bound up with the American avant-garde who was to become director of photography for most of her films of the 1970s, Akerman discovered North American experimental cinema, the minimalist music of Philip Glass as well as New American performance art and dance.

Canadian director Michael Snow's *La Région centrale* (1971), one of the masterpieces of experimental film-making which she first saw at the Anthology Film Archives, the newly opened New York showcase for avant-garde cinema, had a decisive impact on the development of her film aesthetic. Mangolte recalls that she and Akerman spent twelve hours watching the film a total of four times, considering it the most beautiful film they had ever seen (Mangolte 2004: 174). The hypnotic quality of Snow's non-narrative documentary, a cosmic portrait of a barren mountain top in Quebec filmed through a rotating camera anchored to a tripod, revealed to Akerman film's singular power to render the lyrical dimension of time and space without necessary recourse to words or story. The work of Jonas Mekas, Yvonne Rainer and Annette Michaelson, all directors engaged in finding a new film language outside the commercial channels of production, proved similarly inspirational. The avant-garde's subversion of the traditional divide between 'high' and 'low' art, its emphasis on time, duration and perception, most evident in the work of directors like Snow and Andy Warhol, as well as the militant political stance behind the most radical of New York art, especially feminist cinema, profoundly shaped her attitude to filmic represen-tation. The non-narrative stance of many experimental films of the period, moreover, radically altered her outlook on film aesthetics: considering narrative modes as 'obscene', she henceforth privileged more abstract forms of representation in a quest for a pure cinema liberated from representational constraints.

Developed within the minority culture of American underground art and marked by her own marginal position as an exile earning a living from irregular, low-paid work (among other occupations, she worked as a barmaid and a cashier in a porn cinema), Akerman's cinema has from the outset settled on minority issues and developed alternative themes and strategies to the dominant form of production, Hollywood. In analogy to what Deleuze and Guattari, in their seminal study of Kafka, have termed 'minor literature', she calls her practice that of a 'minor cinema', that is, an art form that consciously embraces its own marginality, rebels against the dominance of big production systems and makes exile – from social and linguistic norms, from fixed conceptions of gender and sexuality, from restrictive forms of belonging – one of its central themes. Although it embraces a wide social spectrum, ranging from destitute rural labourers to the gilded Parisian *grande bourgeoisie*, her work has mainly focused on under-privileged and underrepresented groups who are traditionally denied the right of a place in mainstream cinema: the homeless, illegal immigrants, ethnic minorities, displaced people, housewives, adoles-cents, the poor, the elderly. Rather than with the extraordinary lives favoured by commercial cinema, she has concerned herself with the quotidian, the triteness and banality of lower-middle-class life that forms the backdrop to many of her fictions, but which, through her rigorous *mise en scène*, is instilled with an unprecedented potential for drama and tension.

Her films of the 1970s most strongly epitomise this minority position, both thematically and formally, although, as we shall see, the themes of exile and alterity are present in virtually all of her output and resurface strongly in the 1990s, especially in her documentary work. *Hotel Monterey* (1972), her first New York documentary strongly influenced by structural film-making practices, is set in a welfare hotel where Akerman herself lodged for some time during her first stay in the US. A second, unfinished documentary, *Hanging out Yonkers* (1973), originates from her work in a day centre for young delinquents and drug addicts in Yonkers, in the New York suburbs. *Je tu il elle* (1974), produced and directed by Akerman who also plays the lead role, is a remarkable study of adolescent crisis and a milestone in the exploration of fluid sexual identities. *Jeanne Dielman* (1975), the film that was to establish her reputation, chronicles the obsessive routine of a widowed mother and prostitute. *News from Home* (1976) and *Les Rendez-vous d'Anna* (1978), finally, two autobiographically inspired pieces, in different film styles, dramatise wandering and uprooted-ness as forms of personal and artistic exile.

Akerman's output in the 1980s marks a significant departure from her earlier minimalist, single-protagonist narratives and begins an ongoing experiment with more commercially oriented modes of production. Whilst her earlier films are clearly indebted to experi-mental practices, especially in their use of extended duration and their static, fixed-camera work, in the 1980s, she takes inspiration in more popular genres: melodrama, the musical and slapstick comedy. Abandoning the linear narrative of films such as *Les Rendez-vous d'Anna*, the director now experiments with serial structures based on repetition and accumulation. Likewise, the dry documentary style of some of the earlier work gives way to a more exuberant choreog-raphy and to a lighter, more playful tone. The turning point in this development is *Toute une nuit* (1982), a burlesque comedy centred on amorous and sexual encounters during a hot summer night in Brussels. Her next film, *L'Homme à la valise* (1983), in which Akerman once again plays a central role, that of a female director whose privacy is invaded by a male guest, inflects themes of imprisonment and exile in a comic register.

Intermittently, Akerman had embarked on a project of adapting Isaac Bashevis Singer's epic Jewish tales *The Manor* (1967) and *The Estate* (1969), but, unsurprisingly, given her reputation as an experimental director, failed to raise funds from Hollywood for this monumental and costly film. Fascinated by Minnelli's and Cukor's musical comedies, she decided to experiment with the musical, a genre relatively underdeveloped in Europe, but made popular in France by Jacques Demy. Two films result from this venture: *Les Années 80* (1983) and *Golden Eighties* (1985), the former a 'work in progress' documenting the making of the latter. In the first, Akerman's multiplication of performers, scenes and textures (video and film), evinces a distinctly post-modern aesthetics of juxtaposition (Margulies 1996: 185). The second, deploying a more homogenous texture, but showing a similar affinity with post-modern strategies, parodies love and commerce in 1980s consumer culture. Lastly, *Histoires d'Amérique* (1989) seems, on the surface, to return to Akerman's ethnographic documentary style of the 1970s yet, deceptively, this film on New York's Ashkenazi diaspora uses professional actors and applies the comic mode that dominates this period to a more serious and intimately personal topic.

Whilst Akerman's films in the 1980s, at first sight, appear to depart quite radically from her earlier thematic and style, they nonetheless pursue a distinct set of concerns and an ongoing experiment with film form and visual style: deepening the director's exploration of human relationships, of questions of identity and belonging, and of the dramas of everyday life, they at the same time accentuate the burlesque quality that characterises works like *Saute ma ville* and develop her attention to rhythm and performance already manifest in the preceding decade. In fact, the anti-naturalistic choreography of *Toute une nuit* and *Golden Eighties* seems only one step removed from the stylised gestures and dialogues of *Jeanne Dielman* and *Les Rendez-vous d'Anna*. As Ivone Margulies points out, 'the comedy and the musical forms only exacerbate the manic compulsion of the protagonists' behaviour in the earlier films, and they remain vehicles for Akerman's consistent concern with rhythm' (Margulies 1996: 172).

The last twenty years of Akerman's career, that is, roughly speaking, the early 1990s to the late 2000s, have seen a further diversification of her work. On the one hand, she has ventured deeper into the mainstream with movies such as *Nuit et jour* (1991), a much-acclaimed post-feminist story of a Parisian love triangle, the poorly received Hollywood-style comedy *Un Divan à New York* (1996), her adaptation of Proust, *La Captive* (2000), and her burlesque comedy

Demain on déménage (2004). On the other hand, she has produced a remarkable series of experimental documentaries that revert to the minority issues of the 1970s, whilst, at the same time, developing a stronger political edge. The first of a tetralogy, *D'Est* (1993), draws the seismographic portrait of Eastern Europe after the fall of the Berlin Wall and the collapse of the Soviet Union. The second and third parts, *Sud* (1999) and *De l'autre côté* (2002), centre around racism in the American South and the plight of illegal Mexican immigrants in the US respectively. Finally, *Là-bas* (2006), a more autobiographical work set in Tel Aviv, examines Akerman's relations to the state of Israel and to her Jewish identity.

While the documentary series testifies to Akerman's continued social and political commitment, it also foregrounds an aspect crucial to her oeuvre in general, and one which is more directly graspable in these later works: her conception of the cinematic image as a privileged bridge between past and present. The documentary tetralogy takes the form of a quasi-archaeological process by means of which Akerman seeks to uncover traces of the past behind the deceptive banality of the everyday. Her own interpretation of the first three works of the series within a Holocaust framework and her meditation on her relationship with the state of Israel in the fourth signal a more direct engagement with Jewish memory and with her own family history, an engagement that culminates in the autofictional *Demain on déménage* (2004), an unsettling burlesque comedy that, for the first time, directly addresses the relations between and different existential positions of first- and second-generation Holocaust survivors. If the Holocaust and the Jewish Diaspora were omnipresent in Akerman's work from its very beginnings, but were often merely alluded to in the film narrative or were treated obliquely through the tropes of confinement and wandering, the tragedy of the camps has become more explicit in her later work, be it documentary or fictional. In a career stretching forty years, the autobiographically inspired, individualistic portraits on the turmoil of adolescence and the crystallisation of a social, sexual and artistic identity have gradually given way to a greater engagement with collective History, intimately bound up with personal family history.

This panorama of Akerman's oeuvre is far from exhaustive. In addition to the main works mentioned above and discussed in detail in this book, she has authored some twenty more films, many of them in shorter format, on a range of topics and for a variety of outputs: a documentary on Jewish grandmothers for French television (*Aujourd'hui, dis-moi*), art films on Austrian concert pianist Alfred Brendel (*Les Trois dernières sonates de Franz Schubert*), German choreographer Pina Bausch (*Un jour Pina a demandé...*) and French violoncellist Sonia Wieder-Atherton (*Avec Sonia Wieder-Atherton, Trois strophes sur le nom de Sacher, A l'Est avec Sonia Wieder-Atherton*), two remarkable studies of coming of age (*J'ai faim, j'ai froid* and *Portrait d'une jeune fille de la fin des années 60 à Bruxelles*), three autoportraits (*Lettre d'une cinéaste: Chantal Akerman, Chantal Akerman par Chantal Akerman, Portrait d'une paresseuse*), a homage to Salvadorian trade unionist Febe Elisabeth Velasquez played by Catherine Deneuve (*Pour Febe Elisabeth Velasquez*), a filmic appeal against the closure of the Brussels Cinémathèque (*Rue Mallet-Stevens*), and, in 2007, a meditation on East and West in a globalised world (*Tombée de nuit sur Shanghai*).

In virtually all of her output, Akerman has proven a radical innovator and adapter of forms and genres: she has given a phenomenological twist to the documentary, has offered variations on the confession or diary film, has revisited traditional genres such as the romantic comedy and the musical and has ventured from the medium of cinema in the narrow interpretation of the term into the domain of expanded cinema (Païni 2004: 171). As Dominique Païni points out, 'avec Godard, Ruiz et Marker [elle est] l'artiste qui a le plus contribué à émousser les frontières du cinéma vis-à-vis des autres arts'[6] (ibid.). This crossover between the cinema and other art forms is notably manifest in her installation work since the 1990s, some of which is done in parallel with, or subsequent to, her films and which adapts elements from her cinematic oeuvre to a multimedia format. *D'Est: au bord de la fiction*, which she created for the Walker Art Center, Minneapolis, and the Jeu de Paume, Paris, in 1995, and *From the other side*, created for the Documenta, Kassel, in 2000, are examples of this transposition from the projection room to the art gallery or museum environment. A work that centres around her mother's experience in Auschwitz, her installation *Marcher à côté de ses lacets dans un frigidaire vide* (To Walk Next to One's Shoe Laces in an Empty Fridge) created for the Tel Aviv Museum of Art and subsequently shown in the Jewish

6 'with Godard, Ruiz and Marker, [she is] the artist who has contributed most to blurring the frontiers between cinema and the other arts.'

Museum, Berlin, and at the Camden Arts Centre, London, for the first time substitutes imaginary memories with lived ones and, thus, signals an important move in Akerman's work from autofiction to (auto)biography.

At the crossroads between avant-garde and commercial cinema, Akerman has resorted to a wide range of production modes: whilst her early films were self-financed, the critical reputation she acquired with *Jeanne Dielman* has assured her subsidy from both the State and other public sources, in Belgium as well as in her adoptive France. The public funding of her work sharply distinguishes her from the American experimental tradition, which, in financial terms, is largely self-reliant. Like her fellow French film-makers, André Téchiné and Benoît Jacquot, Akerman has moved from a marginal cinema reputed to be hermetic and difficult to a more commercial outlet, even though her brief flirtation with Hollywood has borne no fruit (Philippon 1982: 22). Whilst continuing to work with her own production company, Paradise Films, co-founded in 1975 with her friend Marilyn Watelet, she also collaborates with a range of independent producers as well as with national and European television channels, including Canal+, ZDF and Arte.

Her uniquely personal vision and style and the multiple roles she adopts in some of her films, where she is, at once, director, screenwriter, producer and main actor, resolutely place Akerman amongst the ranks of *auteur* cinema, a concept that emerged with the French New Wave which she embraces wholeheartedly and which, from early on, has won her the support of leading French cinema magazine *Cahiers du cinéma*. She has consistently rejected attempts to assimilate her into a collective discourse – most importantly feminism – and has adopted an individualistic *auteur* stance instead (Margulies 1996: 12). This authorial positioning should, however, not blind us to the fact that her work is a collective enterprise, reliant on the input of a set of, mainly regular, collaborators. The work of cinematographers Babette Mangolte in the 1970s, Luc Benhamou in the 1980s and Raymond Fromont and Sabine Lancelin (amongst others) in the 1990s and 2000s, of editor Claire Atherton and of co-scriptwriter Eric de Kuyper has shaped the changing aesthetics of her films and facilitated the crossover between the experimental and the mainstream. In addition, the presence of three generations of French actresses, the iconic Delphine Seyrig, the enigmatic Aurore Clément and the versatile Sylvie Testud, has allowed her to create her own filmic genealogy. Finally, her truly international output, shaped by both American and European film traditions, and her own status as a transnational director working between France, where she has settled since her return from New York, her native Belgium and the United States, eschew simplistic appropriations of her as a quintessentially Belgian or French *auteur*. Akerman reiterates her liminal position and her sense of non-belonging in many of her interviews:

> Je ne suis pas plus parisienne que belge. Si je devais me sentir de quelque part, ce serait sans doute plus de New York que de n'importe où ailleurs. Je n'ai pas la notion de terre, j'ai au contraire la notion que je ne suis attachée à la terre que là où sont mes pieds. Et même là où ils sont, ça tremble un peu, souvent.[7] (Dubroux et al. 1977: 36)

Whilst in histories and studies of national cinemas she tends to be grouped with Belgian film-makers (unlike Godard, who, despite being Swiss, is quintessential to the French cinematic canon), given her self-proclaimed position of rootlessness, her residing outside her native Belgium, and, most importantly, her status as the daughter of diasporic Ashkenazi Jews, it may be tempting to group her, as Hamid Naficy suggests, under the more elusive, non-national category of exilic or diasporic film-making. Yet, whilst her early New York phase does align her with this category, with which she does indeed share many thematic and stylistic characteristics, her self-chosen exile in a francophone country with close cultural ties to her native Belgium sets her apart from the linguistic and cultural alienation experienced by the many Asian, African or Middle Eastern directors living in the West who are discussed on a par by Naficy (Naficy 2001). Her case throws into relief the deceptiveness of national or transnational labels – after all, the aesthetic category of the avant-garde, within which she is traditionally theoretically framed, arguably, may still be the most meaningful to describe her oeuvre.

Akerman's reception, even at a time when she is acknowledged as one of the leading directors of her generation, remains mixed: whilst the esteem in which she is held critically has continued to grow ever

---

7 'I am no more Parisian than Belgian. If I had to feel that I am from somewhere, it would probably be New York more than anywhere else. I don't feel I belong anywhere. On the contrary, I have the feeling that I am only attached to the land under my feet. And even there the ground is often a bit shaky.'

since the ground-breaking *Jeanne Dielman* – a fact reflected in her numerous exhibitions at the most prestigious international arts fairs, as well as a 2004 retrospective at the Centre Pompidou, Paris, and also her visiting professorships around the globe – her exposure to a broader public remains limited. To date, only *Demain on déménage* has had respectable box-office success. Each of her new films receives substantial coverage in the quality press and in cinema magazines, but her distribution is limited largely to art-house cinemas in a few capital cities. A good selection of her films is now available on DVD (a box set contains all of her major works from the 1970s, others have been released individually), but none of her latest work has had official releases in the United Kingdom. Her name rarely figures in recent histories of French and European cinema[8] and, even in critical reference works, remains associated mainly with a formalist approach. Ivone Margulies' excellent study of Akerman's aesthetic and brilliant contextualisation of her work within American avant-garde traditions and European anti-naturalism, whilst having paved the way for a fuller appreciation of the director's work (and made our own study possible through its manifold insights and minute critical analysis), with its title 'Nothing Happens' and its focus on cinematic form, has, arguably, enhanced the predominant view of Akerman as a 'difficult' director of interest mainly to an elite of professional film critics, academics and 'intellectual' film viewers.

This book seeks to redress this one-sided appreciation of her work. Though close attention will be paid to her evolving film style, it also wishes to pay tribute to the social, ideological and ethical ramifications of her prolific oeuvre. The largely chronological and thematic presentation is intended to show the extraordinary diversity of her output, but also, no less importantly, to capture the dynamics of *ressassement* that we have already mentioned as one of the central driving forces behind her work. Comparable to authors such as Beckett, Thomas Bernhard, Hélène Cixous or Marguerite Duras, who are similarly known for their 'brooding', circular enquiries, Akerman kaleidoscopically reconfigures, behind a multitude of guises, recurrent tropes and preoccupations that haunt her imaginary and find visual form in her

---

8 She is mentioned neither in Rémi Fournier Lanzoni's *French Cinema: From its Beginnings to the Present* (New York, Continuum, 2002), nor in the collective *European Cinema* edited by Elizabeth Ezra (Oxford, Oxford University Press, 2004).

cinematic universe: the loss of ritual and the fluidity of identities – be they social, sexual or gendered; the relationship between self and Other, in family and love relations as well as in the dealings between individuals and nations; the presence of the past and the threat of dehumanisation in the domestic as well as the political sphere. Her intransigent avant-garde style, manifest even in her more mainstream works, in its problematisation of questions of perception, representation and spectatorship, as we will attempt to show, is a direct correlate of as well as an instrument for the profound questions raised by her work.

Chapter 1 will identify the characteristics of her avant-garde work of the 1970s, the period most closely influenced by American structuralist film and performance art. Chapter 2 surveys her work in the following decade in the context of post-modernism, the new aesthetic of kitsch and the emergence of a new hedonism in Western critical discourses. Chapter 3 is dedicated to her documentary work of the 1990s and 2000s, which, in its construction of an archaeology of suffering and its quest for historical traces in the present, sheds light on the central ethical and aesthetic concerns behind her work. Chapter 4, finally, discusses her attempts to penetrate into the mainstream, her renewed engagement with the themes of love and desire, and her further exploration of the permeable boundaries between autobiography and fiction. Whilst greatest attention is given to works that are readily accessible, we will also discuss lesser-known films that are, hitherto, only available in film archives.

Behind the multiple guises of Chantal Akerman, this book seeks to present a cinema that crystallises questions that are at the heart of our post-war, post-Holocaust, post-feminist sensibility, yet succeeds in remaining remarkably timeless, a cinema that is socially committed without, however, pretending to be any form of universal representation. Perhaps most importantly, it will present an oeuvre that, whilst asking probing questions about marginality, exile and suffering, preserves a great sense of humour and is imbued with a profound humanity.

References

Akerman, Chantal (2004), *Chantal Akerman: Autoportrait en cinéaste*, Editions du Centre Pompidou/Editions Cahiers du cinéma.

Bergstrom, Janet (2003), 'Invented Memories', in Gwendolyn Audrey Foster (ed.), *Identity and Memory: The Films of Chantal Akerman*, Carbondale and Edwardsville, Southern Illinois University Press, pp. 94–116.

Dubroux, D., T. Giraud, L. Skorecki (1977), 'Entretien avec Chantal Akerman', *Cahiers du cinéma*, 278, pp. 34–42.

Hoberman, J. (1991), *Vulgar Modernism: Writing on Movies and Other Media*, Philadelphia, Temple University Press.

Mangolte, Babette (2004), 'La Chambre 1 et 2 – Hanging out Yonkers – Hotel Monterey – Jeanne Dielman, 23 Quai du Commerce, 1080 Bruxelles', in *Chantal Akerman: Autoportrait*, pp. 174–6.

Marcorelles, Louis (1976), 'Comment dire chef-d'œuvre au féminin?', *Le Monde*, 22 January, p. 15.

Margulies, Ivone (1996), *Nothing Happens: Chantal Akerman's Hyperrealist Everyday*, Durham, Duke University Press.

Naficy, Hamid (2001), *An Accented Cinema: Exilic and Diasporic Filmmaking*, Princeton, Princeton University Press.

Païni, Dominique (2004), 'Artiste sans modèle', in *Chantal Akerman: Autoportrait*, p. 171.

Philippon, Alain (1982), 'Fragments bruxellois. Entretien avec Chantal Akerman', *Cahiers du cinéma*, 341, pp. 19–23.

1

The 1970s: Anatomy of an avant-garde

The late 1960s and 1970s, during which Akerman established herself as a leading independent director, can be treated as a discrete period in her oeuvre, both in its thematic focus on various forms of minority culture and its crystallisation of an aesthetic indebted to experimental film practices. It is during this decade, considered by many critics as the finest and most representative in a diversified and distinguished career, that the director sets the parameters for her future work and develops the minimalist, hyper-realist style which is often cited as her trademark. This chapter will discuss her rich output in this period in the artistic and cultural contexts in which it emerged and against which it was subsequently assessed, most importantly experimental film, performance art and feminism. To understand Akerman's early work, it needs to be aligned, on the one hand, with the counter-culture of the 1960s and 70s, which vigorously attacked oppressive struc-tures of power and domination and explored new forms of identity, sexuality and desire, and, on the other hand, with the avant-garde practices in film, the theatre and the visual arts that gave artistic form to these interrogations.

Directly influenced by the American avant-garde which she discovered during her first stay in New York, Akerman not only wholeheartedly embraced the political and social preoccupations of her generation but actively propelled them to reach a wider audience. Each of her films in this period can be considered as an example of what Scott MacDonald, subsuming different avant-garde practices, has termed a 'critical cinema', that is, a mode of film-making that thematically and aesthetically positions itself against the dominant form of production, commercial cinema, and the Hollywood entertainment industry in particular. As MacDonald explains, one of the goals of critical film-makers is 'to place our awareness and acceptance of the commercial forms and their highly conventionalised modes of representation into crisis' (MacDonald 1988: 1). The radically new vision and technique of independent film-makers such as Akerman continuously undermines the practices of mainstream cinema as well as the ideologies and value systems that underlie them and for which they become a powerful vehicle. Whilst commercial cinema tends to 'naturalise' social and cultural constructions through its stereotyped presentation of gender, class or race, critical cinema, on the contrary, challenges preconceived ideas and 'denaturalises' what the mainstream presents as the social norm. Whether Akerman films the suicide of a disturbed adolescent, the anonymous lives of residents in a Manhattan welfare hotel or the numbing daily routine of a Belgian housewife-cum-prostitute, her films shun the glamorised fictions based on exceptional characters and situations favoured by Hollywood drama and debunk the often romanticised stereotypes surrounding popular film narratives such as growing up, womanhood and maternity, and heterosexual love and desire. Appropriating the avant-garde practices of, notably, American structural cinema and adapting them to more social concerns, she develops a work which is both politically challenging and aesthetically innovative, or more precisely, a work where formal and thematic innovation go hand-in-hand in offering a new representation of gendered identity, female subjectivity and minority existence.

Coming of age: *Saute ma ville*

The year is 1968. In France, student protests against the shortfalls of mass education have gathered momentum and have turned into a national movement of civil unrest. Universities are occupied, factories have ground to a halt, violent conflicts between revolutionary youth and the forces of order paralyse the capital. During a few weeks of utopian euphoria, the dream of a more egalitarian society where men and women, all social classes, First and Third World enjoy the same rights and freedoms seems to have become a genuine possibility. Though the revolutionary events soon peter out, historians agree that a profound cultural mutation has taken place which will have repercussions well beyond France and Europe and give new momentum to the liberation movements (feminism, gay and lesbian rights, the civil rights movement) that had emerged throughout the world in the course of the 1960s.

In Brussels, eighteen-year-old Chantal Akerman borrows a movie camera, raises a few hundred dollars by selling shares in a planned film on the diamond exchange in Antwerp and, together with a handful of friends, makes her first 13-minute short, an explosive, tragi-comic tale of adolescent suicide. Akerman is at once director, producer and main actress in this autofictional work whose thematic concerns and cinematic style herald the oeuvre to come. The film's setting, captured in the first establishing shots, is an urban no-man's-land, an indistinct zone on the fringes of an unidentified city dominated by the anonymous grey tower blocks of post-war reconstruction and suburban expansion. The forbidding air of the location, accentuated by the greyish tint of the black-and-white film, is intermittently light-ened by the appearance of an adolescent girl, whose graceful figure and romantic apparel, including a bunch of flowers, clash with the stern, dehumanising surroundings.

From the outset, the action is frenzied: the girl picks up the mail, runs through the communal hallway, impatiently hammers the lift button and, when the lift fails to come, makes a quick ascent of the stairs. Her breathless running in the spiral stairway, intercut with fixed-angle shots of the lift going up and down, creates a sense of vertigo. On the out-of-synch soundtrack, a female humming voice, which functions as some kind of interior (though non-verbal) monologue, accompanies the frenetic bodily movement with its shrieked, distraught sounds. Through its changes of volume, rhythm and tone, this inner voice serves to translate the character's mental state, but it also, as Jean-Michel Frodon suggests, evokes the ghostly presence of an Other – an absent lover, the camera, or even death itself – which ominously lingers over the action (Frodon 2004: 172).

The girl's arrival in a flat of which only the kitchen is visible shifts the action from the public to the domestic sphere, a realm intimately associated with the feminine and one of Akerman's preferred film-making territories. Levels of information content are deliberately blurred: cooking and eating are filmed in the same detached way as the girl's locking of the door and her sealing of the doorframe with tape – a routine-like preparation for suicide. The figure of the housewife, one of the most familiar (stereo)types of society, yet rarely shown in her banal everyday life in commercial cinema, becomes the vehicle for a disturbing tale of self-destruction. Akerman parodies domestic cleaning rituals in a burlesque scene of inversion where the tasks habitually associated with creating order result in exactly the contrary: an ever-expanding mess. The girl carelessly flings pots and pans to the floor, floods the kitchen with bucket-loads of water and frantically brushes away all sorts of domestic utensils. A raincoat and scarf, slipped on for the occasion, mark the action as performance – the adolescent mimics the housekeeper in a subversive act of impersonation. Her increasingly dissociated gestures peak in a tragicomic shoe-cleaning scene which ends in her spreading black polish first over her socks, then her lower leg and trousers. The latent aggression already manifest when she brutally throws out the cat is turned against the girl's own body as she vigorously strokes her bare leg with the rough brush. Standard comic devices such as the escalation of routine activities and the use of off-kilter gestures, perfected by actors such as Charlie Chaplin and the Anglo-American duo Laurel and Hardy, here are appropriated for an unsettling portrait of psychic implosion. Revealingly, it is the girl's confrontation with her mirror image – an oft-used cinematic metaphor for self-recognition – that is the catalyst for the suicidal act. The humming voice which had intermittently accompanied the action with its singing, groaning or mimetic sounds ('scratch-scratch' when she lights a matchstick), turns into an animal-like whine when she tapes up the kitchen window. Its shrieking laughter accompanies a wild dance performance, some sort of corporeal last rite during which the adolescent smears herself with mayonnaise, that is abruptly brought to an end by her slapping her own face in front of the mirror – a further hint at self-loathing. The suicide is filmed as a reflection in the mirror. The girl burns the letter she had ominously pinned on the kitchen shelf when entering the flat, turns on the gas and rests her upper body on the cooker, the bunch of flowers hanging from her left hand. Accompanied by the ominous sound of escaping gas, the image goes into freeze frame before cutting to a black leader over which, after a moment which seems unbearably long to the spectator, we hear the sound of an explosion. The voice, which was silent during the suicidal act, hums a few child-like sounds until it becomes gradually extinct.

Akerman's dark comedy of adolescent crisis explosively sets the tone for her subsequent work. In terms of film style, it lays down many of the parameters that will inform the later oeuvre: the co-existence between comic and tragic modes characteristic of the burlesque, the disjointedness between sound and image, and the blending of 'two modes of organization – one geared toward plot (fragmentary as it might seem), the other a phenomenological approach to plot's "uneventful" background' (Margulies 1996: 3). Thematically, the domestic setting and focus on the housewife's daily chores and routine announce *Jeanne Dielman* with which *Saute ma ville* forms a diptych. As in the later works, any conventional character psychology is avoided. The presence of the letter and its romantic linking to the suicidal act suggest an unhappy love affair, but it is less the torments of adolescent love that matter here than the visualisation of a deep inner disturbance rendered above all through the language of the body.

The influence of Godard's *Pierrot le fou*, the film that revealed the possibilities of independent cinema to Akerman, is still tangible in this first work (cf. Margulies 1996: 2–3). Beyond the obvious similarities of the suicide by self-explosion triggered by a troubled love affair, *Saute ma ville* shares with Godard's stylish New Wave piece a 'sense of unassimilated energy' (ibid.: 3), a playful immediacy and a fair degree of adolescent romanticism. Yet, crucially, where Godard's male protagonist sets out on a spree of love, killing and life on the run, the adolescent played by Akerman is bound to her sordid, poverty-stricken environment and confined to the domestic space. Revolt for her takes the form of self-aggression as well as an ill-considered revenge on the similarly disempowered: the town of the title (*Saute ma ville* translates as 'Blow up my town'). The female condition, then, from this audacious first piece, is denounced as one of imprisonment in the domestic sphere, a social form of incarceration tacitly accepted and endured by generations of women, but about to be blown up (albeit in a self-destructive act) by the angry youth of the 1960s.

Flirting with abstraction: *Hotel Monterey*

Akerman would further explore the themes of coming of age, adolescent depression and identity struggle in a variety of projects, most importantly *Je tu il elle*, but, before returning to these topics, she experimented with the more abstract, non-narrative forms of cinematic expression of the American avant-garde, discovered during her first extended stay in New York between 1971 and 1972. Together with San Francisco, New York was the then centre of American independent film, a city rich in artistic experiments and particularly renowned for its underground film culture. The experimental works Akerman saw at Anthology Film Archives alerted her to the possi-bility of alternative modes of film production outside the commercial studio system: experimental film typically is a more 'artisanal' type of film-making that involves individuals or small groups of collaborators producing non-profit-making films that are distributed through film co-operatives and exhibited by film societies, art galleries and univer-sities rather than in standard cinemas. In the course of the 1960s, new forms of cinematic expression were developing in the United States under the labels of New American Cinema and underground cinema.[1] Whilst Akerman had exposure to representative works of these two closely related trends (she recalls having seen works by Jonas Mekas and Stan Brakhage, two of the leading figures of the New York experimental scene), it was another development within the diversified American avant-garde that was to have a lasting influence on her work of the 1970s and beyond: structural film.

As its name suggests, structural film resolutely foregrounds formal aspects of film-making at the expense of narrative and plot. This refusal of narrative is part of the avant-garde's wider challenging of commercial cinema, whose smooth editing style and complex identification strategies aim at drawing spectators into the filmic illusion – a technique referred to as 'suture' in film criticism – thus encouraging them to passively absorb the film image and uncriti-cally indulge in the spectatorial pleasures on offer. The self-reflexive structural approach, in contrast, deliberately undermines tradi-tional viewing habits by putting the very process of perception at the core of its enterprise. Thus, in Andy Warhol's *Empire* (1964), for instance, a provocative 8-hour-long fixed-frame take of the Empire State Building filmed from dusk to dawn from the 44th floor of the neighbouring Time Life Building, narrative and drama are expelled in favour of a 'pure' viewing experience. The most famous example of the structural movement, Michael Snow's *Wavelength* (1967), a film

1 For a history of the American avant-garde, see Sitney (1979); for a detailed study of underground cinema, see Reekie (2007) and Tyler (1995).

composed of a 45-minute gradual zoom through the length of a loft apartment towards a photo on one of its opposite walls, by contrast, hints at various possible dramatic plots as characters enter and leave the frame, but refuses to resolve them as the zoom continues its inexorable progression. Film duration, as is exemplified by these two works, is essential to the structuralist viewing experience. Real-time or near real-time representation are intended to make viewers aware of the physical nature of the viewing process as well as of their own corporeal existence. As Akerman explains in the context of her own work: 'Le temps n'est pas que dans le plan, il existe aussi chez le spectateur en face qui le regarde. Il le sent ce temps, en lui. Même s'il prétend qu'il s'ennuie ... Attendre le plan suivant, c'est aussi et déjà se sentir vivre, se sentir exister'[2] (Akerman 2004: 38). Yet, in her own structurally inspired aesthetics, duration is never merely a formal device; it is intimately linked to a quest for truth which, she asserts, emerges through a sustained looking process: 'la vérité ne se livre pas si simplement, souvent même elle se refuse. Je mettrai la caméra là, en face, aussi longtemps qu'il sera nécessaire et la vérité adviendra'[3] (Akerman 2004: 30).

Akerman's debt to structural film-making practices is most evident in her first documentary, *Hotel Monterey* (1972), a systematic, if somewhat stern, exploration of a New York hotel for 'transients' (the American term for people without a permanent address), located between 96th Street and Broadway. The story of how she raised funds for the film is in itself an amusing example of the subversive practices of counter-culture. In *Autoportrait*, the director reveals that she systematically returned the wrong change to male clients whilst working as a cashier at the 55th Street Playhouse, a cinema which specialised in pornography. The small fortune she amassed from cashing in on one of the most exploitative types of cinema (before being found out and fired by her boss) paid for her documentary on the homeless, a social group of no interest to commercial cinema except as a grim backdrop to more edifying fictions. The film was shot by Mangolte, Akerman's

---

2 'Time is not only in the shot, it is also in the spectators who are looking at the shot. They feel this time, in their own bodies. Even if they claim to be bored ... To wait for the next shot is also already to feel oneself living, to feel oneself existing.'

3 'Truth does not give itself away easily, it even often refuses itself. I will place my camera for as long as is necessary and truth will emerge.'

friend who introduced her to the New York avant-garde and who, as photographer of New American dance performances and collabo- rator of choreographer and feminist director Yvonne Rainer, was herself closely bound up with avant-garde circles. The filmic struc- ture is simplified to the extreme and reflects structural film-making's interest in time and perception: the camera scales the entire hotel building from ground floor to roof, beginning in the main lobby just before sunset and gradually moving upwards during the course of the night. The film ends with a pan taken from the building's rooftop onto a grey New York morning.

Silent and without plot, *Hotel Monterey* constitutes some kind of 'degree zero' of film-making, paring filmic language down to its bare essentials: the syntax of camera movements (fixed camera angles at the beginning of the film, tracking shots as the night progresses and a pan in the morning), colour, composition, framing and editing. Lingering in the communal lobby, lift and, later, corridors and rooms, the camera calmly scrutinises the building's interior and its anony- mous population. In a strategy that paves the way for later works like *Jeanne Dielman*, the director uses the filmic space as her main visual metaphor for the existential condition of the destitute urban class that forms the hotel's clientele. Repeated, barely dissimilar images of neon-lit corridors, sparsely furnished rooms and discol- oured communal areas, shot in fixed camera and frozen in long takes, create an atmosphere of anonymity, claustrophobia and loneliness. The spaces traversed by the camera seem empty and forbidding even when they are populated by the hotel's residents. As the night unfolds, human presence becomes sparse and eventually disappears, but the camera relentlessly continues to track along empty corridors in its upwards progression. The extended duration of the shots, be they static or moving, imbues the film with a hypnotic quality, making spectators painfully aware of the viscous quality of time, yet, by the same token, freezing the action in a suspended temporality: the waiting and inertia that is the residents' lot.

In Akerman's *mise en scène*, the hotel residents are transformed into spectres, the barely individualised members of a dispossessed urban class that commercial cinema condemns to a position of invisibility. Entering and leaving the lift, their bodies are reduced to darkened silhouettes and their faces are barely recognisable under the dim neon lighting. Intercut portraits of individuals in their rooms seem to offer a more privileged access, yet, here also, the camera remains distant and the filmed subjects appear no less anonymous. Unlike the residents in the lift and corridors who occasionally react to the camera – introducing a typical 1970s performance element into the narrative (Margulies 1996: 52) – these singled-out individuals stoically bear the camera gaze without returning it (we will find a similarly 'staged' approach to documentary in *D'Est*, Akerman's 1993 portrait of Eastern Europe after the fall of Communism). Akerman freezes her filmed subjects in still-life-like compositions, whose painterly quality is enhanced by the rigorous framing and the rich, saturated colours obtained by 'push-processing' the film (i.e., by prolonging the time of development to increase its sensitivity). If it weren't for the occasional fluttering of the eyelids, one could mistake the immobile image of a bow-tied, middle-aged man sitting in an armchair for a freeze frame. Shots of a man who turns his back to the camera and of a pregnant woman seen through a doorframe display the same quasi-photographic stillness. The portraits evoke the work of American modernist Edward Hopper who uses similarly formal compositions for his daunting paintings of human solitude and loneliness, a painter with whom Akerman shares an openly declared affinity (Rosenbaum 1983: 35). Beyond their pose and attire, the residents are given no further individuality, but their typicality – pregnant woman alone, well-dressed middle-aged man in a welfare hotel – evokes familiar narratives of social descent and personal tragedy. Like Michael Snow in *Wavelength*, but in an altogether different (less radical) idiom, the film gestures towards drama and stories but leaves them suspended. This narrative element, owing above all to the framing and editing of the non-fiction space, dilutes the boundary between documentary and fiction and introduces Akerman's documentary style 'bordering on fiction' (which will be examined in more detail in Chapter 3).

The rhythmical alternation between human presence and absence situates the work at the threshold between figurative and abstract modes of representation (cf. Margulies 1996: 43). When the camera is placed close to the closed lift door, the image for several minutes dissolves into a pure composition of lines and colours, a lyrical instal-lation with flickering red and white lights. When the lift door reopens, revealing people inside, the image returns to its referential status. Beyond an artistic exploration of the painterly possibilities of the movie camera, this oscillation between concrete and abstract modes serves to draw the viewer's attention to the dual nature of the cinematic image: its function as a window onto reality (the mirror image that opens the film openly alludes to this referential quality) and its more essential status as a projected visual image. Akerman explains this duality, which informs her filmic approach in *Hotel Monterey*, in easily comprehensible terms: 'Quand vous regardez une image pendant une seconde vous saisissez l'information, "c'est un corridor". Mais au bout d'un instant vous oubliez le corridor pour ne voir que du jaune, du rouge, des lignes: et puis le corridor réapparaît'[4] (cit. in Margulies 1996: 43). Like the static camerawork and emphasis on filmic time, this self-reflexive foregrounding of the material character of the film image evinces the director's affinity with a structural aesthetics.

The ending *of Hotel Monterey* scarcely alleviates its pervasive pessimism: when the camera finally emerges from the claustrophobic hotel space out into the open, the images of the surrounding skyline shown in a 360° horizontal pan are as desolate as the interior shots of neon-lit corridors. A grey ashen morning rises over the housing estates of upper Broadway. The iconic New York of glittering boulevards and elegant skyscrapers is a far removed, barely fathomable reality.

Je tu il elle or the time of subjectivity

During her stay in New York, Akerman made two more shorts, *La Chambre*, an experimental portrait of her room shot in a 360° pan strongly influenced by Michael Snow, as well as *Hanging out Yonkers*, an unfinished documentary on a community centre for young delinquents and drug addicts. In 1973, intermittently back in Europe, together with Samy Szlingerbaum, she directed a more individual study of youth, *Le 15/08*, an idiosyncratic portrait of a young Finnish student in Paris. The character's rambling monologue about her daily life in the capital and her shifting moods, delivered in a broken English, as Patrice Blouin points out, posit her as an antithetical double to Eric Rohmer's Nadja, from his 1967 *Nadja à Paris*, an articulate, confident Yugoslav-American who pays homage to the intellectual and artistic

---

4 'When you look at a picture for a second you get the information, "that's a corridor". But after a while you forget that it's a corridor, you just see that it's yellow, red, lines: and then it comes back as a corridor.'

riches of her adopted city (Blouin 2004: 177). Where Rohmer's Nadja leisurely strolls through the capital's famous and lesser-known neighbourhoods (Quartier Latin, Montparnasse, Belleville), Akerman's Chris (Chris Myllykoski) remains confined to her flat, unable to articulate what seems to be an existential malaise. The change of title, from Rohmer's personal *Nadja à Paris* to Akerman's factual *Le 15/08*, signals a radical change of programme reflected in the profilmic events: '[La divergence du titre] indique que c'est pour de bon révolu le temps des petites filles modèles et des récits initiatiques aussi ironiques soient-ils'[5] (Blouin 2004: 177).

In their unconventional representation of the crisis of adolescence, *Saute ma ville* and *Le 15/08* can be considered as a matrix for Akerman's first feature-length fiction, *Je tu il elle*, an ambitious study of a young woman's depression and experimentation with sexual identities, directed on her return from New York to Brussels in 1974. The film was shot in one week, on a shoestring budget. The director once again occupies the roles of producer, scriptwriter and lead actress, but formally distances her autobiographical self from her acting self in the credits where she cites the fictional name 'Julie' as that of the main actress. Margulies reads this playful distancing as part of a wider identity crisis that is dramatised in the film and as a sign of the 'de-individualisation' that is one of the film's main tenets:

> Akerman's process of de-indivualization results from an untenable accumulation of functions in a single body. There is no compromising of one function at the expense of the other. This accumulation creates a fissure in the body's supposed unity, forcing one to read several conflicting registers of identity with equal acuity: that of author, performer, and character. (Margulies 1996: 110)

The film divides into three parts, named by Akerman herself, 'Le temps de la subjectivité', 'Le temps de l'autre ou reportage' and 'Le temps de la relation'.[6] Organised around a journey, a standard film metaphor for self-discovery, it takes the protagonist from a period of self-inflicted confinement (where the 'je' faces herself, but also an anonymous 'tu' to whom she writes letters) to a random encounter

---

5 '[The difference between the two titles] suggests that the time of exemplary girls and initiation stories, however ironic they may be, is once and for all over.'

6 'The time of subjectivity', 'the time of the Other or reportage', and 'the time of relation'.

with 'il', a truck driver who gives her a lift and solicits her sexual favours, and, finally, a reunion with 'elle', a former lover who reluctantly puts her up for the night and yields to her sexual advances. As the title and its spatial distribution in the opening credits suggest, the film conjugates positions of the self's relationship with the Other, be it a personal 'you' or an impersonal 'he/she', indicating the different vectors of the protagonist's sexual experimentation and choice of love object. As Maureen Turim points out, the spatial juxtaposition between 'il' and 'elle' in the title sequence not only announces the central theme of male–female differentiation in the film but hints at the protagonist's sexual mobility, her vacillating desire between members of her own and the opposite sex, that will be explored in a ritual journey of initiation (Turim 2003: 14). The different styles of the three parts – the first is indebted to 1970s performance art, the second to the reportage genre and the third offers an alternative to erotic or pornographic cinema – highlight the various stages of this journey.

Je tu il elle is a quintessential example of what Deleuze has termed a 'cinema of bodies', that is, a film that explores in the greatest possible detail the postures, gestures and attitudes of the body in its banal, yet singular, quotidian (Deleuze 1989: 196). 'The time of subjectivity', in static camera, captures, in a painful and slow anatomy, the language of a female body in distress, swaying between inertia and repetitive, compulsive gestures (moving around furniture, binging on sugar, pinning scattered pages of a letter to the floor). The dissociation manifest in the bodily language is enhanced by a desynchronised voice-over which announces actions to come, describes actions that have been or, more radically, evokes acts that have no correlate in the film image. 'J'ai peint les meubles en bleu le premier jour',[7] declares a childish voice in the initial sequence, yet no such action is ever to be seen. Together with the long takes and the stylised acting, this disjunctive soundtrack distances spectators from the screen image, engaging their awareness of the performative nature of the action and of their own physical presence in the viewing process.

In the absence of any precise start or end point, temporal markers like 'the fourth day' or 'the fifth day', uttered by the voice-over, introduce a sequence but fail to anchor the action in a concrete temporality. Time is conceived as a sensuous subjective experience rather than

---

7 'I painted the furniture blue the first day.'

as an absolute; a subjective female time governed by the woman's menstrual cycle – the voice-over mentions twenty-eight days as a turning point – rather than the objective time of productive, male-dominated society. Fade-ins and fade-outs of the image signalling the passing of day and night reinforce the idea of an instinctual, almost animalistic perception.

The period of self-incarceration and Beckettian waiting involves a stripping process, hinting at a ritualistic liberation from cultural and social conditioning and quest for a more authentic, 'primitive' state of being. First, the young woman gets rid of the furniture that encumbers her studio flat, next of the clothes that burden her. Naked, her body reconnects with matter, but is also threatened to be engulfed by it. In the long fade-outs and fade-ins, the young woman's silhouette, swallowed by darkness, fuses with the contours of the room and becomes an abstract shape (as in *Hotel Monterey*, the film oscillates between figuration and abstraction). This threat of engulfment, in a symbolically charged development, is overcome through the power of the gaze, first, that of a stranger, who looks at the naked girl through the flat's glass door, then, her own lengthy examination of herself in the same reflecting glass. Julie, at this stage of her journey, still depends on the exterior, here male, gaze to constitute herself as a subject. Her abrupt departure through the same door, at once window to the world and mirror of the self, instrument of narcissism and exhibitionism, ends the time of subjectivity and leads over to the time of the (male) other.

If structural film can be considered the main artistic influence behind *Hotel Monterey*, American New Dance, in particular the pioneering work of dancer, choreographer and fellow film director Yvonne Rainer, provides a useful framework for understanding Akerman's formal experimentation in the first part of *Je tu il elle* (cf. Margulies 1996: 102–9). As with film culture, New York quickly established itself as one of the leading centres for experimentation in dance and performance art in the 1960s. Indeed, there was a considerable crossover and mutual influence between these two art forms, as the example of Rainer, a choreographer who incorporated film sequences into her performances and authored some of the most influential feminist films in the 1970s, shows. A classically trained dancer, under the influence of the minimalist aesthetics of, notably, composer John Cage and visual artists such as Donald Judd and Richard Serra,

Rainer developed a new dance language based on the straightforward physical movement of the body in space rather than on the codified techniques of the classical tradition. In her resolutely non-dramatic and non-narrative performances, task-oriented movements based on everyday actions such as walking or changing clothes replace the skills and virtuosity expected from traditionally trained dancers. By suppressing spectacle and emphasising the concrete everyday, Rainer contains the voyeuristic and narcissistic elements inherent in dance and encourages a more distanced relationship between performer and spectator that is devoid of seduction and emotional involvement. *Je tu il elle*'s serialised, cumulative style and use of task-based activities (for instance, when Julie pushes around her mattress) show clear affinities with the minimalist aesthetics of Rainer's choreographies and with the exploration of the body in space and time of 1960s and 1970s performance art more generally. As Margulies explains, '[Akerman] adheres to Yvonne Rainer's move toward a more concrete everyday-ness in performance, to the choreographer and dancer's minimalist mandate that performance emphasize movement at the expense of psychology' (Margulies 1996: 50).

The film's second part, 'The time of the Other or reportage', as its title suggests, experiments with documentary styles of film-making, shifting from the subjective feminine 'je' to the impersonal masculine 'il'. The grainier image and jumpier camerawork, two representational codes associated with the documentary genre and considered as guarantors of the 'truthfulness' of an image, formally signal this move. In the scenes filmed in the moving truck, Akerman occupies the edge of the frame, leaving the centre stage to the driver, who thus appears as the object of the filmic enquiry. In contrast to the feminine time in the film's first part, which was shown as essentially one of waiting and non-development, a circular bodily time governed by the rhythm of day and night and the menstrual cycle, male time here is presented as one of activity and movement. Against the stifling routine of family life and office work, the trucker (Niels Arestrup) has chosen the freedom of the road with its possibility of sexual adventures and random encounters. His self-assured demeanour stands in striking contrast to the female character's timidity and unease culminating in a burlesque scene in a bar where she mimics every single one of his gestures. The voice-over signals the young woman's attraction to the trucker, yet it is he, upholding traditional gender roles, who bluntly asks her to masturbate him, giving precise instructions and commenting on the various stages of his arousal.

Male pleasure, explored in real time through a close-up on the man's upper body, is presented as climax-driven, solitary and altogether impersonal. The trucker's rambling monologue that follows the masturbation, filmed likewise in close-up without the female character appearing in the frame, reinforces the disequilibrium between an active maleness and a passive, submissive femininity. The monologue strings together a series of (often misogynistic) clichés, but is strikingly frank in its articulation of desire, family crisis and personal vulnerability. The young woman, in contrast, remains in the position of observer and listener, her childlike persona enhanced by the almost paternal gesture with which the trucker bids her farewell.

'The time of relation', finally, sees the young woman reunited with her former lover, the suspected 'tu' of her letters (Claire Wauthion). This section further investigates power relations and behavioural modes, this time in a same-sex relationship. The young woman played by Akerman takes on an unexpected agency when she imposes herself on the elfish lover despite the latter's unwelcoming attitude. The parent–child trope we have already noticed in the contact with the trucker is extended in the young woman's demand for nurture followed by the former lover's compliant preparation of food (interestingly Wauthion already played a mother figure in Akerman's *L'Enfant aimé ou je joue à être une femme mariée*, an early autobiographical film disowned by the director). Julie's grabbing and unclothing of the lover's breast indexes a desire for the mother and, through the trope of orality, creates a link between the film's first and third parts. As Turim points out,

> [d]esire for nurturance, linked to desire for breast, is metonymically displaced throughout the film. The focus on the sugar bingeing and, later on, the two sandwiches demanded before any desire for sex is addressed presents orality as a leitmotif connecting the segments beyond their physical trajectory as a journey. (Turim 2003: 15)

Critics have commented extensively on the sex scene that occupies most of the third part, an audacious performance from Akerman and Wauthion and a startling portrait of lesbian sexuality at a time where representations of homosexuality were still largely confined to short experimental works (cf. Margulies 1996, Turim 2003). The love-making is filmed in medium-long shot, eschewing the varying shot angles and close-ups of sexual organs exploited in pornographic film-making. Avoiding any romanticisation of lesbian love, Akerman puts the emphasis on the concrete materiality of the female bodies which wrestle and clash in a choreography of interlocking limbs and floating hair. The amplified sound of crumpling bed sheets underlines the raw physicality of the act. The violence of the first images gives way to more tender scenes of kissing and caressing, filmed from the foot of the bed, culminating in oral sex, shot again parallel to the bed, but from a closer angle. The strongly haptic quality of the images sets the lesbian love-making apart from the brutish, orgasm-driven male masturbation scene. Lesbianism is shown as a genuine alternative to heterosexuality even though the possibility of the renewal of the lovers' relationship is denied by Julie's departure at dawn. The song that accompanies the closing credits, a popular fifteenth-century rondo for children, 'Nous n'irons plus au bois', invites further sexual and amorous experimentation: 'Entrez dans la danse/ Voyez comme on danse/ Sautez, dansez/ Embrassez qui vous voudrez'.[8] Contrary, then, to the two other characters who are fixed in their gender roles (the predatory heterosexual male and the submissive homosexual female), Julie's sexual identity and preference remain suspended throughout the film in a playful embrace of homo- and heterosexuality, a purposeful indeterminacy which, as Margulies points out, privileges mobility over finality (Margulies 1996: 111). For Deleuze, this mobility is part of a wider nomadism that characterises Akerman's work: 'In the same place or in space, a woman's body achieves a strange nomadism which makes it cross ages, situations and places' (Deleuze 1989: 196). In its blowing-up of fixed sexual identities and exploration of the female gest, *Je tu il elle* not only constitutes 'a cinematic Rosetta Stone of female sexuality' (B. Ruby Rich), it partakes in an exploration of female subjectivity that spans Akerman's entire oeuvre and will be brought to perfect fruition in her next work, the monumental *Jeanne Dielman*.

8 'Join the dance/ See how we dance/ Spring, dance/ Kiss whom you please.'

Jeanne Dielman, 23, quai du Commerce, 1080 Bruxelles

Though soliciting considerable critical attention abroad, *Je tu il elle* received predominantly bad reviews at the Brussels Film Festival where it was shown in 1974. One critic commented on what he considered Akerman's failure of applying conceptual art to the cinema in the following terms:

> Réalisant une sorte 'd'anti-cinéma', Chantal Akerman tente l'expérience d'un minutage fidèle de chaque geste posé par un individu. Ainsi, le rasage (soigné) d'un camionneur paraît-il conforme au temps nécessairement imparti ... et la préparation à la dégustation d'une tartine participe de la même volonté ... Chantal Akerman, hantée sans doute par l'expérience du conceptuel dans les arts plastiques veut approprier le système au cinéma.[9] (cit. in Sojcher 1999: 142)

The 'minutage fidèle de chaque geste posé par un individu' which troubled the critic will be explored to perfection by Akerman in what, more than thirty years on, is still considered her masterpiece, *Jeanne Dielman, 23, quai du Commerce, 1080 Bruxelles*. This intellectually challenging and formally sophisticated film made by a twenty-four-year-old director was to epitomise an era with its pressing questions about class, identity, gender and social oppression. It established Akerman as a leading proponent of women's and feminist filmmaking, as well as a director to be reckoned with in European independent cinema.

Having obtained funding from the Belgian Ministry of Culture under the 'avance sur recettes'[10] scheme for independent film-makers, Akerman could for the first time work within the more expensive parameters of a long (200 minutes) colour fiction, employ a bigger film crew and work with well-known actors. The film script, loosely inspired by Godard's *Deux ou trois choses que je sais d'elle* (1966), was written specifically for Delphine Seyrig, one of Europe's most respected

---

9 'Making some kind of "anti-cinema", Chantal Akerman tries to capture faithfully in real time an individual's every single gesture. Thus, a truck driver's (careful) shaving seems to take as much time as it would in real life ... and the preparation of a sandwich shows a similar intent ... Chantal Akerman, probably haunted by the idea of the conceptual in the plastic arts, seeks to appropriate its principles for the cinema.'

10 An interest-free loan either repayable from income or from any grant given to a film.

actresses, perhaps best known for her enigmatic performance in Alain Resnais's *L'Année dernière à Marienbad* (1961). Seyrig brought to the role echoes of European art cinema, the professionalism of an actress who had worked with some of the world's finest directors (Resnais, Truffaut, Buñuel) and an outspoken commitment to women's rights (she directed three works herself, including the 1977 *Sois belle et tais-toi* which addressed sexism in the film industry). The casting of fellow Belgian film-maker Jan Decorte as Jeanne's teenage son, the cameo appearance of Henri Storck, Belgium's most long-standing director, as her first client, and above all the Brussels setting gave the film a distinctly national touch (Fowler 2003: 191). In its espousal of a more traditional narrative form based around conflict and resolution, the film presents a crossover between the structural aesthetics Akerman had discovered in New York and the narrative tradition of European independent cinema. Akerman herself describes it as 'the result of my research, on form in the USA and on story-telling in Europe' (cit. in Kinder 1977: 3). *Jeanne Dielman* was shot between February and April 1975 with the assistance of an exclusively female team including Babette Mangolte as director of photography.

Akerman cites Bataille's 'Tout problème en un certain sens en est un d'emploi du temps',[11] to explain one of *Jeanne Dielman*'s central themes, the compulsive need for order and routine (Akerman 2004: 44). The film, in the greatest possible detail and often in real time, depicts three days in the life of Jeanne Dielman, a middle-aged widow who supports herself and her teenage son by daytime prostitution in her home. The theme of prostitution aligns the film with a distinguished series of works on female sexual exploitation (or empowerment, depending on the vantage point), from Sternberg's *Shanghai Express* (1932) to Buñuel's *Belle de jour* (1967), yet the mundane existence it documents is far removed from the glamour of courtesan life or the erotic titillation of a secret double existence explored in such earlier works. *Jeanne Dielman* is above all a film about the disturbingly banal, the elusive everyday – Maurice Blanchot pertinently defines the quotidian as 'that which is most difficult to discover' (Blanchot 1969: 355) – which, under Akerman's magnifying glass, reveals both its platitude and its potential for drama. 'Le plat', Akerman comments, 'me bouleversait totalement. J'avais l'impression, et je l'ai toujours, que

11 'Every problem, in a sense, relates to how you organise your time.'

c'est là que tout se trouve'[12] (Akerman 2004: 49–52). Documenting in painstaking detail the daily rituals of her protagonist – critics have labelled her approach as 'ethnographic' or 'hyper-realist', Akerman herself prefers the term 'phenomenological' – Akerman not only foregrounds female gestures of the quotidian undervalued by society and relegated to a status of invisibility by commercial cinema, but, in what constitutes a more serious follow-up to *Saute ma ville*, dramatises a woman's conflicting relations to time, the self and the world she inhabits. The film's strictly symmetrical two-panel structure meticu-lously charts Jeanne's daily routine which, once brought out of sync by an unexplained event that occurs in the afternoon of day two (in all likelihood an orgasm she experiences with one of her clients), leads to a gradual disorder culminating in the murder of her third client.

Akerman's disturbing fiction of the everyday forms part of a wider cultural and artistic tradition which needs to be outlined briefly before turning to the film itself. Although shunned by commercial cinema, the quotidian has long fascinated philosophers and artists, rising to particular prominence in European and American avant-garde practices of the 1950s and 1960s.[13] In France, the *nouveau roman* authors, some of whom like Alain Robbe-Grillet and Margue-rite Duras worked in close collaboration with film-makers (Duras also was a film-maker in her own right), proposed a new form of literary expression where plot is no longer subservient to character, but, on the contrary, is driven by the object world around it which is described in uttermost detail. On the other side of the Atlantic, the visual arts, performance art, music and experimental film, as we have already seen to a certain extent, challenged the divide between high and low art, making the quotidian an essential part of their artistic experiments: minimalist composer John Cage performed some of his musical works on ordinary objects; Andy Warhol made real-time filmic portraits of everyday activities such as sleeping and eating (*Sleep*, 1963 and *Eat*, 1964); and performance artists from the New York-based Judson Dance Group integrated everyday gestures like walking, pouring water from one can into another or drawing a line into their works.[14] Perhaps most importantly in the context of

12 'The dull totally shattered me. I had the impression, and I still do, that it is at the core of everything.'
13 For a detailed study, see Sheringham (2006).
14 For the varied experiments of performance art, see Goldberg (1990).

Akerman's work, feminist film-makers of the early 1970s concentrated on women's private sphere in documentaries such as *Janie's Janie* (1971), *Three Women* (1971), and *Joyce at 34* (1972) (Margulies 1996: 4). Yet, never before in the history of cinema had the domestic routine of a housewife become the subject of a feature film and never had 'the materiality of woman's time in the home been rendered so viscerally' (Rich 1998: 170).

At the outset, perhaps the most striking aspect of *Jeanne Dielman* is its bold conflation between the ordinary and the extraordinary, between Jeanne's routine household tasks and her commerce with her clients, which all receive the same de-dramatised attention in the film. The film opens with a kitchen scene: Jeanne is putting potatoes on to boil when the doorbell rings. She slowly takes off her apron, washes her hands and switches off the light before opening the door to let in an elderly man (Henri Storck) who turns out to be one of her clients. The move from kitchen routine to prostitution is seamless and fluid, made with no apparent sign of nervousness or irritation by the protagonist, who performs this parallel thread of her life with the same composed, slightly stylised gestures as her other daily tasks. As in the realm of the domestic, we are in a regime of habit, of repeated everyday activity. Jeanne's clients have their fixed day and hour; they are slotted into the housewife's timetable alongside other chores, apparently sharing the same status in her routine as more mundane tasks in her regulated work pattern: 'Jeanne relegates [prostitution] to the level of cleaning the bathtub or bleaching out a particularly nasty stain: sex becomes a necessary but bothersome choice' (Loader 1985: 335). The interaction with the first client, a grey-haired, respectable-looking man in his sixties or seventies, reveals the paternalistic aspects behind this type of prostitution: from the exchange of hat, scarf and coat, to the seemingly well-meaning pressing of Jeanne's hand when the client takes his leave, the gest evokes a relation between master and servant – exactly the same visual motif of the exchange of clothes is later repeated in Jeanne's interaction with her son, drawing attention to her reproduction of patriarchal codes in the family and thus to her role as a conservative social force. The decapitating middle-range shot that cuts off Jeanne's and her client's heads as she welcomes him highlights the dehumanising nature of the services offered, whilst Jeanne's outstretched hands claiming money as he leaves allude to a far from equal economy of exchange.

Whilst showing in real time what commercial cinema would avoid or compress to mere allusion – all the routine activities that fill the housewife's day, from peeling potatoes and washing dishes to making beds and dusting shelves –, the film withholds the sexual act from the spectator: Jeanne and her client disappear into what we suspect is her bedroom; a few seconds later, the camera cuts and the two characters re-emerge through the same door. The darkened corridor in opposition to the daylight of the previous shot simulates the passing of time. Filmed as an ellipsis, the daytime prostitution of a housewife and mother is presented as the ultimate taboo in bourgeois society, the epitome of the obscene that can only happen behind closed doors, 'out of scene' (Margulies 1996: 76). The sexual act is followed by a complex purification ritual that symbolically and literally effaces its traces: Jeanne removes the towel that protects her bed during intercourse, opens the window to air the bedroom and gives herself and the bathtub a good scrub before preparing dinner for her adolescent son.

The opening sequence establishes some of the narrative and aesthetic principles on which *Jeanne Dielman* is based. The film, from the start, sets up a tension between the seen and the unseen, the images offered to the spectator and those deliberately withheld, which, on the level of the story, mimics the dynamics between public appearance and dissimulation, and on the level of the character, that between consciousness and repression. Whilst the act of prostitution creates narrative drama, this drama is quickly deflated as the film returns to the more mundane activities of Jeanne's life. Traditional narrative codes of suspense, dramatisation and visual pleasure – commercial cinema, as Mulvey argues in her highly influential piece 'Visual Pleasure and Narrative Cinema' (Mulvey 2000), relies heavily on scopophilia, the desire to look – are thwarted and a new visual regime based not on the extraordinary but on the ordinary is set up.

Akerman's minimalist, detached film style and resolutely anti-psychological approach to character construction keep spectators at a distance, obstructing identification with the film characters and thus preventing the passive absorption offered by commercial cinema. Suturing devices such as shot/reverse shot and privileged points of view through zoom-ins and -outs are eschewed. The point of view remains the same throughout the film, clearly designating the position from which the shot was taken, rather than allowing for the 'peeping Tom' voyeuristic perspective that film semioticians have identified as one of the sources of visual pleasure of the cinematic experience. By thus displacing spectatorial pleasures from spectacle – especially the spectacle of a glamorous femininity – to the act of pure seeing, Akerman frees the spectator's gaze and forces it to become more actively involved in analysing the filmic image. The use of long takes encourages viewers to get attuned with Jeanne's rhythm, to scrutinise her daily rituals and to learn to read Seyrig's facial expressions and gestures, the language of the body, which, as in the earlier work, is privileged over speech as an exploration of mental states.

The film's first half (up to the second client's visit) establishes the tightly regulated pattern of Jeanne's existence: the daily routine of preparing breakfast, washing dishes, making beds, shopping and cooking, repetitive gestures performed by millions of housewives around the globe, yet neither recognised nor valued in production-centred capitalist societies, nor traditionally deemed worthy of study or filmic representation. Given the narrative time that is devoted to these activities and Akerman's own repeated comments on her desire to 'montrer la juste valeur du quotidien féminin'[15] and to film 'l'occupation du temps dans une vie de femme rivée à son foyer'[16] (cit. in Siclier 1976: 15), it is tempting to read this aspect of the film as a positive re-evaluation of women's time and domestic routine, a line apparently taken by Luce Giard in her study on 'The Nourishing Arts' (a contribution to the second volume of *The Practice of Everyday Life* co-written by Michel de Certeau), which draws extensively on Akerman. Yet, this would be to miss the morbidity and sense of entrapment that emerges from the film's serialised rendering of the gestures of the everyday and to exaggerate the realist dimension of a film characterised on the contrary by its hyper-realism. Everyday domestic life, in Akerman's film, far from being a privileged space of femininity or an exemplar of a 'feminine time', is shown on the contrary as a fundamentally alienating experience, a series of rituals drained of meaning and performed without any apparent affective investment. It is in its depiction of the quotidian that the unsettling ambiguity of the film and its central character emerges: its documentary aspect, that is, its depiction of a certain social type (the housewife), is constantly undercut by the jarring a-typicality of the main character (highlighted by the very fact that she is also a prostitute),

15 'show the true value of women's daily existence.'
16 'the use of time in the life of a woman bound to her home.'

whose strangeness obstructs easy interpretation and categorisation. Hyper-realism, located above all in Seyrig's stylised, theatrical performance, is the privileged means to render this ambiguity: whilst it allows Akerman to go straight to the heart of reality – 'I did not want to do a kind of naturalism, but rather, with a very stylized image, to attain the very essence of reality' (Akerman cit. in Giard 1998: 154) –, it at the same time foregrounds what, in a pun on Freud, she calls the 'disquietingly familiar' which rapidly emerges as the film's central mood.

Critics have commented on the eponymous character's quasi-patho-logical subjugation to domestic ritual. Jeanne Dielman lives a life of rigid containment and control, devoid of improvisation, spontaneity or creativity: during her working day, she never switches on the radio, reads a book or simply goes for a stroll. Her only distractions are her coffee breaks and daily visit to the café, but these are exactly timetabled like her other activities (including prostitution). Neighbours eager to socialise are politely kept at a distance and interaction with the social world around her is generally kept to a minimum. Akerman offers virtually no insight into the protagonist's consciousness, refusing the standard cinematic means to render a character's subjectivity, that is, point-of-view shots, voice-over or close-up. During the whole first half of the film, Jeanne's face remains quasi-emotionless, a cold, hard mask only occasionally lit up when she interacts with her son, but even then always controlled. A mirror image of the flat she inhabits, devoid of individualising features beyond its easily recognisable petit-bourgeois taste and 1970s style, and the aseptic sexual commerce she engages in, Jeanne Dielman is presented as a figure of sterility, a sexually repressed 'female eunuch'[17] separated from her libido and, as her excessive restraint seems to suggest, from desire more gener-ally. The character ingeniously played by Seyrig seems absent from herself, robotic and automaton-like, incapable of creatively investing herself in the world or of taking a step back, frozen in habit and repeti-tion – an existence reduced to pure functioning. Any confrontation with meaning is avoided, as is comically evidenced in her rehearsal of a Baudelaire poem with her son Sylvain: the words of the poem are parroted without ever elucidating their meaning, their beauty and rhythmical quality being drained by the speaker's hackneyed delivery.

17 The term was coined by Germaine Greer in her influential 1970 book of the same title.

Akerman's minimalist film syntax gives visual form to the protagonist's alienated existence. Static fixed-angle shots and little variation
in the shot (frontally centred images; medium shots for indoor, wide
angle for most outdoor scenes; the same low camera height for all
indoor shots except during the murder scene) create an overpowering
impression of stasis and control. Real-time representation of events
and repetition of the same routine gestures underline their inherent
monotony. As in *Hotel Monterey*, the film aesthetic is heavily indebted
to the visual arts: each shot is a perfectly framed tableau, its careful
composition, warm lighting and rich brown and copper colours
reminiscent of the Flemish old masters (Margulies 1996: 5) renowned
for their intimate portrayals of women in their homes, engaged in
domestic activities or leisure, looking after children or entertaining
visitors. The editing style gives visual form to the character's imprisonment in the domestic sphere: shots frequently open or close on a
section of the flat (corridor, bedroom, kitchen, sitting room) not yet
or no longer inhabited by Jeanne's presence. These cuts on material
space rather than on the placement of Jeanne's figure within the frame,
endow the flat with an overpowering presence, giving it a life of its
own, with 'needs and demands which manipulate Jeanne and structure her day much more substantially than do the needs of either her
living son or once-living husband' (Loader 1985: 331). In the absence
of human voices, the amplified diegetic sound, a chorus of passing
traffic, gushing water in the pipes, creaking doors and cupboards, the
sound of burning gas and the clicking of light switches compulsively
turned on and off by the protagonist, endow the film narrative with
an uncanny dimension further undercutting its deceptive realism.
Together with the flickering neon lights that penetrate Jeanne's sitting
room even when the curtains are drawn, the permanent noise environment builds into a threatening environment of abjection, the whining
laments of closing doors metonymically expressing a distress that
the main character keeps carefully concealed, but also signalling her
impossibility to regulate fully and contain the universe she inhabits.

Though resolutely refraining from any kind of traditional
character psychology and giving the female character little room for
verbal self-expression, Akerman allows limited insight into Jeanne's
mind through the film's sparse dialogues which, in their content and
mode of address, hint at the repressive forces in her life whilst, at
the same time, shedding further light on the function of Akerman's

distanced, detached style. Jeanne's reading of a letter from her sister during the first evening is a crucial example of the wider anti-naturalist strategies at work in the film. Akerman has Seyrig read the letter without any natural breaks or pauses, in a monotonous, blank voice. Trivial information like the sister's description of wintry North America is uttered in the same unemotional tone as a very personal reference to Jeanne's status as widow and single parent. Rather than opting for the naturalising of verbal address practised by mainstream cinema (where dialogues are presented as if they were spoken in the 'real world'), Akerman flattens out language, privileging rhythm and sound over actual communication. With this resolutely anti-illusionist approach, she inscribes herself in a tradition first developed by Bertold Brecht and adopted by modern European directors such as Godard, Duras and Robert Bresson (cf. Margulies 1996: 54–64). In Brecht's 'epic theatre', audiences are made aware of the illusion of spectacle by means of distancing devices such as actors' direct address to spectators, or visual captions that interrupt or summarise the action. Whilst Akerman, to a certain extent, preserves illusion in her film through the use of a realistic set and the presence of a fourth invisible wall that separates the space of action from the space of the spectator – in other words, she never has her characters address the audience directly –, her stylised use of monologue creates an estrangement effect that alerts spectators to the artificiality of the fiction and forces them to scrutinise the letter's content. In tune with Brecht's premise that text should be spoken in a way which reveals its social and historical conditioning, Jeanne's hackneyed delivery of the letter foregrounds its *doxical* content which is, in essence, a series of clichés about womanhood: women should be married, women should make good use of their looks in the marriage market, the condition of a single mother is socially demeaning, and so forth. A second extensive monologue delivered by the neighbour who leaves her baby in Jeanne's care during the lunch break, ironically spoken by Akerman herself invisible behind a doorframe, fulfils a similar function: it is a comic juxtaposition of platitudes, ranging from a burlesque account of food shopping to received ideas about child care and hygiene to a resigned 'on ne peut pas y échapper'[18] that sums up the young woman's entrapment in her role as petit bourgeois housewife and

18 'there's no way out.'

mother. Reduced to parroting received ideas – what Flaubert, the great nineteenth-century master of irony, has called bourgeois 'bêtise' (stupidity) – the female characters in *Jeanne Dielman* are unable to question their condition, let alone take active steps to change it.

The two nightly conversations between Jeanne and her son, awkwardly positioned just before the two characters go to sleep – an example of the non-homogenous distribution of verbal address characteristic of many Akerman films –, give further insight into the conditioning environment which has shaped the protagonist whilst, at the same time, filling the spectator in on some details of her past. Asked how she met her husband, Jeanne gives a revealing account of her compliance with, but also, intriguingly, resistance to, social expectation. Leading a secluded life with her aunts, the orphan Jeanne accepts the common *doxa* that marriage is the done thing ('ça devait se faire', 'c'était dans l'ordre des choses'[19]), but only decides to marry her future husband when he faces considerable financial difficulty, ignoring her family's warnings that she could use her beauty to much greater profit. Jeanne, then, though unquestioning of marriage as such, shows a surprising independence of mind and even defiance when it comes to her final choice of a partner, introducing a critical ambiguity that challenges simple appropriations of her as a victim of bourgeois ideology. Her idiosyncratic logic in the phrase 'il a fait des mauvaises affaires, alors je l'ai épousé',[20] challenges her status as a type and reinforces her strangeness. When questioned by Sylvain whether she didn't mind having sex with a man she didn't love, she responds that sex is just a detail, and, prompted further, affirms her gender difference in lieu of a response: 'Et qu'est-ce que tu peux en savoir? Tu n'es pas une femme.'[21]

The second nightly conversation, an exact counterpart to the previous one in terms of dialogue and setting, further addresses the question of sexuality, in other words, it probes precisely that which the narrative suppresses. The mode of address is once again anti-naturalist. Sylvain, his head turned away from his mother who stands motionless in the background, delivers a lengthy monologue about the violence of male sexuality and his unease about his parents' sexual relations:

19 'it had to be done', 'it was in the nature of things'.
20 'he made a bad deal, so I married him.'
21 'What do you know about it? You aren't a woman.'

> Tu sais, c'est lui [l'ami] qui m'avait tout raconté quand j'avais dix ans.
> Et je lui ai dit: 'Quoi, papa a fait ça à maman?' Et pendant des mois j'ai
> détesté papa pour ça et j'ai eu envie de mourir. Et quand il [le père] est
> mort, j'ai cru que c'est une punition de Dieu.[22]

Akerman here plays with the well-known scheme of Oedipal drama – the adolescent in love with his mother symbolically confronting the rival father –, yet this familiar scheme is defamiliarised through the hackneyed delivery of the speaker's monologue and the violent clash between the habitual communication between mother and son, which turns around dull, mundane preoccupations, and the openly sexual content and confessional tone of the monologue. As in the other mother–son scenes, Akerman refrains from using the more conventional shot/reverse-shot technique which would adopt the characters' point of view and draw spectators into the psychological depths of the action, signalling instead the characters' difficulty in engaging in communication and exchange. When Sylvain tells his mother that, in his nightmares, he wanted to defend her against the sexual assaults of the father, visibly bothered by the intimate nature of this conversation, she laconically responds 'Tu n'aurais pas dû t'en faire'[23] and goes to bed. Sylvain's anxiety about sex, manifest in his metaphorical invocation of sword and fire to describe the sexual act, as Margulies comments, 'exposes the sexual repression operative in Jeanne's household' (Margulies 1996: 160). Yet, what the two nightly conversations, in their (almost comical) insistence on sexuality, reveal also is precisely the impossibility of containing the repressed: the theme of sexuality resurfaces despite Jeanne's (and the film's) careful concealment of the act of prostitution.

The return of the repressed, which symbolically and literally informs the film narrative, begins to haunt the film in its second part, exactly after Jeanne's intercourse with her second client (which, once again, is withheld from view). The spectator is by now familiar with Jeanne's rituals and expects to see them repeated again as the film, twenty-four hours later, completes a cycle. Jeanne and her client re-emerge from the bedroom, yet, unexpectedly, the corridor light remains switched off. Jeanne only hurriedly turns it on again

---

22 'You know, it was he [the friend] who told me everything when I was ten. And I said to him: "What, dad did this to mum?" And for months I hated dad for it and I wanted to die. And when he died, I thought it was a punishment from God.'
23 'You shouldn't have worried about it.'

as the man hands over the money. She deposits the money in the soup tureen on the dining-room table as usual, but fails to put on the lid. The gaping open tureen on which the camera lingers for a moment becomes a visual signifier of the disorder that has settled in. A few shots later, the new positioning of the camera parallel to the oven, which for the first time allows us to see Jeanne entering the kitchen from the inside, further highlights disruption. The editing style changes accordingly: whilst, in the first half of the film, Jeanne is allowed to finish her activities and turn off the light before the camera cuts to another scene, in the second part, it often cuts whilst she is still in the middle of an activity, thus creating a considerably more agitated rhythm (Margulies 1996: 77). Akerman presents the undoing of Jeanne's routine as a series of parapraxes, 'Freudian slips' (cit. in Kinder 1977: 7) as she calls them, in a further play with psychoana-lytical models of interpretation complementary to the Oedipal hints in the dialogues noted earlier. When the potatoes burn, Jeanne doesn't know what to do, walking up and down the kitchen in visible confusion. Later, she is shown struggling to write a response to her sister and abandoning her knitting after a comic thirty-second unfolding and refolding of the garment.

The third day sees an increasing build-up of the disordering process. Jeanne's daily activities and impeccable appearance are compromised: objects fall to the ground whilst she is cleaning shoes and polishing cutlery, her negligently open dressing gown prompts a disapproving comment from her son, the Post Office and shops are still closed as she sets out on her morning tour too early. A dreamy and brooding-looking Jeanne aimlessly wanders about her flat visibly not knowing what to do with herself, picking up objects only to put them down again almost immediately. Repeated looks at her alarm clock confirm that she is out of rhythm. Akerman has spectators share Jeanne's discomfort through long takes of her languidly sitting in her armchair, her hands nervously touching the pocket of her apron, as if some act of domesticity might help her iron out the creases that have appeared in her daily routine. 'The extended duration of the shots no longer points to a nondramatic action but starts to function as the locus par excellence of the drama's eruption' (Margulies 1996: 77).

Time, which was carefully contained in the first part, filled with a myriad of activities and tamed in strictly observed rituals, heavily makes itself felt as the character struggles to keep her composure.

For it is not the monotony of her tightly regulated existence that frightens Jeanne, it is free-floating, pulsating time that becomes her enemy – the Baudelaire poem, revealingly entitled 'L'Ennemi' (The Enemy), that Sylvain rehearses with his mother on the first evening, in a further figuration of the repressed, points to the character's conflicting relations with time in precisely the lines that are omitted: 'O douleur! O douleur! Le Temps mange la vie.'[24] As the regime of habit is disrupted, the reasons for Jeanne's wilful submission to an excessively ordered existence begin to become apparent: ritual for her seems to be, above all, a coping strategy, an attempt to control and displace anxiety. As Akerman explains: 'At the beginning, I thought I was simply telling the story of three days in the life of a woman, but later I realised that it was a film about occupying time to avoid anguish, to keep moving so as not to think about the fundamental thing, which is being' (cit. in Bergstrom 2003: 107).

The film narrative alludes to Jeanne's erupting autonomy, yet leaves her attempts at opening herself up to the world comically flawed: the baby she cradles for the first time screams and struggles against her clumsy befriending gestures. In the haberdashery shop, where she asks for buttons for her son's coat, she gives away intimate family details (a sequel to the Oedipal drama sketched out in the nightly conversations) in front of the politely smiling saleswoman. The uneven, unilateral distribution of address and misjudgement of social context in this scene, which creates a comically jarring effect, is part of Akerman's already observed wider defamiliarisation of speech and, as such, will be used again extensively in *Les Rendez-vous d'Anna*. When Jeanne finally enters the café, her usual table is occupied by another woman. The café scene is interesting for, in its presentation of an alternative view of womanhood, it holds out the possibility of different gender constructions even in a relatively repressive environment. Busily reading, writing and cigarette-smoking, the woman at the next table couldn't be more different from Jeanne: she is short-haired and grey, her gestures are pragmatic and efficient, her dress style is ungendered; she is visibly at ease with herself. Jeanne, on the contrary, with her dyed copper hair, impeccable clothing and mannered gestures, appears as the incarnation of a stifled, rather outdated femininity.

24 'Alas! Alas! Time eats away our lives.'

The film's climax, Jeanne's murder of the third client, addresses the enigma posed by the growing escalation of her routine without nonetheless resolving it. Whilst the inclusion of such a dramatic event (heavily criticised by experimental film-makers like Jonas Mekas) on a surface level makes the film engage with the structures of conventional narrative, the de-dramatised treatment of the event subverts commercial genre conventions and foregrounds their voyeuristic, sensationalist nature. A medium shot shows Jeanne undressing in front of her dressing-table mirror and carefully folding her blouse. The sexual act is clinical and mechanical: Jeanne has kept on her bra and undershirt; the client, on top of her, barely moves, yet her agitated movements, her struggle against the male body and repressed sighs leave no doubt that she has experienced an unwanted orgasm. For the first time, her face becomes intensely expressive, yet returns to its cryptic impassivity after the relief of tension. The next shot, taken through the mirror, shows her getting dressed while the client rests on the bed. She straightens her skirt, gets up, picks up a pair of scissors lying on the dresser, briefly leaves the frame then re-enters it to bend over her client and stab him in the throat. In the composition of the shot, the wedding picture on the dresser constitutes the foreground whilst the agonising man is relegated to the background in a disturbing visual linking of matrimonial life, prostitution and death. The gliding movement from skirt to scissors and the unspectacular depiction of the murder fuse the act into the homogenous depiction of a life where the singular and the habitual, banality and drama, share the same status.

The lack of motivation inherent in the murder scene gives rise to questions all the more vividly debated by critics because the film refuses to provide any answers: is the murder a response to Jeanne's sexual awakening, 'part of a desperate struggle to preserve the status quo in the face of forces that are threatening to change and overwhelm her' (Loader 1985: 336)? An act of liberation and revolt against patriarchal oppression? The abolition of the phallus after a moment of *jouissance* (Johnston 1985: 326)? Akerman herself insists on the murder's neutral status in the film narrative – 'it's neither positive nor negative, it just is. The murder is on the same level as all the other Freudian slips that happen after the visit of the second client' (cit. in Kinder 1977: 7) – but, at the same time, foregrounds its paradoxical status as the only gesture of freedom available to Jeanne: 'c'est sa dernière liberté de ne pas jouir'[25] (Akerman 2004: 88). The last seven-minute shot of a bloodstained Jeanne in the semi-darkness of her sitting room re-establishes stasis. Jeanne's face and body language, though subtly expressive, remain unfathomable, ungraspable, like the flicker that eerily lights the scene.

When the film was released in 1975, it immediately struck a chord with feminist film critics and audiences. In its immediate aftermath, *Jeanne Dielman* has provoked a wealth of feminist readings, focusing both on its subject matter and sketching out of a new feminine film language. The variety of responses, ranging from sociological to semiotic and psychoanalytical, testifies to the shift from first-generation (concerned largely with representations of women in film and their reflection of real life) to second-generation feminism (more concerned with the way woman is constituted in processes of cinematic signification) that occurred in the mid 1970s.[26] Jayne Loader's sociological and stylistic reading which identifies the main character as a victim of traditional bourgeois and patriarchal societies is typical of the first approach:

> [Jeanne] is presented as an automaton, geared for maximum efficiency and functioning perfectly, a victim of both the domestic science movement and the petit-bourgeois Belgian culture that produced her. The compulsiveness of Jeanne's housecleaning, the zeal with which she attacks crumbs and disorder, the serenity with which she accomplishes her tasks all point to a woman who has internalised the principle that 'neglect of housecleaning is tantamount to child abuse'. (Loader 1985: 330)

Within such a framework, Jeanne's compulsive obsession can be recuperated into a wider feminist critique of the alienating nature of housework and the socially and sexually repressive structures of bourgeois societies. It allows us to address Jeanne's ambiguous status as both victim and victimiser, castrated woman and castrating mother, repressive agent and conservative social force both in the home and in her role as a prostitute who 'perpetuates the sexual oppression of other women and leaves them and herself open to other forms of oppression' (Loader 1985: 335). Yet, whilst Loader commends the film's minute examination of housework and of the traditional role of

---

25 'it is her last freedom to not have an orgasm.'
26 For an overview of these shifts, see Kuhn (1994), pp. 72–8.

the mother in male-dominated bourgeois culture, at the same time, she strongly criticises the murder scene, which, according to her, is a 'cheap answer' to the complex social and political problem of female oppression (Loader 1985: 328 and 337–9).

Margulies has convincingly critiqued socially oriented feminist readings of the film in her book *Nothing Happens*. The problem with studies such as Loader's, she argues, is that they impose upon the film a teleology and ideological message which its opacity, circularity and deliberate avoidance of simple cause-and-effect patterns seem to eschew. Akerman's subversive play with type – 'Jeanne's repetitive routine reveals both the general category that she exemplifies (house-wife/prostitute) and the singularities, the individual tics, that make her a unique individual' (Margulies 1996: 143) – and various defamil-iarisation strategies create an 'exceptional typicality' (ibid.: 147) that resists categorisation. The film's complex layering, distanced stance and playful subversion of narrative codes and modes of interpretation signal its critical indeterminacy which eschews any easy interpretation.

For spectators today, rather than the sociological models which freeze the film in a specific historical time frame and social milieu (that is, the post-war petite bourgeoisie with its repressive patri-archal codes and values) and thus reduce the film to the status of historical document, what arguably remains of greater interest is the new representation of women that Akerman proposes in her film and its convergence with more theoretical questionings surrounding the possibility of a new feminine language for the cinema. An important reference point in books on feminist film criticism and women's writing (cf. Kuhn 1994 and Mayne 1990), *Jeanne Dielman* continues to be discussed mainly within the semiotic psychoanalyt-ical framework provided by Mulvey in 'Visual Pleasure and Narra-tive Cinema', published in the same year as the film's premiere at the Cannes Festival. Mulvey's main thesis in this polemical piece is that mainstream cinema heavily draws on the narcissistic and scopo-philic pleasures of the spectator. Aligning point of view with the male spectator, narrative cinema of the Hollywood type reduces woman to the mere status of 'to-be-looked-at-ness' while man is the active bearer of the gaze. Woman's appearance in commercial film is accordingly stylised and eroticised to enhance visual pleasure. Mulvey ends her article by calling for a different film-making practice that does not reduce woman to spectacle:

> The first blow against the monolithic accumulation of traditional film conventions (already undertaken by radical filmmakers) is to free the look of the camera into its materiality in time and space and the look of the audience into dialectics and passionate detachment. There is no doubt that this destroys the satisfaction, pleasure and privilege of the 'invisible guest', and highlights the way film has depended on voyeuristic active/passive mechanisms. (Mulvey 2000: 47)

Although Mulvey does not cite Akerman in the article, and there is no verifiable link between the two works, *Jeanne Dielman* appears like an almost literal realisation of the critic's vision. Whilst its subject matter – the detailed depiction of a woman's quotidian – does of course from the outset set it apart from the glamorous spectacle of mainstream female representation, the detached film style and distanced camera position also, as already mentioned, block spectator voyeurism, shifting the look towards the attitude of 'passionate detachment' Mulvey promotes instead. In her editing style, Akerman deliberately avoids the fragmentation of the female form and voyeurism typical of mainstream cinema:

> It was the only way to shoot that scene and to shoot that film. To avoid cutting the woman in a hundred pieces … cutting the action in a hundred places, to look carefully and to be respectful. You always know what point of view it is. It's always the same way … I didn't go too close, but I didn't go too far away … It was not a neutral look, … but the camera was not voyeuristic in the commercial way because you always know where I am. You know it wasn't shot through the keyhole. (Akerman 1977: 119)

Finally, the denial of privileged points of view through close-ups, zooms or point-of-view shots and the avoidance of shot/counter-shot further block character identification and thus make possible the setting up of a different relation of looking. Apart from its subject matter then, it is above all through its challenging of dominant processes of meaning construction, as critics like Annette Kuhn have shown, that *Jeanne Dielman* offers a new 'feminine language' for the cinema (Kuhn 1994: 174–5).

Whilst asserting that her film has been influenced by the women's movement and is feminist in subject matter and style (cf. Akerman 1977: 118; Dubroux 1977: 35), Akerman has distanced herself from exclusively feminist readings. In an interview with Scott MacDonald, though conceding that the film may have become feminist through

its critical reception, she singles out anxiety and conti
independent of a person's gender, as well as the portraya
existence as its main themes:

> My goal at the time was to show someone who organize
> that there is no hole in her time, because when there *is* a hole, there is
> also anxiety. I could have done that same film about a man, except that
> I was more interested in showing a woman's everyday gestures. I don't
> think it was feminist in the sense that many people have said – at least,
> a film about alienation because of gender was not my goal. Maybe the
> film *became* that, but for me *Jeanne Dielman* ... was more about letting
> everyday gestures exist in a film. (MacDonald 2005: 260)

In an interview with Alain Philippon, she more forcefully rejects
co-optation into a feminist discourse: 'Je ne me suis jamais dit que
j'allais faire un film qui allait servir de porte-drapeau au féminisme.
Mais aux USA, il a été très fort vécu comme ça. Pour moi, c'est
restrictif: le film implique plus de choses que ça'[27] (Philippon 1982: 22).
In conversation with Susan Barrowclough, finally, she states: 'When
people say there is a feminist film language, it is like saying there is
only *one* way for women to express themselves. But there should be
as many different ways as there are different kinds of women making
films' (Akerman 1984: 105). This unease about feminist interpretations of the film does of course not necessarily invalidate its creden-
tials as a feminist work – a film can be feminist tangentially even if
its author did not intend it as such (Kuhn 1994: 10). What it does
highlight, however, is Akerman's profound distrust of collective
representation and cautiousness with regard to essentialist defini-
tions of woman, a resistance to becoming absorbed into political or
theoretical discourses, which is concomitant with her individualistic
auteur stance: 'I am not making women's films. I'm making Chantal
Akerman's films' (Akerman cit. in Martin 1986: 62).

In the interview with Philippon, Akerman offers no further indica-
tions of what the film's 'plus de choses' might be, but one can, in
lieu of a conclusion, advance a hypothesis. Whereas most critics
attribute Jeanne's alienation and anxiety to her internalisation of a
repressive patriarchal order or to an obsessive-compulsive disorder

---

27 'I never said to myself that I was going to make a film which would serve as
standard-bearer for feminism. But in the US, it was very much seen like that.
For me, that is restrictive: the film implies more than that.'

(or both), the film does not in fact give any conclusive clues for such interpretations. Rather, the brief biography Jeanne sketches out for her son in the evening of day one seems to point to a trauma at a young age: at the liberation of Belgium in 1944, Jeanne is an orphan. The cause of her parents' death is not given. In interviews, Akerman has frequently stated that *Jeanne Dielman* pays homage to her mother to whom she wanted to give recognition (Kinder 1977: 3). The film makes no explicit allusion to the camps, yet, eleven years later, in *Golden Eighties*, Akerman casts the same Delphine Seyrig as a Holocaust survivor liberated by an American GI and unhappily married to a businessman. Her name is Jeanne. The autotextual[28] and autobiographical echoes lift the film out of its immediate space-time and endow it with a history which is obfuscated, but nonetheless alluded to from the beginning through the alarming sound of gas which accompanies the opening credits. The anxiety that needs to be contained in a tight ritualistic practice, the repressed that *Jeanne Dielman* so emphatically addresses in its formal politics, as in many of Akerman's later films, then, seems to be implicitly linked to the tragedy of Jewish extermination which, as critics have argued, is itself intimately bound up with the emergence of modernism in film (cf. Frodon 2007). Behind its minimalist style, Akerman's arguably finest *auteur* piece reveals disquieting layers of complexity.

The film-maker as nomad: *News from Home* and *Les Rendez-vous d'Anna*

What does a twenty-five-year-old, hitherto unknown director do after an unexpected international success? Rather than cashing in on the *Jeanne Dielman* formula, Akerman turned even further away from commercial film-making practices, deciding to make a more intimate film, 'hors tout, hors public'[29] (cit. in Dubroux et al. 1977: 35). Shot in New York in 1976, *News from Home* returns to the structural, experimental aesthetics first explored in *Hotel Monterey*, but for the first time closely interweaves a documentary style with an explicitly autobiographical content. An epistolary film and a travel diary, *News from Home* blends images of the city with the voice-over of letters from

---

28 'Autotextual' refers to cross-references in the oeuvre of an artist.
29 'outside everything, outside audiences.'

Akerman's mother translated into English and read by Akerman in a flat, yet rhythmical voice. The translation, as Tijana Mamula points out, is a strategy of appropriating the mother's letters and of deliberately distancing the mother figure (Mamula 2008: 269). The heavily accented voice with which the letters are read foregrounds Akerman's position as an exile, not yet fully assimilated in the US.

A modern 'Symphonie der Grosstadt',[30] indebted to cinema's silent era as much as to the American underground, the film explores run-down and affluent areas, subway tunnels, car parks, street markets and diners, soulless, bleak housing estates as well as the city's commercial and tourist districts. Interior shots in the underground alternate with exterior views of urban scenery, crowd scenes with images devoid of human presence and fixed-angle camerawork with tracking shots. The sound which accompanies the images is frequently desynchronised, adding further to the disjunction between sound and image created by the voice-over. Akerman offers neither a guiding narrative, nor dramatic structure or plot. Her filmed subjects move in and out of frame, trains and cars pass by and disappear, time and space interlock in a pure process of vision and continuous movement. As in *Hotel Monterey*, the highly formal aspect of the film narrative opens itself up to playful chance encounters when a filmed individual intermittently engages with the camera, making room for performance and improvisation. Akerman's own comments on the non-narrative, musical structure of her film intriguingly align her once again with Michael Snow who, in *Presents* (1981), will similarly opt for a rhythmical pattern inspired by music:

> Tu as envie de suivre une fiction parce que tu as été formée comme ça. Tout ce qui fait habituellement fonctionner le spectateur, c'est l'identification au personnage. Or, dans mon film, il n'y a pas de héros et pas de narration classique. Ça fonctionne ailleurs, sur des rythmes, des pulsations, sur le regard, une image en amène une autre, c'est comme dans la musique, tu sais des notes, là tu suis des images, tu ne peux faire qu'une chose, regarder, écouter, et cela te met en question comme spectateur.[31] (cit. in Storti 1977)

30 'Symphony of the Metropolis': the title of Walter Ruttmann's famous 1927 documentary on Berlin.

31 You want to follow a narrative because this is how you have been trained. Identification with the character is all that usually makes the spectator tick. Yet in my film there is no hero and no conventional narration. Things are happening elsewhere, in its rhythms, its pulsations, in the gaze. One image leads to another.

The serial accumulation of images, following no apparent logic or order, gives visual form to what emerges as one of the film's central themes: the absence of a well-defined centre in both the topography of the city and in the life of the director, a nomad between Europe and America, between the Old and the New World. The letters from the mother, written during Akerman's first stay in 1972, form the bridge between the two continents, linking the familiar with the unknown, past and present, home and abroad. The mother's worries about her faraway daughter, her tales of family members and social aspirations reach into the anonymity of the large city (the images we see belong to the daughter's reality, but are also part of the mother's imagination), yet are also constantly threatened with being erased by it. The diegetic sounds of the passing underground and of cars, the swelling concert of the city's multiple voices, repeatedly muffle the maternal voice, reducing it to a sheer soundscape, a spectral chant or lament. As in *Jeanne Dielman*, the flat performance of the address underlines the text's concrete materiality, its rhythmical qualities rather than its content which, like the images of the city, is repetitive and meandering.

Like *Jeanne Dielman* and *Les Rendez-vous d'Anna*, *News from Home* is a film about parental relations, an allegorical tale about the difficulty of emancipation and the weight of family and collective history. The mother's anguish about Chantal's well-being, her worries about her financial situation and her requests for a more frequent correspondence form a leitmotif in this oblique story of coming of age and independence. Her news about the family business's ills and fortunes and the parents' dreams of a small house of their own stand in stark contrast with Chantal's nomadic existence (the letters refer to her frequently changing addresses) and her choice of a life dedicated to art over the bourgeois demand for stability and economic security. The invisibility of the letter's addressee, hidden from the camera, and the defiance of the anonymous New Yorkers who, almost without exception, show a remarkable indifference towards the filming process, become metaphors for the daughter's growing detachment from family ties and gradual absorption into the cosmopolitan city, traditional haven for emigrant communities from all over the world. The increasing mobility of the camera which moves from initial fixed

It is like in music: there you know the notes, here you follow images; you can only do one thing, to look and to listen, and that challenges you as a spectator.'

shots to panning and tracking formally reflects, as Catherine Fowler remarks, Akerman's growing familiarisation with the New York city space (Fowler 2003: 79). The last shot, a long tracking shot from the Staten Island ferry to downtown Manhattan which slowly disappears in the mist, melancholically marks Akerman's departure from her adoptive home, a West–East trajectory inverse to that of her Polish Jewish ancestors, across *la mer* (the sea) to *la mère* (the mother).

The critical reception of *News from Home* was mixed, with a majority of critics complaining about the boredom the experimental film had induced in them, and a minority, including Louis Marcorelles in *Le Monde*, hailing it as another masterpiece. Akerman further developed her exploration of nomadism and exile in her last and most narrative film of the 1970s, the autofictional *Les Rendez-vous d'Anna*. The choice of an international cast, led by the ethereal and enigmatic Aurore Clément, one of Akerman's fetish actresses in the decades to come, and the co-production of French, Belgian and German producers underline the film's transnational theme and outlook. Twenty-eight-year-old Anna is a successful film-maker, a Belgian Jew living in Paris (Akerman does not hesitate to draw parallels with her own life, including the name of the protagonist, Anna, which, as she explains in *Autoportrait*, for a long time, she took to be her real first name [Akerman 2004: 44]) and, perhaps most importantly, a single woman who maintains her autonomy in the face of the more conventional forms of life that family, friends and lovers seek to impose on her. A relentless traveller who shuns domesticity and territorial belonging, Anna is a modern variation of the wandering Jew, a twentieth-century incarnation, as Marcel Marin explains, of a well-known character in Jewish folklore, the 'Luftmensch', a nomad and vagrant incapable of settling down (Marin 1978). Emblematically, the film takes her from Essen, where she is presenting a film, to Paris – a journey from East to West that recalls that of Akerman's family as well as the Ashkenazi Diaspora more generally. The recurrent images of trains, train stations and crowds laden with luggage, more than just marking a 'geography of passage' (cf. Bruno 2002: 100), as in her later documentary *D'Est* (1993), are discreetly haunted by Holocaust memories.

Anna's journey, Akerman insists, is not one of formation or initiation, nor is it a trajectory during which an individual seeks to reclaim his or her territorial roots. It is the journey of an exile, 'une nomade qui ne possède rien de l'espace qu'elle traverse. Qui n'a de relation

de pouvoir ni avec cet espace, ni avec les gens qu'elle rencontre'[32]
(Akerman 1982: 101–2). The locations which punctuate Anna's travels
are in themselves significant: Essen, industrial centre of the Ruhr
and home to the Krupp ironworks, producers of ammunition and
armament in both World Wars (Alfried Krupp's conviction on the
charge of his company's use of slave labour in the Nuremberg trials
and subsequent release and reinstatement during the Cold War is
exemplary of modern Germany's problematic relations to its Nazi
past); Brussels, the director's native city and her parents' adoptive
home; and Paris, Akerman's domicile since the 1970s. Though histor-
ically and autobiographically charged, none of the locations, except
some shots of Paris at the very end, are individualised. 'Non-lieux'
(non-places), as Marc Augé has called the non-distinct, suburban
zones and the soulless public places of transit (train stations, hotels,
motorways) found in all modern cities, they remain stations in the
character's wandering rather than places of grounding and anchoring.
No home is ever entered during Anna's journey: she stays in a hotel
room regardless of whether she is on business, with her mother in
Brussels or with her lover in Paris (cf. Bruno 2002: 100). Even her
flat, with its impersonal décor and sparse furnishings, evokes the
anonymity of travelling life.

At each stage of her journey, Anna meets a character – a German
man, her friend Ida, a stranger on the train, her mother, and her lover
Daniel – who voices his/her anxieties, history and aspirations in the
form of a long monologue and makes demands or projections on the
aloof young woman. It is through these encounters, which follow a
strictly serial, formal pattern, that Akerman meshes the personal with
the political, individual destinies with the history of Europe whose
tormented past and uncertain future form the backdrop to the fiction.
Each of Anna's interlocutors, some exiles like her, others more rooted,
brings to the film the dreams, values and plights of their generation
whilst, at the same time, articulating a deep existential malaise that
hovers over contemporary Europe. Through the combined stories
of Ida, a Polish Jew working in Germany after a period of exile in
Belgium, Anna's mother, who has gained economic prosperity in her
adoptive Brussels but is caught up in the current economic crisis,
an idealistic stranger who is about to settle in France, and Daniel, a

32 'a nomad who does not possess the space she traverses, who has no relation of
   power with either the space or the people she encounters.'

middle-aged man in existential crisis, Akerman draws a subtle picture of emigration and displacement, amnesia ('Il faut oublier l'histoire, tu sais',[33] recommends Ida) and false hopes ('On dit que la Belgique est un pays de cocagne',[34] says the stranger on the train), solitude, marital drama and general disarray. The people Anna encounters are, as Akerman explains, 'au bord de quelque chose',[35] they realise vaguely that the values on which they have constructed their lives are crumbling, yet they hold on to the edge, anguished and eager to share their unease. Their variations of Ida's 'tout ça va mal finir'[36] become a leitmotif of the pessimism of the era.

The encounter with Heinrich (Helmut Griem), a German man who seeks in Anna a new companion and mother for his child, but also a partner who will alleviate his distress and doubts, is the most revealing in historical terms and, to a certain extent, exemplary of the four other encounters. Heinrich has invited Anna for tea in his home in Bottrop, another industrial town in the Ruhr. Standing in the midst of an indistinct, dissociated urban zone, filmed in fixed camera, he delivers a hackneyed, stylised monologue (Akerman has her actors speak in the monotonous, litany-like tone we already know from *Jeanne Dielman*), a lament of his personal destiny as well as a fragmented, clichéd history of modern Germany.

Heinrich's story is that of millions of post-war Germans, critical of the Nazi past, yet unable to find meaning and responsibility in the new state. His platitudinous recital of key dates in German history, from 1920s Communism to Hitler's accession to power, the War, the division of Germany and post-war reconstruction, is a compendium of common knowledge devoid of personal reflection or insight. Symptomatic of a wider refusal amongst post-war Germans to assume responsibility or take up political agency, Heinrich refers to the nation's political leaders with an undifferentiated, impersonal 'ils' (they), whilst Germany is more personally addressed as 'mon pays' (my country). His final 'Qu'est-ce qu'ils ont fait de mon pays?',[37] sums up not only the moral malaise of the 1970s generation but the character's passivity and resignation in the face of rapid socio-economic and

33 'you have to forget history, you know.'
34 'they say Belgium is a land of Cockaigne.'
35 'on the edge of something.'
36 'it will all end badly.'
37 'what have they done to my country?'

political change. The possibility of revolt – after all, the film is set during the German terrorist crisis, the most tumultuous era in West Germany's young history –, evoked through the story of Heinrich's friend forced to leave the country after being accused of 'uncivil activities', likewise is reduced to an anecdotal tale of political injustice (cf. Margulies 1996: 159–60).

As already seen in *Jeanne Dielman*, the uneven distribution between silence and speech and a generalised mismatch between information content and information context (here the fact that Heinrich confides intimate details of his life to a near stranger) is symptomatic of a wider crisis of communication, underlined visually by the refusal of shot/ counter-shot in conversations. Throughout the film, Akerman sets up cliché-ridden 'talk-blocks' (Margulies 1996: 154) in opposition to Anna's silence, mapping through them the commonplaces and *doxas* of post-war Europe in which the young woman risks being trapped, but which she ultimately rejects, offering up instead her mobility and impenetrability as alternatives to the rigid value systems or lofty generalisations of her interlocutors. Anna lends a willing ear to her interlocutors, but refrains from engaging with their stories, and it is precisely her openness and non-judgement of them that makes their self-revelations possible. Her detachment, as Akerman explains, far from connoting indifference, is a refusal to exert power over others, to efface their difference and strangeness:

> Anna accueille [la] parole [de Heinrich] dans sa différence, dans son étrangeté. Elle aurait eu l'air beaucoup plus humaine si elle avait donné quelques signes pour effacer, résorber la différence. Elle aurait pu dire, par exemple, je vous comprends ... Elle aurait alors essayé une prise de pouvoir sur l'autre, je comprends donc je vous prends. Une tentative pour annuler la différence.[38] (Akerman 1982: 101)

Contrary to her interlocutors' persistent demands (married life and motherhood, a less itinerant, more settled life) and projections (the glamour and freedom of artistic life) on her person, Anna simply listens, but refuses to be bound by personal and societal expectations. In the Jewish context, as Margulies explains, her defence of female

---

38 'Anna receives Heinrich's words in their difference, in their strangeness. She would appear much more human if she showed some signs of effacing or reducing difference. She could have said, for instance, I understand you ... But she would thus have tried to take power over the Other: I understand, thus I take you – an attempt to abolish difference.'

independence, refusal of marriage and motherhood, and rejection of transmission, more than a feminist claim for freedom, become a transgression of Jewish tradition and family values (Margulies 2003: 66).

Whilst for most of the film Anna is an echo chamber for her interlocutor's dismay, during her reunion with her mother, she is, for the first time, granted her own voice. Lying naked with her mother (Lea Massari) in a shared double bed, Anna confides her loneliness, her dissatisfaction with casual heterosexual affairs and her adventure with a young woman. Lesbian love, tightly intertwined with the maternal bond in the film narrative – 'j'ai pensé à toï',[39] confesses Anna about her lesbian affair – forms a counterpoint to the repressive male-dominated structures internalised by the other characters, and maps out alternative, non-possessive models of love and sexual desire. The chiaroscuro shot of Anna cuddling up in her mother's arms stands in stark contrast to the coldness and distance of the scenes when Anna is finally reunited with her lover Daniel (Jean-Pierre Cassel) on her arrival in Paris. The hampered communication between the two lovers, modernist décor of the hotel room and towering high-rises seen through the window evoke Godard and Antonioni who, a decade earlier, have drawn similarly desolate portraits of lovers' incommunicability against the backdrop of the modern city. The bleak mood is barely lightened by Anna's recital of an Edith Piaf song ('Une chambre à louer') about two lovers committing suicide in a hotel room. For a brief moment, traditional gender roles and emotional barriers seem to break down – Daniel dreams of a more feminine rhythm in union with nature and his body, and Anna, for the first time, shows genuine concern when fetching medication for Daniel in the middle of the night –, yet the film ends on another scene of solitude: a lifeless, inexpressive Anna stretched out on her bed listening to her answering machine. The voice of an Italian woman, supposedly the lover whom she has been unsuccessfully trying to reach throughout her journey, tenderly asks 'Anna, dove sei?',[40] but the last words are given to a male friend, who complains about Anna's frequent absences. The film's *telos* thus brings no resolution, time is suspended and human communication mechanised, hetero- and homosexuality co-exist as possible relationship models, yet Anna's uncompromising celibacy seems to allow for none of them.

39 'I thought of you.'
40 'Anna, where are you?'

As with so many of Akerman's films, *Les Rendez-vous d'Anna* had a mixed reception: at the international Paris Festival in 1978, part of the audience booed the film – Akerman recalls rescuing the traumatised Aurore Clément from the projection room at the premiere –, but it deservedly received the prize for best *mise en scène*. Too demanding for a commercial public, yet considered by some critics an aesthetic compromise compared to her more experimental work, the film fared well under the somewhat deceptive label of 'European art film'. With the more narrative-oriented, autofictional *Les Rendez-vous d'Anna*, Akerman has certainly come a long way from the earlier structurally inspired works, yet the film's minimalist features (its formal sobriety, narrative structure based on serial accumulation, almost exclusive use of fixed camera with some occasional long tracking shots, continued refusal of reverse-angle shots and anti-naturalistic use of dialogue) are evidence of an uncompromising aesthetic vision that still borders on the experimental. The combination of a greater emphasis on narrative and a style still indebted to avant-garde film practices paves the way for the exuberant experiments of the 1980s.

References

Akerman, Chantal (2004), *Chantal Akerman: Autoportrait en cinéaste*, Editions du Centre Pompidou/Editions Cahiers du cinéma.

Akerman, Chantal (1984), 'Adventures in Perception', *Monthly Film Bulletin*, 51, pp. 104–5.

Akerman, Chantal (1982), 'Entretien avec Chantal Akerman', *Atelier des Arts*, Cahier 1, pp. 101–2.

Akerman, Chantal (1977), 'Chantal Akerman on *Jeanne Dielman*', *Camera Obscura*, 2, pp. 118–19.

Bergstrom, Janet (2003), 'Invented Memories', in Gwendolyn Audrey Foster (ed.), *Identity and Memory: The Films of Chantal Akerman*, Carbondale and Edwardsville, Southern Illinois University Press, pp. 94–116.

Blanchot, Maurice (1969), *L'Entretien infini*, Paris, Gallimard.

Blouin, Patrice (2004), 'Le 15/08', in *Chantal Akerman: Autoportrait*, p. 177.

Bruno, Giuliana (2002), *Atlas of Emotion: Journeys in Art, Architecture, and Film*. London, Verso.

Deleuze, Gilles (1989), *Cinema 2: The Time Image*, trans. Hugh Tomlinson and Robert Galeta, Minneapolis, University of Minnesota Press.

Dubroux, D., T. Giraud and L. Skorecki (1977), 'Entretien avec Chantal Akerman', *Cahiers du cinéma*, 278, pp. 34–42.

Fowler, Catherine (2004), 'Jeanne Dielman 23 Quai du Commerce 1080 Bruxelles', in Ernest Mathijs (ed.), *The Cinema of the Low Countries*, London, Wallflower, pp. 131–9.

Fowler, Catherine (2003), 'All Night Long: The Ambivalent Text of "Belgi-anicity"', in Foster (ed.), Identity and Memory, pp. 77–93.

Frodon, Jean-Michel (ed.) (2007), Le Cinéma et la Shoah. Un art à l'épreuve de la tragédie du 20ᵉ siècle, Paris, Editions Cahiers du cinéma.

Frodon, Jean-Michel (2004), 'Saute ma ville', in Chantal Akerman: Autoportrait, p. 172.

Giard, Luce (1998), 'The Nourishing Arts', in Michel de Certeau, Luce Giard and Pierre Mayol, The Practice of Everyday Life, vol. 2: Living and Cooking, trans. Timothy J. Tomasik, Minneapolis and London, University of Minnesota Press, pp. 151–69.

Goldberg, Rose Lee (1990), Performance Art: From Futurism to the Present, London, Thames and Hudson.

Johnston, Claire (1985), 'Towards a Feminist Film Practice: Some Theses', in Bill Nichols (ed.), Movies and Methods, vol. 2, Berkeley, University of Berkeley Press, pp. 315–27.

Kinder, Marsha (1977), 'Reflections on Jeanne Dielman', Film Quarterly, 30, pp. 2–8.

Kuhn, Annette (1994), Women's Pictures: Feminism and Cinema, London, Verso.

Loader, Jayne (1985), 'Jeanne Dielman: Death in Installments', in Nichols (ed.), Movies and Methods, vol. 2, pp. 327–40.

MacDonald, Scott (2005), A Critical Cinema: Interviews with Independent Filmmakers, Berkeley, University of California Press, vol. 4.

MacDonald, Scott (1988), A Critical Cinema: Interviews with Independent Filmmakers, Berkeley, University of California Press, vol. 1.

Mamula, Tijana (2008), 'Matricide, Indexality and Abstraction in Chantal Akerman's News from Home, Studies in French Cinema, 8, pp. 265–75.

Margulies, Ivone (2003), 'Echo and Voice in Meetings with Anna', in Foster (ed.), Identity and Memory, pp. 59–76.

Margulies, Ivone (1996), Nothing Happens: Chantal Akerman's Hyperrealist Everyday, Durham, Duke University Press.

Marin, Marcel (1978), Les Rendez-vous d'Anna. Dossier de presse.

Martin, Angela (1986), 'Chantal Akerman's Films: Notes on Issues Raised For Feminism', in Charlotte Brunsdon (ed.), Films for Women, London, British Film Institute.

Mayne, Judith (1990), The Woman at the Keyhole: Feminism and Women's Cinema, Bloomington, Indiana University Press.

Mulvey, Laura (2000), 'Visual Pleasure and Narrative Cinema', in E. Ann Kaplan (ed.), Feminism and Film, Oxford, Oxford University Press.

Philippon, Alain (1982), 'Fragments bruxellois. Entretien avec Chantal Akerman', Cahiers du cinéma, 341, pp. 18–23.

Reekie, Duncan (2007), Subversion: The Definitive History of Underground Cinema, London, Wallflower.

Rich, B. Ruby (1998), Chick Flicks: Theories and Memories of the Feminist Film Movement, Durham, Duke University Press.

Rosenbaum, Jonathan (1983), Film: The Front Line, Denver, Arden Press.

Sheringham, Michael (2006), Everyday Life: Theories and Practices from Surrealism to the Present, Oxford, Oxford University Press.

Siclier, Jacques (1976), '"Un film hyperréaliste sur l'occupation du temps"', *Le Monde*, 22 January, p. 15.

Sitney, P. Adams (1979), *Visionary Film: The American Avant-Garde 1943–1978*. 2nd ed. New York, Oxford University Press.

Sojcher, Frédéric (1999), *La Kermesse héroïque du cinéma belge*, vol. 2, *1965–1988*, *Le miroir déformant des identités culturelles*, Paris, L'Harmattan.

Storti, Martine (1977), 'Un entretien avec Chantal Akerman', *Libération*, 20 June.

Turim, Maureen (2003), 'Personal Pronouncements in *I…You…He…She* and *Portrait of a Young Girl at the End of the 1960s in Brussels*', in Foster (ed.), *Identity and Memory*, pp. 9–26.

Tyler, Parker (1995), *Underground Film: A Critical History*, New York, Da Capo Press.

2

The golden 8os:
performance, parody, identity

Akerman has often provocatively declared that films should only be
made with either a very small or a big budget: 'Entre les deux, ça
fait des films ... entre les deux!'[1] (Philippon 1982a: 20). By the late
1970s, having reached such a degree of sophistication in her exploration of a specific style (minimalism) and subject matter (the relations
between time and space, the quotidian, body language) that she
herself could declare she had 'come to an end' (ibid.), she was not
only ready for stylistic and thematic change but eager to reach out to
a wider audience than that accessible to a director of experimental or
art-house movies. Just how radical a break she was envisaging can be
measured in her (unfortunately unfinished) project of adapting Isaac
Bashevis Singer's novels *The Manor* (1967) and *The Estate* (1969), two
epic tales of Polish Jews in the latter half of the nineteenth century,
both rich in psychological, social and historical detail and containing
a wealth of characters, that is, narratives that are placed at the very
antipodes of Akerman's own sparsely populated films. With the
collaboration of Eric de Kuyper (who would later also co-script *La
Captive* and *Demain on déménage*), Akerman prepared a two-volume
script for the planned adaptation, obtained the film rights from
Singer, and flew to Los Angeles in an attempt to raise funding for the
$30 million project (for comparison, *Les Rendez-vous d'Anna* cost a
mere $600,000, but having only been seen by 40,000 people, was a
financial flop). However, once in Beverley Hills, it quickly dawned on
her that not only was she, as a European independent director reputed
for her avant-garde work, a total alien to the industry but that Singer

---

1 'Working between small and big budgets produces ... in-between films.'

also, despite his 1978 Nobel Prize, remained virtually unknown in Hollywood circles (in *Family Business*, a short made for Channel 4, Akerman comically transposes her Hollywood tribulations to a family scenario, whereby in Los Angeles, she is looking for a rich uncle to produce her work).

After three months of unfruitful meetings, Akerman abandoned what she herself ironically calls her *Autant en emporte le vent chez les juifs*[2] (Akerman 2004: 48), but did take to heart a suggestion by Hollywood producer Alan Ladd Jr (the producer of *Star Wars* and some very successful Hollywood comedies) to do a 'little comedy', instead of her epic historical fresco. It is indeed the comic mode, inflected in many different forms, that dominates her feature-length output in the 1980s, from *Toute une nuit* (1982), an effervescent study of urban love, to the musical comedy *Golden Eighties* (1986), her major film of the decade. In between these two milestone films, which form a diptych, the director shot various less ambitious (but no less interesting) works: *Les Années 80* (1983), an experimental film documenting the casting and rehearsing of *Golden Eighties* and intended as a pilot to raise money for the costly musical; *L'Homme à la valise* (1983), an autobiographically inspired burlesque portrait of a difficult cohabitation between the director and a male friend; plus a documentary on German choreographer Pina Bausch, and three shorts – the already mentioned *Family Business*, *J'ai faim, j'ai froid* and *Lettre d'une cinéaste: Chantal Akerman* (all 1984). The decade closes with *Histoires d'Amérique* (1988), a film on Jewish immigrants in New York, which boldly mixes comic and tragic registers.

The fictional work of the 1980s, whilst signalling an important change of mood, also marks a crucial shift in Akerman's cinematic language: as critics have noted, it constitutes a bold departure from the cinema of anti-seduction of the preceding decade towards an exploration of a more narrative-led cinema of attraction (Fowler 2000). Formally, her films in this period soften the rigorous syntax of her earlier output – fixed-angle shots, extended duration, strictly symmetrical compositions of the frame –, in favour of a lighter, more dynamic and supple camerawork. Cross-fertilisation with modern dance, especially the 'dance theatre' of German choreographer Pina Bausch, and the extensive use of music and song, explored to the full

2 'Jewish *Gone with the Wind*'.

in *Les Années 80* and *Golden Eighties*, lend her work a playfulness and spontaneity that sets it apart from the more controlled, minimalist work of the previous decade. In tune with the post-modern sensibility of the period, Akerman wholeheartedly embraces the vivacity of popular culture to create a new cinema of enchantment without, as we shall see, renouncing some of the recurrent formal principles characteristic of her work, notably, serial accumulation. Whether it is in the genres of melodrama, musical comedy, slapstick or docufiction, Akerman confirms herself as a radical innovator of forms who preserves a considerable degree of experimentation even when venturing into more commercial territory.

Fragments of a lover's gestures: *Toute une nuit*

In the interview with Alain Philippon already mentioned, Akerman airs her annoyance with the prevailing depressive mood of the late 1970s and early 1980s and expresses her eagerness to counteract it (Philippon 1982a: 22). The Brussels-based *Toute une nuit*, an upbeat, sparkling comedy on love and desire in the city is her first experimentation with a popular, light-hearted theme and with a less ascetic and controlled film style. Contrary to the earlier works, where all aspects of a film's genesis were carefully planned and mastered, Akerman here, for the first time, works in a more heuristic, improvised fashion. Rather than preparing a full script, the director made use of disparate notes and fragments which she had jotted down in the summer of 1980, but had not initially planned for filmic exploitation. The film was shot and edited intuitively, privileging rhythmical over narrative or structural considerations: 'on a conçu le film très musicalement: on écoutait les images (sans les sons) aussi bien qu'on les regardait'[3] (Philippon 1982a: 21).

Compared to her earlier minimalist formula of films shot 'dans une chambre avec deux personnages'[4] (Philippon 1982a: 20), *Toute une nuit* seems an enormous project, despite its very tight budget: the cast consists of some eighty characters played by professional (including Aurore Clément and Jan Decorte from her earlier movies) as well as

---

3 'We devised the film very musically: we listened to images (without sound) just as much as we looked at them.'
4 'in a room with two characters.'

non-professional actors (mainly friends of the director and members of the crew, but also her mother, Natalia Akerman, who appears in the cameo of a woman enjoying a cigarette in front of her house until she is called back in by her daughter). The frequent change of locations creates the illusion of a multitude of spaces, yet the film is essentially set in three neighbourhoods that reflect Brussels' diverse social geography: the rue des Minimes, a working-class, predominantly immigrant neighbourhood to the north of the historic city centre; the Place de la vieille halle aux blés, a more affluent, but, in the 1980s, still socially mixed area between the Grande Place and the chic Sablons district; and the Valkendal, the middle-class residential suburb where Akerman's parents lived at the time. Most of the domestic interior shots were taken in her parents' house and that of their neighbours, as well as in the art nouveau block of Akerman's producer and friend, Marilyn Watelet, facing the Place de la vieille halle aux blés. Caroline Champetier, the director of photography for *Toute une Nuit*, likens the miracle of the film's protean space to the trickery and cinematic magic of one of the pioneers of the early cinema, Georges Méliès.[5] Akerman herself, stressing the film's departure from realist conventions, describes it as a 'fantasy movie' (Philippon 1982a: 20).

Toute une nuit is a hymn to the night, privileged territory of dreams and the imagination, the proverbial time of the lover and of passion, an alternative time-space where emotions can be lived to the full: 'The night is more unreal, more surreal; at night melodrama can come through, but in the morning, ordinary life starts again' (Akerman 1984: 104). Shot between dusk and sunrise, the film captures the longings and encounters of several dozens of Brussels citizens, a heterogeneous, restless urban crowd animated by an unquenchable thirst for love, passion and adventure. In the domesticity of their homes, in semi-deserted bars and cafés, as well as an array of transitional spaces (dark streets and city squares, public stairwells and lobbies), couples form and separate, strangers awkwardly fall into one another's arms or abruptly take flight. This highly stylised and unashamedly sentimental urban carnival of amorous endeavours unfolds in the course of a sultry summer's night ('*Toute une nuit*') before being brought to a close by a thunderstorm which alleviates the (metaphorical and literal) heat and brings a return to routine and normality.

---

5 'Entretien avec Caroline Champetier, directrice de la photographie', included in DVD *Toute une nuit* (Cahiers du cinéma, collection '2 films de').

In an experiment with alternative forms of narrative construction, Akerman subjects the film narrative to a systematic fragmentation. The wider temporal unit of the night that is the film's frame of reference is shattered into a myriad of micro-narratives, each of only a few minutes' duration, a series of vignettes that dramatise the lovers' experience. It is less the characters, who appear and disappear seemingly at random, than their actions and attitudes – their gestures in the grammar of love – that structure the film narrative and give it coherence. Conventional plot is replaced by serial structures which, with some variation, repeat the same essential motifs of emotional tension: lovers wait impatiently or unite; newly formed couples experience the brief ecstasy of a furtive encounter; women, girls and even children secretly escape into the hot summer's night; sleepless men languish in overheated apartments – so many archetypical situations of love and longing, which, whilst representative of the lover's gest, nonetheless remain intensely personal. These individual dramas of desire, promise, disaffection and new beginnings are organised around three choreographed dance scenes that punctuate the narrative and give it a musical-like feel. Visual motifs like Aurore Clément's bright red attire, later brought to mind in a piece of crimson cloth draped over a tailor's table, create a further network of analogies and echoes.

The fugue-like structure and more rapid, rhythmical editing endow the film with a fluidity in keeping with its effervescent subject matter. As Margulies asserts, in making *Toute une nuit*, Akerman had a double challenge: to give a new lease of life to one of the most celebrated, but also most hackneyed themes in film – love – and to use techniques borrowed from structural and minimal film (serialisation, extended duration, fixed camera angles), traditionally associated with elite intellectual culture, for the expression of a popular subject matter. Shunning the conventional plot structure of conflict, climax and resolution favoured by commercial cinema, Akerman concentrates instead on seminal moments in the lover's experience – embrace, longing, parting – 'rescu[ing]', in the words of the critic, 'singularity and energy precisely where the pressure of convention has turned the representation of love into cliché' (Margulies 1996: 174).

The first establishing shots of the city and its inhabitants seem to promise a narrative where individual stories will eventually interlink and form a unified whole (a model much in vogue amongst

contemporary directors like P. T. Anderson or Alejandro González
Iñárritu) yet, most of the film's characters never reappear, and the
destinies of those who do, such as Aurore Clément in the role of a
woman caught in a love triangle, remain unresolved. No one character
is allowed centrality: even Clément, who is the film's most easily recognisable actor, appears only after four scenes and is granted little more
filmic time than lesser-known or non-professional actors. Where
traditional cinema would carefully weave together a story, Akerman
strips everything back to the bare bones, constructing an anthology
of the loving experience reduced to its most essential moments, the
'highlights' of melodrama and romantic comedy: 'As couples meet
and separate, arrive and depart, fall in and out of each other's arms,
it is like seeing about thirty films, one after another, without all the
conventional elaboration of plot and character to detract from their
cumulative effect' (Barrowclough 1984: 103).

The presence of a multitude of characters of varying social and
ethnic backgrounds, age groups and sexual preferences, as well as
the acute attention to interiors and costumes as predominantly social
signifiers, give the film an exemplary character that, on a surface
level, seems to align it with the ethnographic, social documentaries
developed in France in the course of the 1950s and 1960s by directors
such as Jean Rouch and Edgar Morin under the name of *cinéma vérité*.
Yet, the bold stylisation of the scenes and their exuberant theatricality
belie the purportedly objective format of the documentary genre. The
inclusion of a little girl, leaving the parental home with cat and suitcase
in tow, the last in a series of characters seduced by the lure of the
city and the sultry summer's night, ironically shows that Akerman's
series, though seemingly exhaustive and all encompassing, shun in
fact any form of exemplarity or communitarian representation. As
in *Jeanne Dielman*, we are faced with an 'exceptional typicality': each
individual, though sharing behavioural patterns with others, retains
his or her irreducible singularity and mystery, a fact underlined by the
idiosyncrasies of many of the characters and situations – the second
dance which pairs a tall man in his thirties with a petite, childish-
looking teenager in the old-fashioned décor of a deserted bar exploits
this a-typicality to considerable comic effect.

Toute une nuit, then, playfully flirts with a number of genres: the
social documentary, whose quest for exemplarity it pastiches; structural and minimal film, with which it shares its stripped-down, serial

structure; and the city symphony film, which similarly seeks to render urban multiplicity through an exploded structure (Margulies 1996: 176). Yet, its greatest affinity, manifestly, lies with theatre and dance, or, more precisely, with 'dance theater', the creative fusion between the two art forms invented by German choreographer Pina Bausch. It is no mere coincidence that, one year after *Toute une nuit*, Akerman should complete a television documentary on Bausch's work for the series *Repères sur la modern danse*. Akerman's choreography of longing and passion, her insistence on the crude violence, yet also the lyrical fragility of the lover (kidnapping and harassment are as much part of the lover's gest in *Toute une nuit* as tender affection and timid admiration), the rhythmic oscillation between stillness and excess, repetition and improvisation, share with Bausch a profound interest in the corporeal language of the desiring body. When a man in the Valkendal suburb walks out on his lover, managing to free himself from her grip only to then grab hold of her again, one is instantly reminded of the disturbing couple from *Café Müller* (1978), one of Bausch's most famous pieces, who relentlessly reiterate the same gesture of locking and unlocking bodies.

The soft lighting and dominance of blue and red colour schemes (carrying with them obvious connotations of dream and passion) give *Toute une nuit* a distinctly dreamlike, anti-naturalist feel. In one of the outdoor shots, a lit plaster statue of Cupid, eerily poised in a dark residential garden, with his arrows ready to fly, symbolically inscribes the filmic action in the realm of magic and fable. The graininess of the image (the film was shot on 16mm which, when blown up, looks less finished than 35mm), the fragility of the pictorial frames, and the chiaroscuro lighting, which snatches snippets of vibrant life out of the dark Brussels night, create an impression of 'magic realism' intensified by the diegetic sound (the multi-layered noise of the city, the storm and thunder) which is rendered all the more effective since dialogue is pared down to the essential ('Je vous aime', 'Pas ce soir',[6] etc.). Indeed, some of the film's tensions and dramas are exclusively aural, as, for instance, when we hear a young woman shriek on the Place de la vieille halle aux blés, yet never see her nor discover its cause. Catherine Fowler has helpfully compared the film's aesthetic with Belgian surrealist painting, especially Magritte, with whom Akerman shares

6 'I love you', 'Not tonight'.

the trope of the night and the defamiliarisation of everyday gestures, and with the films of Belgian director André Delvaux which, in turn, evoke the work of the magical realist painter Paul Delvaux:

> Much of the subjunctive mood is evoked through Akerman's use of the night, a trope familiar from Magritte who plays with the concealment which low light offers, and it is this use of the night which lends the film a mood of presence and immediacy. Consequently, the single-couple sequences act like close-ups in which, as in Magritte's images, everyday gestures are enlarged to revue-like proportions, or analysed in intimate detail. Equally, the city is created as a space in which gestures are always grandiose and weighted with emotion, since they are freed from the cold, analytical light of day. (Fowler 2003: 82–3)

When day breaks, the languorous city returns to normality and routine: a middle-aged wife who had left her husband slips back into the marital bed seconds before the alarm clock rings, the character played by Aurore Clément dances with a man she no longer loves and eight times whispers 'oui' (a comic reminder of the film's serial pattern) into the telephone. The swelling noise of the city drowns out the sighs of lovers as the magic blue colour of the night cedes to the ashen grey of morning.

To understand how *Toute une nuit* relates to the broader cultural concerns of the time, it may be useful to briefly frame it in the context of the new discourses of the body and of sexuality that began to emerge on the European and North American philosophical and cultural scenes in the late 1970s and 1980s. Critics have noted *Toute une nuit*'s affinities with Roland Barthes's celebrated *A Lover's Discourse: Fragments* (1977), a 'grammar' of love composed of thematic fragments which analyse seminal moments of the lover's experience (jealousy, the awakening of desire, mourning for the lost lover, etc.) in both personal experience and cultural artefacts, especially literature. The film is also contemporaneous with the first volume of Michel Foucault's *The History of Sexuality* (1976), and with a more widespread interest in the desiring subject and in the body as an object of scholarly enquiry, especially in the academic field known as 'Cultural Studies'. Intellectually, this eruption of desire into Western academic disciplines is one of the signs of the move from structuralism, the system of thought that dominated cultural life in the 1960s and early 1970s, to post-structuralism and, more widely, of the emergence of a post-modern consciousness with its new emphasis on play, eclecticism and self-referential irony. Though structuralism as a movement in film should not be confused with the philosophical movement of the same name, it can nonetheless be argued that *Toute une nuit* holds an intermediary place between a structuralist aesthetics and a post-modern[7] one. The film's more playful, dynamic style announces the exuberant experiments of *Golden Eighties*, yet its ongoing preoccupation with the language of the body and use of serialised structures also signal continuity rather than drastic rupture. As Deleuze suggests, the move from hieratic posture to a burlesque ballad of the loving body points to a new mood rather than a radically new vision in Akerman's work (Deleuze 1989: 196).

The musical as post-modern experiment: *Les Années 80*

Born of the need to raise funds for her costly musical project set in a Brussels shopping mall, *Les Années 80* is both a draft for what, at the time, was still called *La Galerie* and an experimental film in its own right, released three years prior to the finished musical. Though received very positively – Dave Kehr of the *Chicago Reader* called it 'one of 1983's ten best movies', J. Hoberman from the *Village Voice* hailed it as 'Akerman's most playful, purely pleasurable film' – it remains one of Akerman's lesser-known works owing largely to the fact that it is not available on DVD. Though in principle a 'making of' *Golden Eighties*, *Les Années 80*, in a reversal of the habitual order, was released *before* rather than with or after the finished product – Gwendolyn Foster, drawing on post-modernist philosopher Baudrillard, calls it a 'simulacrum', that is, a copy without an original (Foster 2003: 132); Jerry White describes it as a 'deconstruction' of *Golden Eighties* (White 2005: 56) – and was directed by Akerman herself, rather than by a third party, as is the convention for this type of film (in comparison, the documentary on the making of *Jeanne Dielman*, included in the box set of Akerman's films from the 1970s, was shot by Sami Frey). Only superficially concerned with documenting the genesis of *Golden Eighties*, *Les Années 80* is, above all, a film about cinematic process, the moulding of reality into fiction which the director herself has

7 Post-modern cinema, like post-modern literature, is characterised by self-referentiality, a playful dialogue with past forms and genres, as well as an increased use of parody and pastiche and a blurring of high and low art.

signalled as the film's nexus: 'Comment, entre le scénario toujours irreprésentable et sa future représentation, vont peu à peu s'organiser les différents éléments du réel jusqu'à donner un film? Comment, avec du réel, on arrive à la fiction'[8] (Akerman 1983).

The film opens on a black screen. An unseen actress rehearses a line: 'A ton âge, un chagrin, c'est vite passé'.[9] Akerman, in voice-over, gives detailed instructions on how to perfect intonation and delivery. This coaching scene involving the director and one of her lead actors, from the outset, highlights the self-reflexive nature of the enterprise – a film whose main content is its own coming into being – whilst at the same time presenting its thematic focus as one of the oldest and most popular narratives of the cinema: love and loss. We are literally in the midst of a rehearsal (revealingly called *répétition* in French), but also, metaphorically, in the domain of the repeated: the *déjà vu* and *déjà entendu* of the love story, whose language and grammar the director will set out to playfully deconstruct. The presence of the black screen, which disturbingly denies visual pleasure to the viewer, from the outset points to the film's subversive approach, suggesting, as Lucy Fischer has argued, that, 'in *The Eighties*, the notion of theatrical spectacle will be revised' (Fischer 1989: 162).

The film's first part, shot in video, consists of footage of auditions and rehearsals for *Golden Eighties*. Apart from a sequence revolving around Aurore Clément reading out love letters whilst selling drinks and ice-cream in a snack bar, there are no settings yet, though it is evident from the dialogues and songs that the film will be set in a shopping mall. The second part, a mere fifteen minutes at the end entitled 'The Project', offers key scenes and fully choreographed song and dance numbers, shot in 35mm, that serve as a showcase of the planned musical to potentially interested producers. Typical of a 'behind the scenes' approach, the first part foregrounds what conventional narrative film endeavours to dissimulate: the collective work effort and substantial coaxing behind the smooth and perfect fictions sold by the Hollywood dream factory. Whilst offering fascinating insights into Akerman's precise and highly involved style of direction, this 'creative laboratory' part thus also playfully debunks the

---

8 'How do the different elements of the real, between the always unrealisable screenplay and its future realisation, organise themselves until they build into a film? How with elements of the real is fiction fashioned?'

9 'At your age, sorrows are soon over.'

illusory nature of film entertainment, which is traditionally offered to the spectator in the form of a seamless, perfect spectacle, highlighting instead process, performance and simulation.

The audition and rehearsal part of the film deals a blow to the star system by showing that actors are almost as easily exchangeable as roles, props and costumes: the slender, blonde Aurore Clément, who was initially cast as the romantic owner of the mall's snack bar, gives as moving a performance as the curvaceous brunette Myriam Boyer who eventually replaced her in *Golden Eighties*; Robert, the film's central male love interest, is at times played by a self-important and mannered-looking actor in his mid-forties, at others by an attractive youngster; the actress for the Lili character is in turns auburn, blonde or dark-haired, in her twenties or thirties, but Lili is always played as a *femme fatale*, a type rather than individual. Contrary, then, to what the Hollywood star system would make viewers believe, there is no natural match between actor and role. The director's considerable creative input into aspects of characterisation and delivery – her involvement goes as far as to record songs in her own voice as a model for her actors – furthermore belies the idea that the lead actor is the driving force in a film and gives the musical, a film form naturally associated with the Hollywood studio system, a distinctly *auteurist* slant.

The film's fragments, though hinting at a story, do not yet build into a coherent narrative. When the singer Lio, who holds one of the lead roles in both the 'making of' and the finished feature, repeats 'Je l'aime, je l'aime tant ... C'est elle qu'il aime',[10] we understand that the film will revolve around a love triangle, yet the indexical pronouns ('il, 'elle') have no direct equivalent in the narrative. The isolated gestures, poses and dialogues, rather than serving traditional plot and character construction, above all, playfully foreground the highly codified nature of the romantic musical, whose emotional excess and melodramatic bent Akerman will both adopt and lay bare. In an early statement of intent for the film, the director states: 'While leaning on "sociologically precise" facts, we have not hesitated to push situations towards the melodrama – to use old vaudeville procedures such as recognitions, pursuits, confusing quarrels, quid pro quos ... but we are also intent on tearing away the cliché' (cit. in Margulies 1996: 185).

---

10 'I love him, I love him so much ... It's her that he loves.'

Like *Toute une nuit*, *Les Années 80* unashamedly foregrounds sentimentality through a camp aesthetics of excess. In the rehearsal with Lio, Akerman pushes the young woman to 'faire passer l'émotion'.[11] Close-ups on the actors' faces render visible the hyperbolised gestures of the loving body, whilst schmaltzy love ballads celebrate the intensity of the lover's emotion ('Plus rien n'existe, plus rien ne compte ...'[12]) and gritty chorus pieces warn of the dangers of amorous infatuation and make ironic the choice of love object ('c'est une tigresse, elle roule les fesses', 'il est beau, c'est un idiot'[13]). In the song rehearsals, it is always less the quality of the singing (which is often shaky) than the emotion that is put into the delivery that matters (Margulies 1996: 189). Akerman herself joins in this performance of excess when directing an actress during the recording of a song, gesturing wildly, humming in tune and spinning round on her toes. When she herself records the same song, her performance is similarly invested with affect and burlesque intensity. As we will see in greater detail in the finished musical, at the heart of the film lies once again Akerman's critical engagement with recycled ideas and modes of being: male and female behavioural codes; received ideas and expectations about love, womanhood and the relation between the sexes; social stereotyping and cultural conditioning. The repeated acts and mechanics of rehearsal, as Foster has pointed out, not only playfully debunk the conventions of melodrama and romantic musical, they foreground the constructed nature of gendered performance, thus giving a feminist slant to the highly codified musical form (Foster 2003: 132–3). J. Hoberman similarly draws attention to the film's feminist dimension when he describes *Les Années 80* as 'a movie about how women learn to play their roles – as lovers, workers, "women", and movie directors ... No less than *Jeanne Dielman*, *Les Années 80* is a film about the female condition' (Hoberman 1991: 149). Yet, the deconstructive enterprise is double-edged as indicated in Akerman's statement of intent above. *Les Années 80* both parodies and draws on the conventions of the romantic musical: it playfully lays bare the recycled nature of language, thought and behaviour, but also celebrates the intensity of the lover's emotion, instilling a camp humour into the over-codified genres of the melodrama and the musical, and giving a new lease of

11 'transmit the emotion.'
12 'Nothing exists anymore, nothing counts.'
13 'she's a tigress, she rolls her bottom', 'he's beautiful, he's an idiot'.

life to the outdated genre of the love ballad. Pleasure – visual, narrative and aural – is not denied at all, but, typical of Akerman's approach
in general, finds alternative forms of expression in an unorthodox
dialogue with the dominant film form against which she continues
to position her work.

Les Années 80 eschews easy classifications and transcends fixed
genre boundaries: somewhere between documentary and fiction,
'making of' and commercial pilot, experimental and deconstructive
film, it foregrounds above all its own hybridism, manifest visually
in the move from video to 35mm in the last fifteen minutes which
transforms the rehearsal into a simulacrum of the finished product.
In its self-reflexive debunking of the mechanics of illusion, its bold
mixing of formats, eclectic juxtaposition of rough draft and polished
product, deconstruction of stable notions of character and gender
and, perhaps most importantly, its flirtation with popular culture
(love life in a shopping mall) and popular genres (the musical and the
melodrama), *Les Années 80* reveals a distinctly post-modern sensitivity.[14] Its setting in a mall, the quintessential space of 1980s consumer
culture, and its explicit linking of love and economics further align it
with post-modernism, the new aesthetic and philosophical paradigm
that emerged in the wake of post-war, post-industrial societies and
which, as critics like Fredric Jameson and Mike Featherstone have
argued (Jameson 1992; Featherstone 1990), is inseparably bound up
with consumerism and late capitalism.

Les Années 80 ends on a panning shot of Brussels at dusk, with the
director thanking contributors and listing the film's credits in voice-
over, which establishes an implicit link with the beginning of *Toute
une nuit*. The former ends where the latter takes off: day and night,
public and private spheres constitute the two panels in Akerman's
playful diptych of the lover's experience. Yet Akerman's closing words
'Next Year in Jerusalem', the traditional conclusion of the Yom Kippur
service and the Passover Seder, announce a Jewish dimension to the
film that will be unveiled only in *Golden Eighties*.

---

14 For a brief but excellent survey of the characteristics of post-modernism, see
   Peter Brooker's introduction to the volume of essays *Modernism/Postmodernism*
   (1992).

Paranoia as comedy: *L'Homme à la valise*

In 1981, the Institut National de l'Audiovisuel commissioned from various film-makers, including Chantal Akerman, sixty-minute feature films for its series 'Télévision de chambre'. The film-makers had free play in their choice of subject, except for one constraint: the fiction should be set in one single space. Akerman decided to present an anecdote from her own life, her involuntary cohabitation with a friend who had failed to vacate the flat she had lent him while she was away from Paris. The film's title, *L'Homme à la valise*, whilst introducing the idea of nomadism which is one of its central themes, also alludes to the eponymous English television series, a spy story in thirty episodes that was broadcast in France in the early 1970s.

The film mimics classical drama in its strict observation of the unity of place (the director's flat), time (twenty-eight days of cohabitation) and action (no subplots). Characters are reduced to a minimal two: Akerman playing herself and the American actor Jeffrey Kime in the role of the friend Henri who continues to squat in her flat after her return. In its blending of autobiography and fiction (the director playing herself, her friend being played by an actor) and its distanced approach to the self (Akerman plays a caricatured version of her own persona rather than her real self) the film once again blurs genre boundaries and foregrounds the fluid interface between lived reality and cinematic representation. The fact that it is set in the same apartment as the closing sequence of *Les Rendez-vous d'Anna* – thus creating a self-conscious autotextual link between the two works – renders the film's representational status even more complex: as some sort of a sequel to the earlier film, *L'Homme à la valise* offers another incarnation of Akerman the film-maker, at once closer to autobiography, in that the director herself plays the lead role, yet also distanced through the chosen film style of burlesque comedy. The elegant Aurore Clément in *Les Rendez-vous d'Anna* and the deliberately clumsy female character in *L'Homme à la valise* appear as two versions of the director, one idealised, the other comically distorted – performative doubles of the self which Akerman playfully recreates in an autofictional mode.

The film begins with an intertitle reminiscent of the conventions of silent movies, but also of Godard's anti-illusionist counter-cinema strategies: '1er jour. Après deux mois d'absence pendant lesquels j'avais prêté mon appartement à un ami, je rentre chez moi pour travailler'.[15] The first shots show Akerman returning to her (fictional) flat and re-appropriating the domestic space in a series of ritualistic actions: she opens the shutters, curtains and windows, puts down her bag, takes a bath and examines the kitchen. This reclaiming of territory is presented essentially as a corporeal act: the body, step by step, readapts to a space that has become unfamiliar and rediscovers the gestures to inhabit it (Tomasovic 2004: 192). Objects that have been left by the friend are examined with caricatured suspicion (Akerman sniffs butter in the fridge) and comically disposed of (she throws a towel out of the bathroom window). Scenes from *Les Années 80* which she watches on a video screen in the sitting room – another playful autotextual and autobiographical reference – indicate to the spectator familiar with her filmography that she is preparing her musical *Golden Eighties*. Having reconquered her living space, the director puts paper in her typewriter, ready to get back to her working routine.

The second intitle explicitly announces her project: '2ème jour, Je me prépare à écrire'.[16] An identical sequence to that of the film's beginning shows Akerman about to open the flat's main door. Yet just as she puts the key into the lock, the door is opened by a tall man who greets her with an embarrassed smile. This encounter triggers a frantic series of actions that become increasingly deranged as the narrative unfolds. Akerman, filmed in accelerated mode, changes around furniture, installs a temporary desk, rescues the typewriter and takes refuge in her bedroom. Her reappropriation rituals have been in vain. Unable to write until the friend is gone, she starts a comic warfare against the intruder.

Like *Saute ma ville* fifteen years earlier, *L'Homme à la valise* adopts the language of slapstick comedy. As in a Laurel and Hardy piece, the film's comic effect is produced first and foremost through the contrast between the two characters' physical appearance and behaviour: the female character is petite and plump, the male tall and thin; he is bright and cheerful, she passive-aggressive and visibly disturbed; he is elegant in dress and demeanour, she, unstylish and awkward. He, the intruder and foreigner, is visibly at ease in the flat, whilst she has become a stranger in her own home.

15 '1st day. After two months' absence during which I had lent my flat to a friend, I come home to work.'
16 '2nd day. I get ready for writing.'

The conventions of slapstick and silent film are furthermore evoked in the film's formal strategies: use of intertitles, caricatured, over-expressive acting, speeded-up motion, as well as an exaggerated contrast between silence and noise. Margulies draws attention to the importance of off-screen sound for the 'depiction of a paranoid sensibility' (Margulies 1996: 164). Aligned to the woman's point of view, the spectator learns to listen with her for signs of the man's presence: the sound of his cleaning rituals in the bath, keys in the lock, cracking floorboards and, above all, the clicking noise of the typewriter (for, ironically, he hammers away whilst she is the victim of writer's block), all become acute reminders of the male's colonisation of the woman's space.

The female character's pathology as well as the gradual escalation of her actions which the film traces in minute detail align *L'Homme à la valise* with *Saute ma ville* and *Jeanne Dielman* which both inflect similar themes in a different register. During the twenty-eight days of cohabitation, the female character devises increasingly complicated strategies for avoiding the friend (the intertitle for day four reads, 'S'arranger pour jamais le rencontrer';[17] for day seven, comically, 'Dieu se reposa, mais pas nous'[18]) rather than simply talking to him. On day three, she barricades her bedroom door with her mattress, spies on the corridor and notes the precise time when Henri leaves the house. On day five, she draws up an exact timetable which records every single one of his activities (his getting up, shaving, having breakfast, etc.) together with the precise time of their occurrence. The typewriter, formerly in the service of creativity, becomes a weapon in her warfare against the male intruder. On day nine, she installs a movie camera outside her window to keep watch over Henri's comings and goings.

Even when the friend has left for a full seventeen days, the woman is incapable of getting back to her work and routine. Barricaded in her bedroom, she waits for his return. As Alain Philippon remarks, the film plays on the ambivalent attitude of the female character who, whilst doing everything to protect herself against the man's intrusion, seems to nonetheless desire his presence (or at least, one may add, needs to keep control over him) (Philippon 1984: 79). With its video screen and hermetically closed shutters, her room resembles a watch-tower or a prison cell, the character's self-imposed confinement

17 'I make sure never to meet him.'
18 'God had a rest, not us.'

evoking the concentrationary universe which is present in so many of Akerman's films independent of their tone and style.

When the friend finally returns on the twenty-sixth day, he engages in a period of frantic writing activity which extends over two days. The woman, by contrast, slumbers in her trashed room that is littered with rubbish and overturned furniture. On the twenty-eighth day, finally, we hear the man packing, moving furniture and closing the door. When Akerman ventures into the corridor, the suitcases and suits which for four weeks were a visual reminder of the male presence have disappeared. The man with the suitcase has left. Akerman enters the light and spacious sitting room where the man had slept and sits down at the table in front of the typewriter in exactly the same position as in day two. She finally begins to write.

A droll and apparently light-hearted comedy, *L'Homme à la valise* works through many of the issues we already observed in earlier films and which are recurrent concerns in Akerman's oeuvre: the problem of a troubled routine and the difficulty of adapting to change; a female character's wilful imprisonment and conflicting relations with the outside world; the desire for control and order which, once disturbed, provokes exactly the contrary, namely, entropy and mess; the need to control others for fear of losing oneself. In its invocation of and simultaneous distancing from autobiographical indices, the film, moreover, reflects, in a comic mode, on the porous boundaries between lived experience and fiction (boundaries which, in the same period, were being explored in literature by writers such as Marguerite Duras and Georges Perec) and on the nature of film-making more widely. The fact that Akerman turns her own video camera into the instrument with which she spies on her friend ironically hints at the film-maker's voyeuristic relation to his/her filmed subjects, the 'peeping Tom' position that characterises the filmic process.

Finally, the film recasts in a different form the theme of exile already explored in earlier works, especially *News from Home* and *Les Rendez-vous d'Anna*. Here, exile is no longer geographical or cultural but (as to a certain extent in *Les Rendez-vous d'Anna*) gendered and artistic. Akerman becomes an exile in her own flat, unsettled by the male presence which renders artistic creation impossible. It would, of course, be tempting to read *L'Homme à la valise* as a comic enactment of the war between the sexes and an affirmation of the director's own lesbian identity against the heterosexual couple, which becomes an object of phobia in the film. Such a reading would, however, blatantly ignore the performative aspect of the film which *plays* on stereotyped oppositions between man and woman, male assertiveness and female hysteria, without becoming complicit with them. Rather than falling into any reductive binary opposites, or playing one party against the other, Akerman, in a convincingly comic and self-ironic performance, lets her own body act out the symptoms stereotypically associated with female hysteria in a burlesque rite of exorcism, drawing attention to the constructed nature of gender identities, but also figuring, once again, a self in crisis on the verge of mental implosion.

Golden Eighties: love in the time of consumer culture

With releases on the Champs-Elysées and in the Paris suburbs, *Golden Eighties* is Akerman's most commercial film of the decade. It signals an intermittent crossover from alternative modes of production to the mainstream, yet also demonstrates, as we will see, that a popular genre and subject matter are by no means irreconcilable with the strategies of a 'critical cinema' identified in Chapter 1. When the director was finally in a financial position to shoot the film, some of its parameters had changed: lead actors like Aurore Clément were no longer available, roles had been merged in an attempt to keep the budget down, and French actors had replaced Belgian ones to reduce production costs. The overall tenet of the project, however, remained the same: a musical comedy set in a Brussels shopping mall which interlocks the loves and destinies of nine main characters against the backdrop of 1980s consumer culture threatened by a global recession. The spatial axis is simplified to the extreme: four locations in the mall (Sylvie's snack bar, the Schwartz's clothes store, Lili's hairdressing salon and the local cinema) provide a dynamic, permeable setting for dance, singing and performance acts. Akerman's choice of name for the setting, the *Galerie de la Toison d'or* (Mall of the Golden Fleece), apart from its obvious mythological echoes, also carries strong autobiographical overtones, for it is here that her parents, shopkeepers like the Schwartz of the film, had their leather goods store.[19] Temporally, the comedy divides into three symmetrical panels: 'day one', 'the

19 The mall was recreated in a studio in Paris.

following day' and 'three months later', with the action becoming increasingly frenetic towards the end.

Young hairdresser Mado is in love with Robert Schwartz, the son of the shopkeepers in the mall, but Robert loves Lili, the attractive manageress of the salon. Lili is 'kept' by Monsieur Jean, a married man of dubious business practices, whom she secretly betrays with Robert. Pascale, one of Lili's employees, still loves ex-boyfriend Robert, but her loyalties are torn because she is also Mado's best friend. Robert's mother, Mme Jeanne Schwartz, is courted by the love of her youth, the American Eli, but cannot bring herself to leave her husband. Finally, Sylvie, the owner of the snack bar, is waiting for letters from her lover who has left for Canada to make his fortune. These are, in short, the amorous predicaments of the main characters, serial variations on that most popular theme in literature and the cinema: the love triangle. The first shots of a trainee hairdresser kissing two boys and rapturously declaring 'Je l'aime, je l'aime'[20] with regard to each of them set the scene for the film's burlesque intertwining of passions and desires, love found and lost, romantic hopes and brutal betrayals.

In the tightly structured film narrative, individual stories echo and interfere with one another, as is signalled by the occasional completion of characters' monologues by their interlocutors, and the commenting of the action by a malicious chorus of trainees and a group of loitering boys, post-modern incarnations of the chorus in classical Greek drama. *Golden Eighties*, formally and thematically, is a comedy of echoes and resonances, an exuberant ballet of confidences and rumours, where gossip goes round as quickly as the nimble twirling feet of the trainees. A scene in the film's first part, where the news that a gentlemen has come to the ladies' salon for a shave is whispered from ear to ear by the giggling hairdressers, serves as a visual metaphor for the transmission of banter that is the mall's main social function. Actions in the mall, as Cathy Fowler remarks, 'are constantly overheard or overseen by other people, and events are relayed via gazes in the fictional world' which, in turn, invite spectator identification. 'The shopping mall exists, then, as a space which makes spectators of everyone and which emphasises display and artificiality' (Fowler 2000: 113, 112).

20 'I love him, I love him.'

Akerman's talent for choreography and sensitivity towards setting and costume are used to remarkable effect in this exuberant, camp comedy. The cheerful primary colours of *Golden Eighties* stand in striking contrast to the bluish evening light of *Toute une nuit*, the (almost) silent ballet of amorous desire with which this celebration of the human voice and body forms a diptych. *Golden Eighties* is a perfect anthology of 1980s style: the satin skirts of the trainee hairdressers, Lili's red, low-cut dress and dangling jewellery, the large, tightly fitted belts, pink and pale-blue plastic raincoats, permed hair and red lipstick, all accessorise Akerman's hyper-stylised recreation of 1980s consumer-culture chic. With its colourful costumes and setting, bright lighting, rapid editing and quickly alternating song-and-dance numbers, the film displays an aesthetic of excess in stark contrast to the director's minimal, sober style of the preceding decade. *Golden Eighties* is a charming exercise in viewer seduction, an unashamed spectacle of femininity and a bold pastiche of melodrama and the musical, the two genres which, as we have already seen in the context of *Les Années 80*, it uses as its thematic and aesthetic foil.

It is, above all, in the European rather than the American musical tradition, and especially in the line of Jacques Demy's musical comedies of the 1960s, that the film self-consciously positions itself. Demy, as Jill Forbes explains, 'first realised that the enclosed space of a gallery and its symmetrical design is the perfect foil for a musical, with the constraints of the setting justifying and shaping the choreography of the formation dancing and making the musical romanticism seem more fantastic in contrast' (Forbes 1987: 145). In *Golden Eighties*, references to Demy's work abound: not only does the *Galerie de la Toison d'or* appear as a post-modern avatar of the nostalgic turn-of-the-century passageways in his *Lola* (1961) (revealingly, in *Les Années 80*, Lili is still called 'Lola') but Sylvie's wall-less coffee bar resembles the bar-aquarium in his *Demoiselles de Rochefort* (1967);[21] with Sylvie herself evoking Mme Yvonne in the latter film, who prefers living in her dreams rather than confronting reality (Fowler 2000: 110). The conflict between the commercially oriented parental generation and their offspring in quest of love, freedom and self-discovery, moreover, is reminiscent of Geneviève's (Catherine Deneuve) fate in *Les Parapluies de Cherbourg* (1964). In its self-conscious echoing

21 Cf. Charlotte Garson, 'Les deux galeries', DVD *Golden Eighties* (Cahiers du cinéma, collection '2 films de').

of sets and themes, and its heightened melodrama and unashamed sentimentality, *Golden Eighties* pays homage to Demy's musical films. Like Demy, who raised ordinary spoken language to the status of song, Akerman makes extensive use of popular and youth culture in her self-scripted lyrics which are ingeniously set to music by Marc Herouet. Schmaltzy love ballads quickly alternate with the *a cappella* mock songs of the group of 'bad boys' and the shampoo girls' giddy comments on passion and betrayal. The chorus deflates the romantic clichés that are lived and repeated by the central characters, its malicious comments distancing the spectator from the spectacle on display. More 1970s chanson than 1980s pop, the soundtrack nostalgically evokes Akerman's own youth at a time when the tunes of French composers and singers such as Michel Berger (author of the highly successful rock opera *Starmania*) and his wife, the Eurovision Song Contest winner France Gall, enjoyed international popularity.

If Demy and, more generally, the French tradition of using the emotional affect of song in modern cinema (Margulies 1996: 191) can be considered as crucial inspirations behind *Golden Eighties*, the film also engages in a playful dialogue with the Hollywood musical whose conventions and values it playfully subverts. The traditional American musical, one of the most successful genres produced and marketed by the Hollywood studio system, follows a set rule of codes and strategies which, as Rick Altman and Richard Dyer have shown, underpin a coherent, subliminal ideology (Altman 1981 and 1987; Dyer 1985).[22] Though rich in variations, the dominant model that emerged during the musical's heyday, roughly between 1930 and 1960, is characterised by a conservative social and sexual politics and a marked patriotism, manifest in its celebration of communal stability, advocacy of gender fixity and promotion of American wealth and, more generally, of the merits of capitalism. Traditionally based on a set of opposites – sex, age, social origin, temperament, values –, it works through these binary oppositions with a view to abolishing difference in its resolution. Vincente Minnelli's *Gigi* (1958), as Altman has shown (Altman 1981), is characteristic of the musical's paradigmatic structure: the marriage between the young, economically feeble Gigi to the older, wealthy Gaston that closes the romantic comedy merges what first appeared as irreconcilable opposites into a harmonious ending,

22 See also Susan Hayward's very informative entry on the musical in *Cinema Studies: The Key Concepts*, London, Routledge, 1996.

promising prosperity and happiness for both lovers. Complicit with bourgeois value systems, the Hollywood musical advocates marriage – Altman calls it an 'ode to marriage' – as well as the traditional alliance of (male) wealth and (female) beauty. 'The ecstatic, uplifting quality of the musical's final scene', in the words of Altman, 'permits no doubt about the permanence both of the couple and of the cultural values which the couple simultaneously guarantees and incarnates' (Altman 1987: 51).

In a playful subversion of classic Hollywood codes, Akerman puts marriage at the centre of her fiction, making it a constant topic of gossip and excitement in the mall, yet, at the same time, deconstructs the romantic resolution of more commercial productions: at the end of the film, the bride (Mado, played by Lio) walks away in her wedding dress, relinquishing her fiancé to the femme fatale (Lili, played by Fanny Cottençon) who has returned the day before the wedding. The latter, object of desire and bearer of the gaze amongst the mall's heterogeneous population (Akerman deliberately sets her up as the object of 'to-be-looked-at-ness' and thus as female spectacle), bursts out laughing when Robert proposes to her, visibly bemused by the very idea of marital ties. Marriages are made and dissolved at the speed of lightening and lovers taken and discarded *ad libitum*: in Akerman's witty take on 1980s consumer culture, the heart is just another commodity.

The legendary wealth of North America, another trope of the Hollywood musical, is relegated to the domain of the mythical ('le Labrador et ses mines d'or'[23] is the refrain of one of the songs), belied by the lover's letters from Canada, which document his struggle to find work and implicitly comment on the price of industrialisation (the same song mentions millions of tons of asbestos). Rather than celebrated, American capitalism is denounced as a form of cultural imperialism through the presence of posters in the mall's cinema promoting American blockbusters *Gun Crazy* and *Green Ice* as well as through the film's English title which eventually replaced the French *La Galerie* (in America, the film was released under the somewhat misleading title 'Window Shopping'). Far from being optimistic about the future, *Golden Eighties* evokes the spectre of economic recession that will bring an end to unbridled consumerism: 'Si ce n'est pas

---

23 'Labrador and its gold mines.'

celui-là, ce sera un autre ... et puis tant qu'on a encore à manger',[24]
says Jeanne Schwartz trying to console Mado over the loss of her
fiancé at the end of the film.

Love itself, though the prime driving force behind the characters'
feverish activity, is questioned by its most desirable figure, Lili:
'L'amour, l'amour, il n'y a que ça dans la vie?'[25] she asks her lover,
the sleazy Monsieur Jean, and, later, reflecting on her emotional
torments, 'C'est affreux l'amour'.[26] Finally, even music and stardom
are derided in Akerman's parodistic take on the musical. Internation-
ally renowned pop icon Lio is given one of the lead roles, but is cast
against type: ironically, contrary to all other characters, she is not
allowed to sing once.

Beneath its baroque effervescence and apparent light-hearted-
ness, *Golden Eighties* raises profound questions about the nature of
love and desire, the destiny of memory and the experience of trauma.
Sylvie's anonymous lover emphatically declares the worthlessness
of the world's riches compared to being with his beloved, but Sylvie
herself (Myriam Boyer) doubts that he will ever return from the land
of (dreamed) opportunity and happily renounces a shared existence
for the romanticism of distance. Monsieur Schwartz (Charles Denner)
sings the praises of his wife to his son (Nicolas Tronc), yet his incongruous juxtaposition of 'nous avons bien travaillé ensemble' and
'[c'est] un vrai mariage d'amour'[27] belies the discourse of romantic
love and reveals the more pragmatic, economic stakes behind their
union. Most importantly, through the figure of Jeanne (Delphine
Seyrig), a Polish Jewess liberated by the American GI Eli (John Berry),
Akerman, for the first time, directly addresses the horrors of the
camps, thus giving her musical comedy a grave historical dimension,
tempered only partially by the gaiety of the surrounding spectacle.
Eli's return to Europe after forty years to meet the woman he cared
for after the Liberation and with whom he is still in love brings back
painful memories of destitution and horror. In choosing Delphine
Seyrig for the role of the Holocaust survivor and giving her the name
'Jeanne', as we have already alluded to in Chapter 1, the director

24 'If it's not him, it will be another one ... anyway, as long as we still have something
     to eat.'
25 'Love, love, is that all that there is to life?'
26 'Love is awful.'
27 'we have worked together well', '[it's] a true love marriage'.

seems to link up the story lines of *Jeanne Dielman* and *Golden Eighties*, hinting, retrospectively, at a possible past for the mysterious Jeanne Dielman and, perhaps, at a clue for her dissociation and compulsive need for order (Eli says to Jeanne, 'tu me disais ton cœur était mort, tu ne pourrais plus jamais rien ressentir après ce que tu avais vu dans ces camps'[28]).

As we have already seen, with regard to *Les Années 80*, *Golden Eighties* continues, albeit in a different cinematic style, Akerman's persistent work on stereotype and cliché as forms of social conditioning and discursive gender construction. Pascal's advice to Mado, 'si tu lui dis que tu l'aimes tu es foutue',[29] M. Schwartz's praise of a married life devoted to the accumulation of wealth, and Sylvie's lover's swooning letters, all belong to the realm of the *déjà entendu*, to the discourses of love and bourgeois morality that, as Roland Barthes has shown in a literary context, naturalise convention into general wisdom (Barthes 1975). As in her earlier work, Akerman signals cliché by merely repeating it, letting the commonplace denounce itself through a typically post-modern use of pastiche. Yet, there is a marked difference between the hackneyed anti-naturalist delivery of the sister's letter in *Jeanne Dielman*, for instance, and Sylvie's enchanting recitals of her lover's missives in *Golden Eighties* which turn each letter into a moving prose poem. Cliché, here, though omnipresent, is tempered and embellished by the rhythm and lyricism of the songs. Re-recycled by the director in a playful reappropriation, cliché is the very fabric out of which the film's complex discursive tissue is woven.

The conflict between repetition and authenticity which lies at the heart of cliché is rendered visible by the choreography, which, especially in the dance numbers of the trainee hairdressers, oscillates between robotic, repeated movement on the one hand and anarchic exuberance on the other. The scene in the film's second part entitled 'Le Lendemain' (The Following Day) where the trainees comment on Robert's betrayal of his fiancée as they work, giddily dancing around with their clients and creating havoc in the salon, is a bravura piece in this respect. The young women perform the same movements, but their slightly desynchronised gestures, as in a Pina Bausch performance, gradually build into a crescendo of burlesque revolt. The

28 'you told me your heart was dead, you could never feel anything again after what you had seen in those camps.'
29 'if you tell him you love him, you've had it.'

trainees' violent massaging of their clients' heads and brandishing of hairdryers and sprays like weapons endow the scene with an anarchic power, enhanced by the belligerently (stereotypical) anti-male content of the songs ('les hommes c'est tous des salauds'[30]). In Akerman's ambivalent filmic universe, the hairdressing salon, that archetypal haven for gossip and confidences and locus of a gendered femininity, is both a space of mechanical repetition and of possible female empowerment. Given its potential threat to the patriarchal order, it is only logical that it should be destroyed by Monsieur Jean (Jean-François Balmer) at the end of the film's second part and replaced by yet another consumer temple for the discerning female customer (the title sequence's criss-crossing of female feet on the mall's marble tiles, as Forbes points out, reminds us that women are the main clients of shopping centres and thus a crucial 'locomotive of the economy') (Forbes 1987: 145).

Confined to the claustrophobic atmosphere of the mall, the characters' lives and passions, as in *Toute une nuit*, are subjected to the sweltering summer heat (the mall ironically has none of the air conditioning usually associated with the comfort of the modern shopping experience). Only in the last scene are three of the characters – Monsieur and Madame Schwartz and Mado in her wedding dress – allowed to emerge into the open where they run into Eli and his new (considerably younger) wife. Monsieur Schwartz, clumsily trying to console Mado over the loss of her fiancé, gets embroiled in a comic comparison between the fickleness of hearts and people's desire for new clothes whilst his wife gazes nostalgically at the disappearing couple. 'Si les gens sortaient tout nus, on ne ferait plus d'affaires'[31] are his closing words in an increasingly absurd tirade. The discourse of love and the discourse of commerce in *Golden Eighties* remain intimately interlinked until the end.

Memories of exile: *Histoires d'Amérique*

The first travelling shots of *Histoires d'Amérique*, Akerman's 1988 film about Jewish immigrants in New York, taken from a boat crossing the sea, from the outset designate the film as a narrative of arrival. Polish

30 'men are all bastards.'
31 'if people went out naked, we wouldn't sell anything anymore.'

and Yiddish voices whisper in voice-over whilst, in the blue evening mist, iconic images of the New York skyline appear: the Statue of Liberty, distant and fragile, followed by the graceful constellation of Lower Manhattan skyscrapers floating in the frame. In their bluish haze, the images are weightless and immaterial, ciphers of an imaginary city of dreams and hopes rather than the busy late twentieth-century metropolis to which the director returns for the shooting. The privileging of time over space and the mirage-like images of the city 'characterise this crossing as storytelling' (Margulies 1996: 196). The languorous musical accompaniment, Max Bruch's *Kol Nidrei* arranged and played by cellist Sonia Wieder-Atherton, imbues the opening sequence with an air of nostalgia. Contrary to *News from Home* which ended on a departure scene associated with one individual (the director), *Histoires d'Amerique* evokes a collective, iterative journey, the East–West crossing made by generations of Jewish immigrants from the Old World to the New, a passage heavily charged with hopes, anxieties, regrets and aspirations.

As the camera captures a ship gliding into New York harbour, we hear Akerman, in voice-over recite a Jewish legend in heavily accented English:

> A rabbi always passed through a village to get to the forest and there, at the foot of a tree, and it was always the same one, he began to pray and God heard him. His son, too, always passed through the village to get to the forest, but he could not remember where the tree was, so he prayed at the foot of any old tree and God heard him. His grandson did not know where the tree was, nor the forest, so he went to pray in the village and God heard him. His great-grandson did not know where the tree was, nor the forest and not even the village, but he still knew the words of the prayer, so he prayed in his house and God heard him. His great-great-grandson did not know where the tree, nor the forest, nor the village were, not even the words of the prayer, but he still knew the story, so he told it to his children and God heard him.

And she adds: 'My own story is full of missing links, full of blanks and I don't even have a child'.

This unusual incipit marks *Histoires d'Amérique* as a film concerned with the problematic nature of remembrance and transmission. The Jewish legend laments the loss of origins and the gradual transformation of rite into tale, of religious practice into family anecdote, but, at the same time, asserts that transmission – keeping the story alive – not only allows diasporic Jews to remain in touch with their past but also with their God. Akerman's own addendum, on the contrary, whilst placing herself in a long line of Jewish ancestry, signals the incomplete passing-down of history in her own family (as we have seen in the Introduction, she frequently mentions her parents' reluctance to talk about the past, especially her mother's silence about Auschwitz) and, by positing herself as the last in a family line, conjures up the threat of total oblivion. *Histoires d'Amérique* can be read as an attempt to rescue memory, collective and personal, from effacement and annihilation and as a commitment to ensure, through art, a transmission that can no longer be guaranteed in the individual private sphere.

The film is based on both fictional and documentary sources, taking inspiration from the Jewish tales of Isaac Bashevis Singer as well as from letters from Jewish immigrants published in the Yiddish newspaper *The Jewish Forward*, which Akerman rewrote and fictionalised (Bergstrom 2003: 95). The imaginary memories in *Histoires d'Amérique*, as she explained herself when the film was complete, make up for the void in her own family history, but the film also transcends the purely personal in its wider reflection on memory, exile and displacement:

> Au lieu de connaître mon histoire par une transmission directe de parents à enfant, il m'a fallu passer par la littérature et lire Isaac Bashevis Singer par exemple. Mais cela ne suffisait pas. Ses souvenirs à lui ne pouvaient pas être tout à fait les miens. Alors d'un emprunt à l'autre, je me suis constitué des souvenirs imaginaires. Et ce film [*Histoires d'Amérique*] est un travail sur le souvenir, mais des souvenirs inventés.[32] (cit. in Bergstrom 2003: 113–14)

Like Georges Perec and Robert Bober's *Récits d'Ellis Island* (1979), a two-part documentary which examines the stories and captures the traces of the sixteen million European emigrants to the United States from the late nineteenth century to the 1950s, *Histoires d'Amérique* constitutes what French historian Pierre Nora has called a 'lieu de mémoire',[33] all the more important here since, as Nora remarks, the

32 'Instead of knowing my history by having it passed down directly from parents to child, I had to resort to literature and read, for instance, Isaac Bashevis Singer. But that was not enough. His memories could never be really mine. So, from one borrowing to the next, I built up imaginary memories. This film [*Histoires d'Amérique*] is a work on memory, but invented memories.'

33 'realm of memory.'

Jewish tradition, 'has no other history than its own memory' (Nora 1989: 16).

Histoires d'Amérique is composed of a series of self-contained tableaux: medium-shot portraits of individuals who tell their stories alternate with sketches of Jewish humour, both culminating in an extended al fresco dining sequence which brings together the various characters we have seen previously. As in *Toute une nuit*, the structure is permutational and serialised and most of the film is shot during the night which, once more, dramatically ends in a thunderstorm. Rather than opting for genuine testimony by authentic witnesses, which would place her film in the documentary genre, Akerman has professional Jewish actors deliver imaginary, yet starkly representative, stories of Jewish immigrants' experiences in the United States. Temporal markers are as fluid and shifting (the stories cover about a hundred years of Jewish immigration) as the largely unidentified locations: anonymous residential quarters, building sites and a highly poetic, somewhat surreal outdoor dining area in the first part of the film shot at night; an inner-city wasteland as the night turns into day. The only recognisable monument, Williamsburg Bridge, as well as connoting the multi-ethnic borough of Brooklyn with its significant Jewish population, just like the urban wastelands and the suitcases characters randomly carry around with them, serves as an index of transition, a filmic metonym for the emigrant's straddling two worlds and cultures – East and West, old and new – and for the uprootedness of the diasporal Jew more generally. The bilingual title *Histoires d'Amérique: Food, Family and Philosophy* further signals this liminality which emerges as one of the film's central concerns.

In contrast to her work of the 1970s, where human emotion was explored largely through the language of the body, with *Histoires d'Amérique* Akerman creates a more vocal, polyphonous work made of a chorus of voices, old and young, male and female, rich and poor, but who all share the same predicament: the alienation of the immigrant in his/her host country and the burden of a traumatic history. The film style reconnects with the work of the previous decade through the largely static camerawork, direct verbal address and the privileging of open form which allows characters to walk in and out of frame, but also continues the more recent exploration of filmic magic through the expressive use of lighting, occasional song performances and choreographed group scenes. The frontal camera position adopted for individual portraits creates a Brechtian distancing effect, yet the affect and sentimentality of many of the stories deliberately draw the spectator into the narratives. Akerman's casting of little-known actors, some of them intimately linked to the emergence of a new theatrical practice in the 1970s, brings to the film echoes of New York counter-culture and underpins its representational code of 'life as theatre'. The following are among the better known of the film's recurrent charac-ters: George Bartenieff, the co-founder of the *Theatre for the New City*, known for its radical political plays and community commitment; Judith Malina, co-founder of the *Living Theatre*; Roy Nathanson (who is also responsible for parts of the soundtrack) from the jazz group *The Lounge Lizards*; and, perhaps most movingly, the young Eszter Balint, closely associated with the New York avant-garde theatre group *Squat Theatre* founded by her father (Reynaud 2004: 200). '[T]he fact that the performers are of Jewish or Eastern European origin, some of them having acted in the old Yiddish theatres of the Lower East Side', in Margulies' words, 'literalizes the displacement of the temporal frame in which this immigration account is set' (Margulies 1996: 195).

The filmic portraits and sketches conjure up archetypal situations and fundamental problems that face the displaced person: the culture shock of arriving in a foreign country and difficulty of belonging in a new society; the conflict between traditional and modern values and the guilt and rootlessness that may be the other side of the coin of secularisation; the growing rift between first-generation immigrants and their Americanised children; the difficult negotiation of multiple cultural identities; the loss of illusions and the longing for a common origin, faith and culture. Whether it be the story of an atheist scientist who finds happiness in the Talmud, of a young girl who loves two men – one of them a Gentile, the other a Jew – and cannot decide which to marry, of a suicidal young man whose family has perished in the camps, or of an elderly immigrant eager to return to his native Warsaw, the tales, in fictional mode, echo the multifarious dramas of more than a hundred years of Ashkenazi emigration. Behind them, evoked diffusely, but no less insistently, lurk the traumas of the pogroms and the Holocaust, centuries of persecution and annihila-tion that constitute the Jewish communities' shared history.

Histoires d'Amérique, as several critics have noted, is a film about phantoms and about absence. The stories, which trace an Eastern European Jewish community that is no more, 'de ce pays yiddish entre la mer Blanche et la mer Noire, avec sa langue, sa littérature, ses films'[34] (Boltanski 2004: 202), are haunted by the spectres of those that have perished and by a culture that has been eradicated. In Akerman's *mise en scène* of death, the immigrant characters also, with their outdated costumes reminiscent of the 1930s and 1940s, their stilted mannerisms, tales of slaughters and famine, and their diaphanous silhouettes eerily cast against the dark New York sky, become ciphers of an irretrievable past. 'Maybe we are ghosts,' speculate two men during the outdoor dining sequence. 'But ghosts from where?', asks one, to which the other replies, 'That I don't know, and I certainly don't want to go back there.' The sparse lighting of the scenes, use of coloured filters, flickering streetlights and softly swinging light bulbs suffuse the film with a ghostly atmosphere enhanced by the equally spectral city space, a derelict part of Williamsburg whose half-decaying houses and overgrown nature give the scenery an oneiric, fantastic touch. Akerman has chosen New York as the setting for her film, as Bérénice Reynaud remarks, 'non seulement parce que c'était encore, à la fin des années 80, la ville du rejet, du déchet, de la saleté, des terrains vagues envahis d'herbe et des coins de rue plongés dans la pénombre, mais parce que *c'est une ville qui n'existe plus*'[35] (Reynaud 2004: 201). Just as the former Jewish ghetto of the Lower East Side evoked in some of the film's sketches has long disappeared in the process of modernisation, the very locations of the filmic fiction have fallen victim to Mayor Giuliani's gentrification projects of the 1990s.

Though archetypical in their characterisation (the Jewish bride, the starving emigrant family rescued by American philanthropists, the wandering Jew, the young women raped in a pogrom, etc.), the stories often have unexpected twists which, together with their stylised delivery, resist easy readability. The spectator watches with considerable unease as a young woman tells her story, which first seems to be about a husband who has left her, but quickly reveals itself as a tale of this same husband's death, before eventually slipping into a lament about her kissing the husband's best friend on their way back from the funeral. Tragic and comic registers intersect in the

---

34 'of this Yiddish land between the White and the Black Seas, with its language, literature and films.'

35 'not only because New York, in the 1980s, was still a dirty city full of rubbish, with pieces of overgrown waste land and badly lit street corners, but because *it is a city that no longer exists*.'

portraits themselves as well as in their alternation with the sketches of Jewish humour. This juxtaposition of traumatic tale and burlesque performance, at first disturbing to the spectator, is in fact essential to the Jewish experience the film seeks to capture. As Akerman explains in *Autoportrait*, sadness and laughter are inseparably linked in Jewish culture and Jewish humour – that oft evoked quintessentially Jewish trait – is directly born out of the horrors of History:

> [C]es blagues n'existent qu'à cause de la tragédie. C'est une manière par la dérision de nier ce qui arrive, de s'en moquer. Non pas tout à fait. C'est surtout une mise à distance pour apprivoiser l'insupportable, l'insoutenable même parfois. Quand l'Histoire ou les histoires deviennent difficiles à supporter, il ne reste plus qu'une chose à faire, se mettre en scène dans son propre malheur et rire.[36] (Akerman 2004: 166)

Humour in *Histoires d'Amérique*, then, as in Jewish culture more widely, can be understood as a distancing strategy, a way of domesticating the unbearable and a gesture of resilience in the midst of breakdown and destruction. But, perhaps more importantly, in Akerman's meditation on memory and transmission, it also takes on the function of a cultural link, a shared practice many thousands of years old that constitutes the diasporic Jew's common language. Beyond the stereotype and the archetype, which are recuperated in her fiction, Akerman presents Jewish humour as a trace that links immigrants to their origins and that defiantly rings out in the face of annihilation. The song numbers, self-deprecating jokes and vaudeville-style performances that punctuate the film, in a self-reflexive homage, seem to celebrate the contribution of Jewish comedians to American culture and the entertainment industry in particular, which recruited some of its finest talents from the Eastern Jewish Diaspora.

Histoires d'Amérique, just as it began, ends on a story: an elderly man enters a butcher's shop in Warsaw. Standing before the increasingly irritated butcher, he orders a long series of meats that are no longer on sale. When he leaves, empty-handed, the butcher comments: 'What a fool! But how well he remembers! How well he remembers!' The man's longing for a past that is no more and the

---

36 'These jokes only exist because of the tragedy. They are a way of denying, by means of derision, what is happening, of laughing at it. Not exactly. They are above all a distancing strategy to tame the unbearable, even sometimes, the intolerable. When History or histories become difficult to bear, there remains only one thing to be done: to stage oneself in one's own misfortune and laugh.'

litany-like list of fine foods, each a slight variation of the former, are emblematic of the film's theme and style: a serial accumulation and permutation put into the service of a complex reflection on loss and remembrance, where the personal and the collective – 'la petite et la grande histoire'[37] – are inseparably intertwined. Akerman's haunted and haunting film, at once poetic and uncanny, as Reynaud remarks, is a touching attempt to respond to one of post-war cinema's most pressing questions: 'comment peut-on faire du cinéma – après Auschwitz?'[38] (Reynaud 2004: 201).

References

Akerman, Chantal (2004), *Chantal Akerman: Autoportrait en cinéaste*, Editions du Centre Pompidou/Editions Cahiers du cinéma.

Akerman, Chantal (1984), 'Adventures in Perception', *Monthly Film Bulletin*, 51, pp. 104–5.

Akerman, Chantal (1983), Dossier de Presse: *Les Années 80*.

Altman, Rick (1987), *The American Film Musical*, Bloomington and Indianapolis, Indiana University Press.

Altman, Rick (1981), 'The American Film Musical: Paradigmatic Structure and Mediatory Function', in Rick Altman (ed.), *Genre: The Musical*, London, Routledge and Kegan Paul, pp. 197–207.

Barrowclough, Susan (1984), 'Toute une nuit (All Night Long)', *Monthly Film Bulletin*, 51, pp. 103–4.

Barthes, Roland (1975), *S/Z*, trans. Richard Miller, Hill and Wang.

Bergstrom, Janet (2003), 'Invented Memories', in Gwendolyn Audrey Foster (ed.), *Identity and Memory: The Films of Chantal Akerman*, Carbondale and Edwardsville, Southern Illinois University Press, pp. 94–116.

Boltanski, Christian (2004), '*Histoires d'Amérique* et *D'Est*', in *Chantal Akerman. Autoportrait*, pp. 202–3.

Brooker, Peter (ed.) (1992), *Modernism/Postmodernism*, London, Longman.

Deleuze, Gilles (1989), *Cinema 2: The Time-Image*, trans. Hugh Tomlinson and Robert Galeta, London, Athlone Press.

Dyer, Richard (1985), 'Entertainment as Utopia', in Bill Nichols (ed.), *Movies and Methods*, Berkeley, University of California Press, pp. 220–32.

Featherstone, Mike (1990), *Consumer Culture and Postmodernism*, Sage.

Fischer, Lucy (1989), *Shot/Countershot: Film Traditions and Women's Cinema*, London, MacMillan.

Forbes, Jill (1987), 'Conservatory Blues: *Golden Eighties*', *Sight and Sound*, 56, p. 145.

Foster, Gwendolyn Audrey (2003), 'The Mechanics of the Performative Body in *The Eighties*', in Foster (ed.), *Identity and Memory*, pp. 142–9.

37 'small and big history.'
38 'how can one make films – after Auschwitz?'

Fowler, Catherine (2003), '*All Night Long*: The Ambivalent Text of "Belgianicity"', in Foster (ed.), *Identity and Memory*, pp. 77–93.

Fowler, Cathy (2000), 'Harnessing Visibility: The Attractions of Chantal Akerman's *Golden Eighties*', in Bill Marshall and Robynn Stilwell (eds.), *Musicals: Hollywood and Beyond*, Exeter, Intellect, pp. 107–16.

Hoberman, J. (1991), *Vulgar Modernism: Writing on Movies and Other Media*, Philadelphia, Temple University Press.

Jameson, Fredric (1992), *Postmodernism or the Cultural Logic of Late Capitalism*, Durham, Duke University Press.

Margulies, Ivone (1996), *Nothing Happens: Chantal Akerman's Hyperrealist Everyday*, Durham and London, Duke University Press.

Nora, Pierre (1989), 'Between History and Memory: Les Lieux de mémoire', *Representations*, 26, pp. 7–24.

Philippon, Alain (1984), 'L'Homme à la valise', *Cahiers du cinéma*, 360–1, p. 79.

Philippon, Alain (1982a), 'Fragments bruxellois. Entretien avec Chantal Akerman', *Cahiers du cinéma*, 341, pp. 19–23.

Philippon, Alain (1982b), 'Nuit torride: *Toute une nuit* de Chantal Akerman', *Cahiers du cinéma*, 341, pp. 24–6.

Reynaud, Bérénice (2004), 'Histoires d'Amérique', in *Chantal Akerman: Autoportrait*, pp. 200–1.

Tomasovic, Dick (2004), 'L'Homme à la valise', in *Chantal Akerman: Autoportrait*, p. 192.

White, Jerry (2005), 'Chantal Akerman's Revisionist Aesthetics', in Jean Petrolle and Virginia Wright Wexman (eds.), *Women and Experimental Filmmaking*, Urbana and Chicago, University of Illinois Press, pp. 47–68.

1 Delphine Seyrig (Jeanne) in *Jeanne Dielman, 23, quai du Commerce, 1080 Bruxelles* (1975)

2 Magali Noël (Ida) and Aurore Clément (Anna) in *Les Rendez-vous d'Anna* (1978)

3 *Toute une nuit* (1982)

4 *Golden Eighties* (1986)

5 *Histoires d'Amérique* (1988)

6 Guilaine Londez (Julie) and Thomas Langmann (Jack) in *Nuit et jour* (1991)

7 Sylvie Testud (Ariane) and Stanislas Merhar (Simon) in *La Captive* (2000)

8 Sylvie Testud (Charlotte) and Aurore Clément (Catherine) in *Demain on déménage* (2004)

9 *D'Est* (1993)

10 *Sud* (1999)

11 *De l'autre côté* (2002)

3

The archaeology of suffering

A radical innovator in fiction film, Akerman also has a distinguished career in the genre of the documentary which forms an integral and important, though relatively neglected, part of her filmic oeuvre. Over a career of more than forty years, the director has produced a dozen documentary works on a plethora of subjects ranging from modern dance to music, and from self-portraiture to international politics. Whilst her documentary work of the 1970s and 1980s (with the exception of *Hotel Monterey* and *Un jour Pina a demandé...*) is mainly in short format and is thematically very diverse (focusing on the destitute urban class as well as on renowned artists Pina Bausch, Alfred Brendel and Sonia Wieder-Atherton), in the course of the 1990s and 2000s, the director embarked on a series of feature-length works on a particular geographical region which, although not initially planned as such, retrospectively imposed themselves as a tetralogy: *D'Est* (1993), a stylised, painterly portrait of Eastern Europe after the fall of Communism; *Sud* (1999), a harrowing enquiry on racial conflict and hatred in the American South; *De l'autre côté* (2002), a moving study on the plight of illegal Mexican immigrants who attempt the crossing to the US; and *Là-bas* (2006), a minimalist meditation on life in contemporary Israel.

Each of the four films portrays a region caught in political and social instability and torn between the traumas of a not-so-distant past and the uncertainties of an explosive present. Whilst the artist pursues in these works her reflection about minority cultures, exile and displacement developed in the 1970s films and in *Histoires d'Amérique*, she also continues her enquiry into the encounter between the self and others, both on a personal (the film-maker and her filmed subjects) and on a collective (society's dealings with the foreign) level. In the first three works of the tetralogy, Akerman increasingly shifts her camera away from the urban and interior settings that characterised her earlier films to open spaces and the outdoors. Place itself becomes the main protagonist of these films, and landscape, as we shall see, takes on an important role as a locus of manifold inscriptions and a repository of memory. Though more overtly political than her earlier work, the documentary tetralogy continues to bear the artist's signature experimental style, showing her sustained commitment to avant-garde practices and her espousal of the long and rich tradition of French film-making (led by directors such as Godard and Chris Marker) that puts experimental film language in the service of ethical and philosophical enquiry. Labelled as 'experimental ethnography' by critics, the four films revert to the minimalist syntax of the 1970s, which they refine, extend or, in the case of *Là-bas*, radicalise.

Because of their strong thematic and formal similarities and their crucial, but altogether underrated, place in Akerman's oeuvre, we have regrouped the films that constitute the tetralogy in a separate chapter. It would, however, be erroneous to think of her documentary output as a genre that is totally distinct from the rest of her oeuvre. Not only do documentary and fiction film run parallel in Akerman's work, they often, as we have already seen to a certain extent in *Histoires d'Amérique*, overlap to such a degree that conventional genre categories are exploded and transgressed. As the director explains herself:

> Après le documentaire tourné, et monté s'il n'ouvre pas une brèche dans l'imaginaire, s'il ne s'y glisse pas de la fiction, alors pour moi, ce n'est pas du documentaire. Quand à la fiction, s'il ne s'y glisse pas du documentaire alors, j'ai du mal à penser que c'est un film de fiction.[1] (Akerman 2004: 98)

Especially *D'Est* offers an interesting example of Akerman's documentary practice 'bordering on fiction'.

1 After a documentary is shot and edited, if it does not open a breach into the imaginary, if fiction does not slip into it, then, for me, it is not a documentary. As for fiction, if no documentary aspects slip into it, then I find it difficult to think of it as a fiction film.'

Two of the films, *D'Est* and *De l'autre côté*, were later adapted into video installations of the same title, testifying to a further expansion of genre boundaries (from film to the visual arts), but also witnessing an important new shift in Akerman's career since the early 1990s: her experimentation with video and other media in the context of a museum or gallery space rather than in the sole confines of a cinema.

Travelling in time: *D'Est*

In the late 1980s, Akerman was approached by the Museum of Fine Arts, Boston, about a commission for a multimedia installation on the coming together of the European Community. While immediately attracted to the project, the director 'proposed a look at what was left out of this union as well, and at the concomitant rise of nationalism and anti-Semitism' (Halbreich and Jenkins 1995: 8). A first trip to Russia in 1990 to prepare a film about the poet Anna Akhmatova (a project which, unfortunately, was never brought to fruition), made her want to further explore a region with which she felt a deep personal affinity and to film the countries of Eastern Europe, 'while there's still time' (Akerman 1995: 17), that is, before their impending absorption into the uniformity of global capitalism. *D'Est*, her elegiac portrait of Eastern Europe after the fall of Communism, was shot during two consecutive journeys; the first to East Germany and Poland during the summer of 1992, the second across Russia to Moscow, where the majority of the film is set, during the winter of the same year.

For Akerman, the daughter of Holocaust survivors and a descendent of the Polish Jewish Diaspora, this voyage east inevitably carried strong personal resonances. Yet, whilst not denying that emotional reasons may have come into play when she accepted the project, the director says she carefully avoided an explicit autobiographical approach – for example, she did not make a travel diary about her quest for her family roots – for fear of restricting her vision and prejudicing her neutral eye:

> There might also be personal reasons for going, and there are. My parents are from Poland. Since the thirties, they've been living in Belgium, where they feel very much at home [...] And yet, even if the personal reasons are real, I don't want to make a 'back to my roots' kind of film because ... she who seeks shall find, find all too well, and

manipulate things a little too much in order to find them. (Akerman 1995: 20–2)

The same refusal to control and shape in advance the material to be filmed made her opt against a more conventional, narrative-based documentary about the disintegration of the Eastern Block and the disarray of its citizens. Rather than fixing Eastern Europe into a series of exemplary images, as would be the danger of an 'expository' type[2] of documentary, she wished to film 'sans pré-pensée',[3] to capture life in its unobstructed flow without any pre-established principles of argumentation and selection and without imposing any authoritative argument on the spectator. This observational, or, rather, phenom-enological approach to documentary film-making is, as she explains in interviews and *Autoportrait*, a constant of her filmic practice: less a director in the conventional sense of the word than a seismograph, an archaeologist and an analyst, Akerman conceives of her documen-taries as an echo chamber, an experimental ethnography or a perfor-mance piece where unforeseen events and chance encounters are allowed to happen.

D'Est opens with a fixed long take of a highway at night over which the film's opening credits appear. The noise of cars is heard in ampli-fied sound, yet, for the greatest part of the shot, the passing traffic remains invisible. The two horizontal bands, one green, the other orange, which divide the image, give it an almost abstract feel. The following shot, taken through the window of a café, shows a quiet country road and, in the background, open countryside. A German song is heard on the radio whilst cars are passing by slowly. In a later shot of the same sequence, the camera moves for the first time. Tracking from right to left, it follows an elderly woman walking on the pavement. Her body is intermittently blocked from view by parked cars in the foreground. This first sequence of shots, as Michael Taran-tino explains,

set[s] up a rhythm for the entire film, one which will be based on shifts between stasis and movement. Both the fixed-frame and the moving shots Akerman uses adhere to a particular formal character: the former often resemble the spaces of painting (carefully composed

2 Critic Bill Nichols defines the expository mode as 'emphasis[ing] verbal commentary and an argumentative logic' (Nichols 2001: 33).
3 'without thinking in advance.'

> still lives or landscapes) while the latter – for the most part, extended
> lateral tracking shots – are uniquely cinematic in their manipulation
> of time and space. (Tarantino 1995: 48)

Each of the shots is self-contained, forming a micro-narrative or
tableau, but in their serial accumulation, these fragments, which, over
the course of the film, form distinct motifs that echo one another,
build into a lyrical and increasingly hypnotic portrait of post-communist Eastern Europe.

As in Akerman's fictional work, the quotidian is privileged over
extraordinary personal or historical events and is filmed in real time:
families frolicking by the sea, a young man sitting on a bench, his
upper body bent and his eyes forlorn, an elderly woman carrying out
rubbish and other such scenes are recorded by the calm, unobtrusive
gaze of the camera. The film offers no authorial voice-over commentary for the images that unfold before the spectator's eye, nor does it
have recourse to the interview format that, despite the many debates
surrounding documentary representation, is still largely considered
as a guarantor of objectivity or, at least, an attempt at creating a partici-
patory dynamic between the film-maker and his/her filmed subjects.
More radically, the filmed subjects are given no voice at all and thus
no possibility of verbal self-representation. The film-maker and her
crew remain invisible; their filmed subjects are reduced to a quasi-
muteness. Side-stepping language as the main vector of communication, the film thus once again shifts the focus of attention to the
body, whose posture and gestures are examined in minute detail in
Akerman's customary long takes, and to the human face, which the
camera scrutinises like an expressive landscape.

Eschewing conventional narrative and plot, *D'Est* signifies above
all through its filmic syntax, which is structured around a rigorous
set of formal and thematic oppositions: interior scenes (homes,
waiting rooms, cafés) alternate with exteriors (streets, fields, bus
stops); portraits of individuals with crowd scenes; day with night;
and, as already mentioned, fixed-frame with long tracking shots.
'Neither documentary nor fiction, *D'Est* systematically transgresses
the formal and narrative economy of both these genres by creating
a rhythm that is constantly on the verge of imploding' (David 1995:
59). Geographical anchoring is pared down to a minimum. In the
absence of any recognisable monuments, landscapes or borders, the
film's spatial parameters are reduced to mere linguistic hints: East

Germany is discreetly signalled by a commercial sign containing the word 'Berlin', the entry into Poland by the murmuring of Polish voices in the non-synchronised soundtrack and the entry into Russia by a street sign in Cyrillic script. A visual metaphor for the frequent territorial changes the region underwent in its tormented past, this lack of spatial demarcation, together with the film's disjointed narrative structure, creates a sense of disorientation that, from the outset, taints the viewing experience.

If there is no clear division between the three countries, the voyage East, which constitutes the film's central movement, is nonetheless clearly manifest through changes in landscape, architecture, dress and, above all, season. The summer scenes of cyclists and bathers in East Germany and Poland are gradually replaced by images of harvest, situating the action in the autumn, by fields and streets covered in frost and, finally, by the almost incessant snowfall of the Russian winter. The vivid colours of exterior scenes at the beginning of the film fade in the later parts shot in Russia, giving way to almost monochromatic tableaux melancholically tinted in bluish grey or sepia by way of coloured filters. Whilst Akerman's work generally verges on the pictorial in its emphasis on duration and its formal concern with composition, in the latter parts of the film, as we penetrate deeper into the East, the crossover between film, the quintessential art of time *and* space, and the visual arts, essentially defined by space, becomes even more apparent. The filmed subjects become increasingly more sculptural in their hieratic poses and outmoded clothing, their arrangement in solitary public groups or still-life compositions in their homes evoking, at times, the existentialist paintings of Edward Hopper, at others, the art of European expressionism.

The soundtrack, recorded live, but remixed in the studio, adds to the film's poetic anti-naturalism. Defiant of any realist conventions, the sound often carries on beyond the image or else stands in no clear signifying relation to it. Strongly amplified or, on the contrary, lowered sound create dramas and tensions that form an independent subtext in the film, compensating to a certain extent for the silence of the filmed subjects and gesturing towards stories that are not told visually. Snippets of voices that invade the image with their chant-like whispering tone in languages that are never translated, most notably perhaps a long monologue in Russian that accompanies the tracking shot of a suburban setting, imbue the film with a ghostly presence.

Rather than illustrating the narration and stitching it together, as is the common function of sound in mainstream film-making, the soundtrack contributes to the overbearing feeling of emotional and physical disorientation in the film. As Catherine David remarks:

> Just as any voice-over commentary or subtitled translation (which might have been used when bits of conversation or words emerge from the crowd's murmuring) is absent from the film, the sound track offers no pretense of realism. The extreme precision and volume of sounds serve to anticipate or prolong the duration and effect of the images, which they color emotionally and affectively ... The sound restores the emotional, mental, and physical experience of the subject in much the same way that color and light work in the film ... rejecting the impossible transparency of 'statement', Akerman offers instead a 'mise en scène of visibility [which] involves a stylisation and concreteness that rubs against conventions which require a prior, ideational, figuration'. (David 1995: 60)

About one fifth of the way into the film, images of expressionless individuals laden with baggage, marching in groups along bleak country roads or, more strikingly, across snow-covered fields, begin to invade the narrative – archaic scenes out of sync with other images of Moscow city dwellers that have a more contemporary feel. Places of departure (train and bus stations), public transport and the omnipresence of bundles of belongings take on a heavy metaphorical charge in this meticulous *mise en scène* of a region in limbo. Suspended between past and future, between the collapse of Communism and an as yet uncertain new order, Eastern Europeans, in Akerman's cinematic language, become a community of wandering souls, nomads without a fixed destiny.

That this harrowing portrait of an errant humanity carries more than just contemporary resonances becomes evident in one of the film's central scenes set in a Moscow railway station. Situated almost exactly two thirds of the way into the film, this portrait of yet another place of departure reinforces the nostalgic tone that dominates the filmic language since the crossing over to Russia. The shot begins with passengers entering the station through a set of doors filmed in fixed angle. The camera recedes slightly and starts a long panning shot from right to left, the only circular camera movement in the film. Amidst the anonymous crowd appears a paraplegic who makes his way through the hall on an archaic construction on wheels, a figure of suffering who taints the image with a dark mood. The camera follows the man, eventually overtakes him and completes its 360° movement. The Stalinist architecture of the station, with its high ceilings, vast arcades and statues of political leaders, dwarfs the crowd entering and leaving the frame.

After a second full circle, the film cuts to a tracking shot of the waiting room, filled with a vast crowd of people of all ages, wrapped in coats, fur hats and scarves, once again laden with luggage. The general atmosphere that emerges from this collective portrait is one of stoic resignation. Clearly conscious of the presence of the camera, the filmed subjects nonetheless rarely return its gaze. A few minutes into the shot, Massenet's *Elegy* (sung in Russian) rings out in the soundtrack, its yearning, post-romantic tones suffusing the scene with a profound melancholy. The sequence ends on a series of individuals whose heads are decapitated by the camera, and more sinister still, on the immobile silhouettes of men lying against the balustrade of the central stair, their bodies piled up against one another, faces hidden.

In the course of these scenes, coloured in nostalgic sepia, a discomfort invades the spectator, haunted by other such images of a heteroclite crowd awaiting departure for an unknown destination, of tired, haggard, fleeting faces and piled up, torn, immobile bodies. The earlier shots of people walking with suitcases on wintry roads, incongruous amidst the more realist surrounding tableaux, the portraits of waiting crowds, slightly archaic in their brownish colour and in their emphasis on bundles of belongings, the amplified cry of a child hovering over one of these scenes, retrospectively show their inherent duality. Behind the image of a contemporary community awaiting an uncertain destiny lurks the spectre of a century of atrocities – deportation, the Holocaust, the gulag. Suggested through the allusions to wounding and death (the paraplegic, the decapitated men on the balustrade) as well as through the movement from right to left which, in Occidental culture, signals a return to the past or even a movement towards death, the horrors of the past are allowed to surface beneath the images of the present.

D'Est, then, like the two following titles of the tetralogy, effects a complex oscillation between past and present, memory and contemporary reality, the visible and the invisible. It opens up a rift in the image where memory is allowed to inscribe itself through a complex layering process. In Akerman's aesthetic of the palimpsest, contemporary Eastern Europe is invaded by echoes of its past, echoes that imbue the film with a fluid temporality. Not dissimilar to Proust's famous concept of involuntary memory, where everyday objects conjure up flashes of the past, Akerman's work on the traces of memory summons the dead through the images of a contemporary community in disarray. The word 'image' here as Stéphane Bouquet points out, regains its original meaning, since 'imago' first designated a funeral mask before acquiring its current sense (Bouquet 1995: 44).

Akerman has repeatedly stated that she was not aware of the film's multi-layered dimension whilst shooting it and that it was only once she saw the edited product that its deeper meaning revealed itself to her: 'When I made the film, I – who was born after the war – often wondered why I shot this and not that. I didn't know. But afterwards when the film was finished, I understood that those particular images were already in my head, and I was looking for them' (cit. in Carvajal 2008: 16). Unlike Claude Lanzmann's approach in *Shoah* (1985), then, which still sets the ethical standards for representations of the Holocaust, her uncovering of traces of an erased past behind contemporary reality is not the fruit of a deliberate cinematic strategy. Rather, the dual images that collapse past and present seem to have emerged from the director's unconscious, or perhaps, more interestingly, if one believes in a collective unconscious that haunts the cinema post-1945, they seem to be part of a complex symptomatology that extends even to films not directly concerned with the Holocaust.

Two years after its official release, *D'Est* was adapted for a three-part installation revealingly entitled *Au bord de la fiction* and shown in galleries and museums across America and Europe, including the Walker Art Centre in Minneapolis, the Jewish Museum in New York and the Jeu de Paume, Paris. The first room of the modular installation shows the film in its entirety. The second room contains eight blocks, each with three video screens which loop three-minute-long extracts from the film, the twenty-four monitors evoking the pattern of twenty-four frames per second that is characteristic of the cinema. The last part of the installation, entitled *The Twenty-Fifth Screen*, is composed of a single video monitor, which projects an image of a nocturnal Moscow street from the film. In voice-over, Akerman reads, first in Hebrew and then in English, an excerpt from the book of *Exodus* on the prohibition of idolatry plus a text of her own which offers a retrospective commentary on the film:

whether from long ago or still to come, old images that are barely concealed by other more luminous, even radiant ones: old images of evacuation, of people with packages marching in the snow toward an unknown place, of faces and bodies placed side by side, faces that vacillate between a strong life and the possibility of a death that would come to strike them without their having asked for anything.

And it's always like that.

Yesterday, today, and tomorrow, there were, there will be, there are right now, even, people that history (without a capital H) comes to strike. People who are there, rounded up in herds, waiting to be killed, hit, or starved; people who walk without knowing where they're going, in a group or alone.

There's nothing to be done; it's obsessive and it obsesses me.

Despite the cello, despite the cinema.

The film finished, I say to myself, *that's* what it was: once again *that*. (cit. in David 1995: 63)

D'Est is arguably Chantal Akerman's most complex and representative work on time, space and memory. Expanding traditional boundaries of the documentary with her stylised images bordering on fiction and letting echoes of the past haunt her portrait of the present, the director creates a multi-layered work which collapses past, present and future into a hallucinatory vision; a work replete with memory, but which eschews explicit commemoration and one which, through its haunted images of destitution, warns of humanity's fragility before the vagaries of History. Akerman, as we have said earlier, did not finish her project of a film on Anna Akhmatova, yet it is in *D'Est*, a work subtly traversed by the great Russian poet, that she creates her own *Requiem*.

The banality of evil: *Sud*

At its release on the international film festival circuit in 1993, *D'Est* met with almost unanimous acclaim. Critics praised the sensitive portrait of the former Eastern bloc drawn by the director, the love and respect she affords her filmed subjects, as well as her questioning of objectivity in ethnographic film-making and her bold transgression of the traditional boundaries between documentary and fiction. The influential journal *Artforum* rated the film amongst the best works of the 1990s. Akerman carried out preparatory work for another documentary, this time on the Middle East (the project's provisional title was *Du Moyen-Orient*[4]) during an extended trip to Syria, Lebanon and Jordan in 1997, but eventually had to abandon the project because of a lack of funding.

It was only at the end of the 1990s, in the wake of a teaching stint at Harvard University, that the director returned to the investigation of place and memory that *D'Est* had so forcefully opened up. Inspired by the literature of William Faulkner and James Baldwin, two American authors who, though in many ways antipodal to one another, are deeply concerned with race, questions of identity and the weight of the past on the living, she undertook a journey to the South of the United States in preparation for a film focusing on racial violence and exploitation and the traces these have left in the region's landscape. She explains:

> J'ai aussi envie d'aller voir là-bas à quel prix se passe le miracle améri-
> cain, sur le dos de qui se crée en ce moment même le plus grand
> amoncellement jamais vu de richesses mais aussi et surtout si ce
> paysage garde les traces ou le souvenir de quelque chose d'autre que
> de leur propre beauté.[5] (Akerman 2004: 164)

The project was conceived as a counterpart to *D'Est* with which it shares the specific geographical locus (reflected in the title) as well as the dual focus on past and present and the interest in landscape as the repository of a collective history.

The director had already travelled to the Southern States of Alabama, Mississippi, Louisiana and Georgia, all members of the Confederacy in the American Civil War and former defenders and practitioners of slavery, when she read the news of the brutal lynching of a black man, James Byrd Jr, in the small town of Jasper, Texas. The forty-nine-year-old musician and father of three was beaten up by three young white men, stripped naked and chained

---

4 '*Of The Middle East.*'
5 'I also want to go there and see at what price the American miracle is happening, on whose back, at this very moment, the greatest wealth ever seen is accumu-lated, but, also and above all, if the landscape preserves the traces or the memory of something else than their own beauty.'

to a pick-up truck then dragged to his death along several kilome-
tres of a quiet country road. When the murder was discovered the
following day, body parts of the victim were littering the street.
Deeply shocked by the crime, Akerman decided to set her film in
Jasper, her aim being less to uncover the reasons and circumstances
of the murder, but, rather, in her own words, to see 'comment
celui-ci vient s'inscrire dans un paysage tant mental que physique'[6]
(Akerman 2004: 233).

Formally and structurally, *Sud* replicates the principles explored
to perfection in *D'Est*: alternation between fixed-angle camera shots
and long tracking shots, use of extended duration, and a relatively
systematic juxtaposition between images of urban landscape and
nature and portraits of individuals or groups. The narrative unfolds
at the rhythm of these encounters, following no pre-established structure and, once again, eschewing traditional expository devices such as
voice-over commentary and shot/counter-shot. Despite its similarities with her portrait of post-communist Eastern Europe, *Sud* does,
however, display two significant variations that signal a noteworthy
difference in the cinematic language and overall approach. First and
foremost, unlike in *D'Est* where the filmed subjects were reduced to
silence, in *Sud* they are given ample opportunity for self-representation, their comments on the murder, its circumstances and, more
widely, on the history and continued reality of racial conflict and
hatred in the region playing an integral and indispensable part in the
film. Second, and closely related to the first point, Akerman opts for
a less stylised, more bluntly realist approach, refraining from the use
of colour filters and non-diegetic, non-synchronised sound as well as
from the painterly approach to the cinematic image that gave *D'Est*
its singular lyrical power. Visually, *Sud* verges on the reportage genre,
even though its disjointed syntax and restrictive cinematic vocabu-
lary resolutely signal its status as an experimental work. As director
Vincent Dieutre comments, 'l'image de *Sud* est d'autant plus impar-
tiale, métallique, qu'elle a perdu son grain pittoresque d'image pelli-
cule. La caméra ne peint plus, elle témoigne, elle veille, elle glisse'[7]
(Dieutre 2004: 211).

6 'how it inscribes itself in a mental as well as physical landscape.'
7 'The image in *Sud* is all the more impartial and metallic since it has lost the
picturesque grain of a film image. The camera no longer paints, it testifies, it
keeps watch, it slides.'

Before the first images appear on screen, the sound of crickets that accompanies the opening credits sets the tone for the film. 'This sound alone makes the heat palpable, and with it a sense of seductive languor and natural beauty that is at once enveloping and oppressively suffocating' (Schmuckli 2008: 21). A long fixed-angle opening shot of a black man mowing the lawn in front of a church alludes to the importance of religion for the region and, in combination with other shots of black people carrying out lowly paid activities, points to its continued racial inequality. A series of tracking shots, alternating between left to right and right to left movement, scans row after row of run-down, almost identical houses. The camera scrutinises the urban landscape, imposing its slow-paced rhythm onto the spectator, the monotony of the images creating an atmosphere of paralysis, deceptive banality and boredom.

As in *D'Est*, tracking shots of urban and natural scenery are intercut with fixed-frame portraits, or more precisely here with testimonials made before the camera. The film advances in narrowing concentric circles, beginning with an elderly woman's account of black people's dire working and living conditions before the 1960s Civil Rights movement before moving on to the description, by a black man, of how the body of James Byrd Jr (who is not named at this stage) was found and then, finally, the account, by a white man, of the gruesome circumstances of the murder. A tracking shot of the road taken from the back of a car, inserted between the two witness accounts, visually evokes the murderous act.

The fact that direct testimonies of the murder are considerably delayed in the progression of the film narrative, and that the film's central subject is only gradually unveiled, creates an element of suspense in the film narrative. The uncommented juxtaposition of testimonials from various members of the community (the local sheriff, an expert on the white supremacist movement, relatives of the victim and people who knew him), translates into cinematic language the multiple point-of-view technique characteristic of modernist writers like Faulkner and Proust, who are a constant reference point for the director (incidentally, *Sud* was released in the same year as her adaptation of Proust, *La Captive*). Different accounts complete, confront or contradict each other in a complex web of stories that spectators are left to piece together and whose veracity and intent, in the absence of any authoritative voice-over commentary, they must assess for themselves.

Whilst there seems to be general agreement among witnesses that the murder was racially motivated, official voices are keen to stress the good relations between black and white citizens in Jasper. The local sheriff emphasises the integrated nature of the community and implicitly makes economic problems, rather than racial hatred, responsible for the crime. The preacher, addressing the congregation at a memorial service for the victim, likewise asserts that the crime is not representative of a more widespread racism. The true extent of racial hatred in the South is revealed by a former FBI agent who elaborates on the considerable growth of the Aryan Nationalist movement over the last fifteen years and the re-emergence of Ku Klux Klan groups under the new banner of 'Christian identity'. A young man's tale of the beating, bombing and castration of black people confirms the brutal reality of white supremacist violence, and a black woman's memories of the shooting and dragging to death of black people at the hands of white farmers alerts spectators that the horrific way in which Byrd was put to death is, in fact, characteristic of Southern lynching practices.

These gruesome testimonies of racial violence together with other tales of racial oppression gradually taint the images we see and change our perception of them. Shots of black prisoners working in fields supervised by white men on horseback almost inevitably conjure up the memory of slavery abolished little more than a century ago. Even pastoral images of lush nature gradually become instilled with memory in a complex resonance between past and present. Akerman explains:

> Je voudrais faire des images qui évoquent presque trop de bonheur. Presque de l'écœurement. Et puis ce paysage va se mettre à bourdonner. Et par le ressassement, toujours le ressassement, j'espère vous faire valser du plaisir que peut procurer la nature, la partie de campagne, le plaisir et son frémissement. Jusqu'au doute même de ce plaisir, jusqu'au sentiment de l'horreur et même du tragique dans un silence de plomb.[8] (Akerman 2004: 164)

8 'I would like to make images which evoke almost too much happiness. Almost nausea. And then the landscape will begin to buzz. And through turning-over, always turning-over, I hope to make you waltz with the pleasure that nature, a trip to the country, can give, pleasure and its thrill. Until you start having doubts about this pleasure, until there emerges a feeling of horror and even of tragedy in a leaden silence.'

The extended duration of shots that is the director's trademark is instrumental in this second project on memory traces. Akerman has always insisted that long takes are necessary to stir the spectator from a state of passivity and to divest the quotidian of its familiarity. If the camera rested only thirty seconds on a tree, she explains, all the spectator would see is a tree. If, however, it is allowed to hover long enough, spectators can remember that, not so long ago, on other such trees, African-American men and women were brutally lynched (Akerman 2004: 36–7). The long take, in other words, renders visible the invisible and allows the past to inscribe itself in the present. As in the poem by Abel Meeropol, set to music and made famous by Billie Holiday, cited by Akerman in the context of *Sud*, 'Southern trees bear a strange fruit'.[9]

Sud, then, like its predecessor *D'Est*, is an archaeology of suffering, a memory-space where shadows of the past haunt the deceptively anodyne quotidian. The two works attempt to come to terms with horrific events whilst at the same time acknowledging the difficulty of finding an appropriate language with which to express the horror. Faced with a similar representational (and ethical) problem, Claude Lanzmann, in his monumental *Shoah*, which we have already mentioned in the context of *D'Est*, decided not to use archival footage, evoking the Holocaust instead by juxtaposing present-day images of the camps and their surrounding countryside with witness accounts. Although Akerman states that she has never seen *Shoah*, her formal strategy in *Sud* is comparable in that she also alternates between the places where the crime has happened and witness accounts, and refuses to use footage of the murder. News footage, she explains, risks foreclosing spectator reflection instead of encouraging it. Her cinema, by contrast, solicits a more active engagement and seeks to communicate on an affective rather than on an intellectual level (MacDonald 2005: 265).

The film's last scene, a seven-minute-long tracking shot of the road on which the victim was dragged to death, is exemplary of her more oblique, distilled approach to the cinematic image. The camera, fixed to the back of a car, meticulously scans the stretch of road and its surrounding countryside. Blue circles drawn on the tarmac by

---

9 'Southern trees bear a strange fruit/ Blood on the leaves and blood on the root/ Black body swinging in the Southern breeze/ Strange fruit hanging from poplar trees.'

the police to circumscribe the places where personal possessions and body parts of the victim were found come into sight. Though not in any way graphic, this is arguably the most violent scene in Akerman's entire oeuvre. For spectators, the horror is all the more intense because our imagination has to supply the images of suffering the director withholds from view. Ultimately, invisibility becomes the most powerful strategy in a film that, from the outset, sets up a tension between what is and what isn't shown or said and which actively implicates the spectator in its summoning of the dead.

In an interview, Godard once teased Akerman by saying that she always referred to her film-making in literary terms like 'inscription' or 'writing' whilst he opted for a language more appropriate for the cinema. Akerman dryly replied, 'I say that, yes, there are images already inscribed, and it is exactly *under* those that I work: over the inscribed image and the one I would love to inscribe' (cit. in Margulies 1996: 20). It is apposite to relate her poetics of inscription articulated in this exchange to Walter Benjamin's theory of dialectical images, all the more so since Akerman herself stresses her affinity with the German philosopher in the context of *Sud*.[10] In *Autoportrait*, she cites Benjamin: 'La manière dont le passé reçoit l'empreinte d'une actualité plus haute est donnée par *l'image* en laquelle il est compris. Et cette pénétration dialectique, cette capacité à rendre présentes les corréla-tions passées, est l'épreuve de vérité de l'action présente'[11] (Akerman 2004: 44). For Akerman, as for Benjamin, the truth of an image lies, above all, in its capacity to make visible, in a dialectical process, the connection between past and present. *D'Est* and *Sud* partake in this dialectical process by lifting elements of everyday life out of their original context and rearranging them in a new constellation that instils them with new meaning. The imbrication between different temporal strata makes possible the recognition of the past's relevance for the present. Shifting the focus from the more autobiographi-cally charged Eastern Europe to the American Deep South, in *Sud*, Akerman thus once again works through what she herself calls the

10 Alisa Lebow similarly links Akerman's project to Benjamin in a sophisticated reading of *D'Est* without, however, talking specifically about dialectical images (cf. Lebow 2003).
11 'The way in which the past receives the imprint of a higher present event is determined by the *image* in which it is contained. And this dialectic penetration, this capacity to render present past correlations, is the test of truth of the present action.'

'primal scene' of her cinema: 'l'Histoire, la grande et la petite, la peur, les charniers, la haine de l'autre, de soi et aussi de l'éblouissement de la beauté'[12] (Akerman 1999: 3).

Phantoms of the wall: *De l'autre côté*

The busiest international frontier in the world, the US–Mexico border is subject to about 250 million legal crossings per year, plus an estimated 1 million illegal ones of which around 80% are by Mexicans. Some 10,000 patrolling agents of the US federal government guard an almost 2,000-mile-long stretch of land, extending over the four border states of California, Arizona, New Mexico and Texas. Steel fences with high-intensity lighting, motion sensors and watch-towers, currently extending over seventy-four miles, but likely to be expanded in future years, further serve to curb illegal immigration and drug-trafficking. As border enforcement has been strengthened in urban sections such as San Diego and El Paso that have the highest number of illegal crossings, immigrants increasingly divert to the more remote desert and mountain areas, especially in Arizona, leading to a significant number of deaths. According to the Migration Policy Institute, there were 473 migrant deaths at the border in 2005, over 260 alone on the Arizona border.

It is the condition of Mexican illegal migrants as well as the attitude of American citizens and the US government to illegal immigration that interests Akerman in the third part of her tetralogy on place, memory and identity, *De l'autre côté*, arguably the masterpiece of her documentary work and the best exemplar of her cinema as 'une forme qui pense'[13] (Frodon 2002). Following a diptych structure (the first part is dedicated to the Mexican side, the second to the American), her experimental reportage alternates testimonies of citizens from both sides of the border with scenes of daily life and arresting images of nature, filmed in the by now customary combination of fixed-angle and tracking shots. Loosening the rigorous ascetic principles of the earlier documentary works, the director slides from the role of mere observer into that of occasional participator, one who facilitates testimonials

---

12 'small and big History, fear, mass graves, the hatred of the Other, of oneself and also of dazzling beauty.'
13 'a form that thinks.'

with short questions or encouraging comments in the language of the interviewees (Spanish and English). The barrier between film-maker and filmed subject is thus broken down even though Akerman never appears on screen. In the same vein, the anonymity of the filmed subjects that characterised *D'Est* and *Sud* is relinquished in favour of a more personal approach that allows individuals to introduce themselves to the spectator.

The film starts with a prologue that unravels before the film's title: a young man, filmed in medium shot against a door frame, with a window conspicuously present in the background, tells the story of his brother, who nearly lost his life when the 'coyote', that is, the human trafficker paid to take illegal immigrants across the border, abandoned his group in the middle of the desert. Almost all died from dehydration and starvation, some survived. The man's moving tale is accompanied by a melancholic Monteverdi cello duet that blends with the chirping of crickets and the voices of children in a bold mixture of diegetic and non-diegetic sound. The first part of the diptych, shot exclusively on the Mexican side of the border, in Agua Prieta and little border villages, gathers further such testimonials from illegal immigrants and their relatives who tell of the loss of loved ones and of the multifarious dangers and deprivations that await the clandestine along the perilous crossing and beyond, 'de l'autre côté', the land of their collective dreams and hopes.

Akerman films the witnesses in their familiar environment, using the frontal address with which we are already familiar. The careful framing and fixed camera angle gives the images an almost photographic still-ness and perfection – Philippe Azoury compares them to the Canadian photographer Jeff Wall whose work has affinities with both painting and the cinema (Azoury 2002) –, yet there is nothing aestheticising about her portraits of ordinary people who, in the privileged intimacy of the listening situation, speak of their grief, mourning and sorrow. With reference to French philosopher Emmanuel Levinas, Akerman states that, in bringing the spectator face to face with the Other, the frontal shots create a situation of trust and respect: '"quand on voit le visage de l'Autre, on entend déjà le mot *Tu ne tueras point*", dit Levinas ... Ce rapport à la frontalité renvoie à l'autre, au spectateur.'[14]

14 '"when you see the face of the Other, you already hear the phrase *Thou shalt not kill*", says Levinas ... This relation towards frontality relates back to the Other, the spectator' (www.arkepix.com/kinok/Chantal%20AKERMAN/akerman_annexes.html).

In her statement of intent for the film, Akerman asserts that she wishes to avoid any simplistic binary opposites between poor Mexico 'avec une vieille culture qui a aussi sa cruauté, sa corruption, mais qui est dans la vie'[15] and the rich US 'où rôdent la mort, l'acculturation'[16] but concedes that, in the end, taking sides may be inevitable, though it should happen in an oblique way (Akerman 2004: 90, 93). Whilst any overt bias is indeed avoided, the selection of testimonials and the attention to *mise en scène* nonetheless reveal an empathetic point of view that indirectly informs the film narrative. Brightly coloured interiors (most striking in the shot of a boy leaning against a pink wall, a candle flickering on a cast-iron shelf beside him) exude a warmth that is echoed in family members' loving reminiscences about lost relatives and their humble hopes for improving the living conditions of their community. The recurrent motif of the window or the open door, present in many of the portraits, serves as a visual metaphor of hope and faith (Ottmann 2008: 34). By contrast, a television, DVD player and stereo propped up on a coffin-like, plastic-covered table, obtrusively present in the background as a mother tells how her son and grandson perished whilst attempting to cross the border, allude to the price to be paid for access to consumer culture and modernisation.

Intercut between the testimonials, first shown fleetingly, but increasingly more present, appears the wall that divides the two countries and which gradually emerges as the film's central protagonist. Built in wood or in steel, completed or under construction, traversing rural and urban settings, omnipresent, the wall transcends the specific context of the film and becomes an allegory of all the barriers that have divided and continue to divide humanity, from the Berlin Wall to the Gaza Strip.

The danger that faces illegal immigrants is rendered palpable in a series of scenes showing the US border guard at work. The camera laterally tracks stretches of grassy borderland and barbed wire plunged into eerie blue and white by high-voltage lighting whilst we hear the footsteps and voice of the patrolling agents in search of illegal trespassers (all in amplified sound). Akerman affectively draws spectators into the drama of this 'daily war', as one of the patrolling

---

15 'with an old culture which is also cruel and corrupt, but which is anchored in life.'
16 'where death and acculturation roam.'

agents terms the guarding of the border, with these visceral images, vacillating between abstract and realist modes, whose sound, lighting and point of view combine in communicating the terror felt by the immigrant tracked down by dogs, guards and helicopters.

The emotional centrepiece of the Mexican diptych is the reading of a text by illegal immigrants whom Akerman and her crew found whilst shooting along the Mexican side of the border and to whom they gave a lift to nearby Naco. Read in a calm and dignified voice, this collective text tells of the plight of illegal immigrants who, alone and in danger of losing their lives, are betrayed by those who promised to help them (the group were taken by their 'coyote' to a place where the Mexican police robbed them), 'treated worse than a criminal' if they are caught, and suffer discrimination in both countries. Yet, the letter, though outspoken about injustice and inequality, is never accusatory or vengeful, but rather imbued with a deep humility and faith. It ends on a prayer to God to forgive Americans and Mexicans, 'for there are some who have everything and others nothing'.

This moving scene closes the series of testimonials on the Mexican side of the border. The crossing over to the US is announced by tracking shots of traffic jams and soulless suburbs, but the actual border crossing is withheld from view – the camera, like the illegal migrant, sidesteps the official crossing point, 'essentially "smuggling" sights, voices and scenes' (Zanger 2006: 39). The Arizona desert, a 'Dead End' as is ominously indicated by a road sign placed in the middle of nowhere, offers no refuge for the illegal immigrant. Its sculptural mountains, enhanced by orange-coloured filters, steel-blue skies and elemental forces – a desert storm, rendered in amplified sound, violently sweeps clouds of sand across the barren soil – are as inhospitable as the unambiguous warning printed on another road sign: 'Stop the Crime Wave! Our Property and Environment is Being Trashed by Invaders'. A series of testimonials, including a Mexican councillor who explains the lethal impact of border reinforcements in urban zones, a sympathetic restaurant owner who tells of the many perils that await the immigrant on the other side, a couple of ranchers concerned about the consequences of illegal immigration, and a sheriff, explaining the rural population's fundamentalist defence of private property, are intercut with further shots of patrolling agents, forbidding deserts and mountains and drab interiors draped with the omnipresent American flag.

Akerman states that, unlike in *Sud*, in *De l'autre côté* she also wanted to give a voice to poor white people 'qui sont pris dans ces discours fascistes dans le vide de leur vie'[17] (Akerman 2004: 94). Asked by the director whether they think the events of 9/11 will change something in their country, the two ranchers, husband and wife, express their fears about a Mexican invasion spreading terror and disease and adamantly defend their right to use guns to protect themselves from trespassers. Their words echo an article Akerman cites in an interview with Scott MacDonald as her initial incentive for making the film:

> I wanted to go to the Mexican-American border because I read an article in the newspaper and was struck by the words used by one of the Americans who was quoted in the article: one word he used was 'dirt' – 'We don't want that dirt' – 'They're going to bring dirt.' That made me think of other times in history when the word 'dirt' was used: for example, for the Jews – 'dirty Jews'. (MacDonald 2005: 267)

What emerges here is, once again, a broader frame of reference for the film that extends the problematic of the US–Mexico border to a wider enquiry about society's dealing with the foreign, the Other, and implicitly links it to the Holocaust. Unlike in the two earlier works, Akerman opts for a more hybrid cinematic strategy to give visual expression to the themes of exclusion and alterity that are mediated in *De l'autre côté*: diegetic is mixed with non-diegetic sound, classical with Mexican folk music, and a range of film formats, including Super-16 material and DVD, are utilised. Moreover, transgressing her own dogma of 'purity', Akerman for the first time has recourse to archival footage, first in the sequence of the border patrol and, later again, when she uses aerial views of the border and its illegal crossers. Whilst this deliberate hybridism makes the film less emblematic about a particular place – Akerman cites the use of the Monteverdi cello duet that serves as a leitmotif in the film as a deliberate strategy of broadening its geographical scope (MacDonald 2005: 268) –, it also self-consciously echoes the fear of 'impurity' and 'contagion' that underpins so many racist discourses. Akerman's aesthetic of impurity proudly reclaims hybridism and appropriates it as one of the central formal devices in her denunciation of intolerance, exclusion and xenophobia.

---

17 'who, in the emptiness of their lives, are caught up in these fascist discourses.'

The last scenes partake in the film's double focus on here and there, past and present, self and Other. The penultimate sequence, one of the film's most visually striking, is composed of aerial images taken by the infrared camera of a US patrolling helicopter. The camera's viewfinder, strongly reminiscent of the sight of a gun, scans the ground until it falls upon a line of white silhouettes (the image is in negative), marching one behind another. In their weightlessness and distance, the human figures are phantom-like, apparitions of the past, vulnerable and without defence. The shrieking, scratching noise of the surveillance machine creates an atmosphere of terror, enhanced by the target finder that remains focused on the human subjects (the video-game-like aesthetic reinforces the impression of a deathly hunt). When the group reaches a structure of barbed wire (a section of the wall), the plaintive Monteverdi duo is heard again and the camera cuts to a black leader. 'La violence du film, outre l'enchaînement des plans, c'est de nous rendre spectateur de cette image, au même titre que ceux qui s'en servent comme arme'[18] (Charpentier 2004: 213).

The film's final scene, shot from inside a car on a Los Angeles highway whilst Akerman, in voice-over, tells the story of David's mother, who managed to cross the border but who disappeared without a trace on the other side, acts as a coda for the movie. The woman's landlady believes she once saw her in a Mexican area of Los Angeles, but quickly dismisses this sighting as a mirage. On the other side also, the illegal migrant remains a phantom, untraceable even for the son who has followed her. This tale of separation, loss and memory, like the earlier images of watch-towers, barbed wire and floodlights once again takes on a heavy metaphorical charge beyond the context of illegal Mexican immigration, enhanced by the fictional name of the boy, David.[19] To a lesser degree than in *D'Est*, but still manifest in *De l'autre côté*, a post-Holocaust imaginary taints the images of contemporary reality.

Like the first part of the tetralogy, *De l'autre côté* was adapted into a three-part video installation, first exhibited at the Documenta in Kassel in 2002. A year later, the last part of this installation was exhibited in a Paris gallery under the title 'Une voix dans le désert' (A voice

18 'The film's violence, in addition to the sequence of shots, lies in the fact that it makes us spectators of this image, just like those who use it as a weapon.'
19 In an interview with *Libération*, Akerman admits that the story of David's mother may be fictional (Akerman 2003).

in the desert). Based on the last two sequences from the documentary, projected upon a large screen erected on the Mexico–US border and filmed in DV, this installation imports images of the border into the gallery space. As night gives way to dawn, the countryside in which the screen is implanted becomes visible whilst the projected images gradually dissolve into whiteness. The installation, in staging the agony of an image, powerfully evokes the dissolution of the American dream, as 'l'aurore lave l'écran de toute image, jusqu'au blanc défini- tif'[20] (Azoury and Lebovici 2004: 222). The looping of the images draws attention to the impossibility of any kind of simple closure and thus solution to the problems raised in the film.

Israel through the window: *Là-bas*

Through the windows of a flat, shrouded in semi-darkness, appear a row of modernist apartment blocks, their contours shaded by lowered matchstick blinds. The image shot in fixed angle is almost still, a combination of verticals, horizontals and colours, but for a man moving about on his roof terrace, gesticulating and tending to his plants. The interior of the apartment from which the shot is taken is barely visible, reduced to a still-life-like composition of chairs, a vase, and a fruit bowl; the use of shallow space makes the exterior perceived through the large glass front appear flat. The outside world penetrates the inside in the form of an atmospheric sound environment of chirping birds, children's voices and passing cars that filters into the muffled interior where the camera is positioned. A few minutes into the shot, footsteps, the rattling of coffee cups and the sounds of a gas cooker being lit evoke a part of the apartment and a human presence that remain off-screen.

From the outset, *Là-bas*, Akerman's last (and most radically experi- mental) part of her documentary tetralogy on time and space, revolves around this dialectic between inside and outside, introspection and projection outwards, visibility and invisibility. The location of the film is Tel Aviv, yet, beyond the immediate vicinity of the apartment, which offers a limited window on the world (a self-reflexive metaphor for the filmic process), the city is not shown. Likewise, Chantal Akerman, the film-maker and inhabitant of the flat, remains invisible, except

20 'dawn washes the screen of all images, until total whiteness.'

for a shot towards the end of the film when her silhouette furtively appears reflected in a mirror. Over a staggering 118 minutes, the camera varies the angles and the distance from which the outside is perceived, matching the window with the frame of the shot, reclining slightly into the interior of the apartment, looking down onto the street or sideways to a neighbouring building. The matchstick blinds remain hermetically closed for the greatest part of the film, but small gaps between them or between the window and the half-open terrace door occasionally offer unobstructed views, always on the same neighbouring blocks of flats. Somewhere between Hitchcock's *Rear Window*, Edward Hopper's urban scenes and Mondrian's geometrical creations, the film creates a painterly universe of great visual perfection, where each shot constitutes an experiment with composition, lighting and exposure as well as an exploration of different camera angles (high-angle, low-angle shots) and types of focus (deep focus, shallow focus). As Bill Arning explains:

> As the camera cannot properly balance both the overexposed exterior and the murky, shaded interior, the outside world is a blindingly bright, stippled, distant, flat representation of itself. We are often aware of the play of the director's hand manipulating the camera's features within the confining enclosure, seeing what the device on its own can do without requiring its master to venture outside. (Arning 2008: 42)

To a certain extent, the film's troubled genesis explains the formal strategies at work in this highly minimalist and distilled film. Xavier Carniaux, the producer of her documentaries, had urged Akerman for some time to make a film about Israel, which would complete her study of time, place and memory and which he felt was particularly apposite from a director of the diaspora concerned with questions of Jewish heritage. To Akerman, this idea initially felt 'downright repulsive' (cit. in ibid.: 41), yet, whilst on a visit to Tel Aviv in 2005, in connection with a teaching appointment at the University, she became intrigued by a particular shot cut out between the window and the door in her sublet apartment and started filming and jotting down thoughts. Back home, together with her editor Claire Atherton, she edited the film in the intuitive manner that characterises her documentary practice. *Là-bas* self-consciously exhibits her reticence about and difficulty in tackling the project. Rather than making a film about Israel, a task she deemed impossible because of the multiple conflicting discourses surrounding the state of Israel, Akerman decided to make 'un film sur quelqu'un de la diaspora qui se rend là-bas'[21] (Akerman cit. in Vermeersch et al. 2007), that is, a film about her own relations to the country.

An exploration of the boundaries of visibility, the film priori-tises telling (voice) over showing (image), interiority over exteriority. Rather than sounding out a country and its citizens as she had done in the three previous works, the director locks herself away in her apartment, submitting to the kind of self-imposed isolation we last saw in *Je tu il elle* and *L'homme à la valise*, two films in which she similarly held the positions of main character and director, albeit in a fictionalised mode. Insistent telephone calls from friends and family enquire about her well-being or tempt her to come into the open, to no avail. Only two sequences by the sea, inserted between the interior shots, interrupt the monotony of what, as in the earlier works, appears like a pathological confinement thinly disguised as a rigorous work routine ('c'est difficile de sortir de prison, surtout de sa prison',[22] comments a visitor from the university on seeing her isolation).

The confined space of the flat with its human presence that remains off-screen becomes a visual metaphor for Akerman's interi-ority, an interiority explored and revealed by the director's charac-teristically husky voice. Mixing the trivial with the exceptional, the private with the collective, here with there, past with present in the meandering stream of consciousness characteristic of her writing and of the verbal address in so many of her films, Akerman tells stories of her family, complains about bad health, meditates on her Jewish upbringing, broods, reflects or simply stays silent. In the domestic space of the apartment, which appears as both prison and fortress, even historical and political reflections are subsumed into a family narrative where the collective – the history and troubled status of Israel – can ultimately only be grasped through the personal.

Akerman may well reassure friends and family members who phone her that she is well, but her voice-over monologue tells a different story: not only is she physically weak, recovering from a recent illness, but she seems to be in the grip of a profound existential malaise. 'Je suis déconnectée de presque tout ... je ne sais comment vivre ... il y a quelque chose en moi qui a été abîmé, mon rapport au

21 'a film about someone from the diaspora who goes there.'
22 'it's difficult to get out of prison, especially one's own.'

réel',[23] she confesses in a crucial passage, attributing this dissocia-tion from the world to her relationship with Israel and, by extension, to her condition as an exile and a Jew. Depression haunts the film through the darkened interior and insistent figuration of confinement and imprisonment, but also, more directly, through the intertwined stories of the suicides of Akerman's aunt, Ruth, in Brussels and that of the mother of Israeli writer Amoz Oz in the newly formed state of Israel. These two deaths, together with Oz's acclaimed *A Tale of Love and Darkness* (2002), an autobiographical tale of the creation of the state of Israel which acts as a literary prism in the film, spur Akerman to reflect on the diasporic Jew's ambiguous relation to Israel, which, whilst being a 'terre promise'[24] for European Jews after the Holocaust, also became 'une nouvelle terre d'exil'[25] (Akerman cit. in Vermeersch et al. 2007). Akerman implicitly raises the question whether any land or physical space can offer lasting refuge and peace in the wake of such a tragedy.

'Il faut bien un jour regarder Israël en face',[26] she asserts, yet this evaluating gaze literally does not extend any further than 'en face', to the scenery that is immediately opposite, to what is visible from the safe haven of her abode. The voice-over (self-ironically) articulates the difficulty the artist has in making sense of modern Israel and in coming to terms with her family history and identity. She mentions that she reads many 'complicated' books about Jews without always understanding their intricacies. She has lost, several times over, her notes for her planned film on Israel, but makes no attempt to retrieve them 'par manque de désir'.[27] The ideas she has jotted down whilst in the country fail to articulate clearly what she would like to express. The voice-over monologue, in a process of brooding (the *ressassement* we encounter so often in her films) insistently returns to the difficulty of (and perhaps resistance to) understanding, manifest in the almost symptomatic loss of documents.

Akerman is acutely aware of her status as an outsider in the Jewish state, a mere passer-by (as the repeated references to her imminent

---

23 'I am disconnected from almost everything … I don't know how to live … something in me has been damaged, my relationship to reality.'

24 'promised land.'

25 'another land of exile.'

26 'We'll have to look Israel in the face one day.'

27 'through lack of desire.'

departure from Tel Aviv remind us) who fails to grasp the bigger
picture. She says she still remembers the Hebrew word for 'pioneer',
a crucial term in Oz's fresco and one central to the country's collective mythology, yet neither she nor her family belong to the race
of pioneers who built modern Israel. Her grandfather, she reveals,
before leaving with his family for Belgium in the 1930s, was intent on
settling in Palestine, but, after talking to a settler who had returned
from there, became discouraged by the hostile climate and barren
nature of a country yet to be shaped. Akerman dwells on the fundamental implications this alternative departure could have had for
her family – 'on serait peut-être encore tous là'[28] – and speculates
how 'là-bas', as Israel is called by her family, could have changed her
own upbringing and sense of belonging and rootedness. The opposition, between her confinement in the flat and the buzzing world
that continues outside that forms the film's visual core, symbolically
relates the differing attitudes of 'those who stayed home – in Belgium,
for Akerman's family – and those who left for Israel, enthralled by the
pioneer spirit, when it was a new country with an unknown future'
(Arning 2008: 43).

Halfway through the film, Akerman's disembodied voice tells us
that, whilst fetching cigarettes outside, she learnt of a nearby bomb
attack that left four dead and more than fifty wounded, some of them
seriously. The embedding of this event into the trivia of the director's quotidian and her comment on the civilians' calm reaction to the
attack brings home the realities of a country under a permanent threat
since the outbreak of the second intifada. Akerman does not ask who
has committed the attack and why, nor indeed does she make any
attempt to dwell on the Israel–Palestine conflict. As Philippe Azoury
comments, '[Akerman] a tout vu en Israël, mais elle ne dit rien. Elle
fait semblant de n'avoir rien à en dire. Sinon cette difficulté à dire,
cette impossibilité à donner un avis, qui devient progressivement le
centre du film'[29] (Azoury 2006).

What power does the image hold in view of complex politics and
longstanding ethnic and religious conflict? What is the status of the

28 'we'd perhaps still all be here.'
29 '[Akerman] has seen everything in Israel, but she doesn't say anything. She
pretends that she has nothing to say. Except this difficulty of saying something,
this impossibility of giving an opinion, which progressively becomes the centre
of the film.'

cinema, oft-evoked modern-day avatar of Plato's cave and creator of simulacra?[30] What is the value and role of documentary representation? Akerman's film metaphorically asks all these questions, but resolutely refuses to explain, to theorise, analyse and, above all, to take a position. Like the shot through the window that is emblematic of the dilemma with which the film-maker is faced, it can only put in perspective, cut out a slice of the world which, of necessity, is always the subjective gaze of one person, a meditation between inside and outside and an indirect reflection of reality. Although distinctly more self-reflexive than the earlier films in its critical reflection on the nature of the cinema and the limitations of documentary film-making, *Là-bas,* like the earlier work, situates the documentary in the realm of the emotions rather than of reason, privileging an affective, embodied perception (hence perhaps the repeated references to the director's health and ailments) of reality over an intellectual one.

Shortly before the film's end, the still, urban landscape opposite the director's window suddenly comes to life: images unfold in accelerated motion, as the camera, situated on the balcony of the apartment, tracks rapidly between the sky, blocks of flats and the street. Coloured filters bathe the horizon and the domestic interiors in a menacing red, whilst the noise of aeroplanes and cries of children, heard in amplified sound, imbue the scene with terror. In just over a minute, Akerman, mimicking the rhetoric of the disaster film, simulates war before returning to the normality of life on her doorstep. Is it a genuine attack on Tel Aviv that is being staged here or just a nightmarish vision born of the director's fear? Is the context the Israel–Palestine conflict or is this stylistic exercise a reminder of the horrors of war and terror more generally? As in the rest of the film, no answers are given.

No longer a travel diary but more a journey through the mind, *Là-bas* exerts a singular visual power. Closer perhaps to installation art than to conventional documentary film-making practices, the work serves as a self-reflexive critique of documentary's pretence at veracity as well as a meditation on the film-maker's impossibility in coming to grips with a complex political situation. 'C'est un film impossible

30 Film critics have stressed the analogy between the shadows cast onto the wall of the cave in Plato's *Republic* and cinematic images and, thus, between the chained prisoners to whom these shadows appear as reality and modern cinema spectators. Deleuze, in *Cinema 2*, dedicates a chapter to cinema's 'power of the false'.

à faire, il n'y a rien à attendre de moi sur Israël',[31] Akerman warned her producer before her departure for Tel Aviv. *Là-bas* displaces the Arab-Israeli question and turns it into a personal meditation about belonging, relatedness and exile. The refusal to engage with politics does indeed spare the film from the potential pitfalls of over-simplification and authorial bias, just as the director had wished, yet her insistent withdrawal into the private sphere, compulsive self-revelation, and complaints about personal ailments, especially in view of the genuine deaths and suffering that form the filmic backdrop, risk compromising the ethical dimension that so forcefully informed the earlier work. In *Là-bas*, the focus has shifted from the Other to the self, from the silent, sympathetic restraint and listening that made human encounters possible to a noisy refusal to see and let speak.

References

Akerman, Chantal (2004), *Chantal Akerman: Autoportrait en cinéaste*, Editions du Centre Pompidou/Editions Cahiers du cinéma.

Akerman, Chantal (2003), 'J'étais inconsciente des images que je cherchais', *Libération*, 4 June.

Akerman, Chantal (1999), *Sud. Notes de production*. Paris, Doc et Co.

Akerman, Chantal (1995), 'On *D'Est*', in *Bordering on Fiction: Chantal Akerman's D'Est*, Walker Art Center, Minneapolis, pp. 15–45.

Arning, Bill (2008), '*Down There (Là-bas)*', in Terrie Sultan (ed.), *Chantal Akerman: Moving Through Time and Space*, Blaffer Gallery, the Art Museum of the University of Houston, pp. 40–9.

Azoury, Philippe (2006), '"Là-bas", voyage en appartement', *Libération*, 25 October.

Azoury, Philippe (2002), 'Akerman fait des mirages', *Libération*, 24 May.

Azoury, Philippe and Elisabeth Lebovici (2004), 'Une voix dans le désert', in *Chantal Akerman: Autoportrait*, p. 222.

Bouquet, Stéphane (1995), 'Ce qui revient et ce qui arrive', *Cahiers du cinéma*, 497, pp. 42–5.

Carvajal, Rina (2008), 'Visions in Passing: *From the East (D'Est)*', in Sultan (ed.), *Chantal Akerman*, pp. 10–17.

Charpentier, Caroline (2004), 'De l'autre côté', in *Chantal Akerman: Autoportrait*, p. 213.

David, Catherine (1995), '*D'Est*: Akerman Variations', in *Bordering on Fiction*, pp. 57–64.

Dieutre, Vincent (2004), 'Sud', in *Chantal Akerman: Autoportrait*, p. 211.

Frodon, Jean-Michel (2002), 'Guerre sans nom aux frontières de l'Amérique', *Le Monde*, 26 May.

31 'It's an impossible film, one shouldn't expect anything from me on Israel.'

Halbreich, Kathy and Bruce Jenkins (1995), 'Introduction', in *Bordering on Fiction*, pp. 7–12.

Lebow, Alisa (2003), 'Memory Once Removed: Indirect Memory and Transitive Autobiography in Chantal Akerman's *D'Est*', *Camera Obscura*, 18, pp. 35–82.

MacDonald, Scott (2005), *A Critical Cinema: Interviews with Independent Filmmakers*, Berkeley, University of California Press, vol. 4.

Nichols, Bill (2001), *Introduction to Documentary*, Bloomington, Indiana University Press.

Ottmann, Klaus (2008), '*From the Other Side (De l'autre côté)*', in Sultan (ed.), *Chantal Akerman*, pp. 28–39.

Schmuckli, Claudia (2008), '*South (Sud)*', in Sultan (ed.), *Chantal Akerman*, pp. 18–27.

Tarantino, Michael (1995), 'The Moving Eye: Notes on the Films of Chantal Akerman', in *Bordering on Fiction*, pp. 47–55.

Vermeersch, Laure, Pierre Zaoui and Sacha Zilberfarb (2007), 'Là-bas ou ailleurs: entretien avec Chantal Akerman', *Vacarme*, p. 39.

Zanger, Anat (2006), '*From the Other Side:* On Borders in the Films of Chantal Akerman', in Edna Moshenson (ed.), *Chantal Akerman: Spiral Autobiography*, Tel Aviv Museum of Art, pp. 36–51.

4

Love and intimacy
in a post-lapsarian world

Chantal Akerman is not a director commonly associated with the
depiction of love and romance. Her stern minimalism of the 1970s
and her preoccupation with themes of imprisonment, alienation
and forms of marginality and exile have given her the reputation of a
'serious' and difficult director concerned with grave human questions
at the expense of what is generally considered as the more light-hearted
subject matter of love and intimacy (even if inflected in a negative
key). And yet, desire, love and relationships have played an important
part in many of her works, ever since the rebellious *Saute ma ville*
with its suggestions of an unhappy adolescent infatuation. Whilst
in the work of the 1970s, mutual, fulfilled love is largely presented
as an absence or an impossible aspiration in the life of protagonists
condemned to a life of solitude or errant desire by their nomadism or
psychological difficulties, in the lighter output of the 1980s, love and
romance emerge as the main driving forces of Akerman's burlesque
dramas, even if the possibility of romantic or shared love continues to
be (this time more playfully) called into question. Finally, in the narrative work of the 1990s and 2000s with which we shall be concerned in
this chapter, love relationships are once again scrutinised and probed
in a variety of combinations, from heterosexual love triangles to
adolescent bisexual attraction and transatlantic romance across class
and national boundaries.

   As we have seen throughout this book, a tension between commercial and experimental forms of film-making informs Akerman's work
from an early point in her career. The demon of the mainstream, she
explains in *Autoportrait*, has been haunting her ever since the success

of *Jeanne Dielman*, when friends and cinema professionals encouraged her to 'faire des entrées',[1] and has become more acute over the years, especially since, now in her fifties, she increasingly considers herself a veteran of the cinema rather than a young innovator of the avant-garde: 'Je pense aux entrées. Pas en les faisant, mais c'est là. Et je n'y arrive jamais à faire des entrées. Et c'est une douleur ... Je voudrais ne fusse [*sic*] qu'une seule fois faire des entrées avec un film. Une seule fois. Pour mon père, mon producteur et pour moi'[2] (Akerman 2004a: 111). Since the 1990s, her work has increasingly developed along two avenues: on the one hand, in documentaries and installation art, she explores further the experimental film language which established her reputation as one of the most innovative directors of her generation; on the other, her fictional output pursues the attempts at audience seduction first begun a decade earlier. Her post-feminist romance *Nuit et jour* (1991), the Hollywood-style *Un divan à New York* (1996), the acclaimed adaptation of Proust, *La Captive* (2000) and the burlesque comedy *Demain on déménage* (2004), all, to varying degrees, constitute further ventures into the mainstream. Her autofictional portrait of youth, *Portrait d'une jeune fille de la fin des années 60 à Bruxelles* (1993), by contrast, marks a counterpoint to this tendency in that it operates within the more limited budget of a television commission and employs the spare formal language of her minor cinema. The more popular themes of these films – love, adolescence and young adulthood, the dynamics of desire and the experimentation with different forms of pleasure –, their narrative-driven plots as well as their attractive casts of talented young actors (Guilaine Londez, Thomas Langmann and François Négret in *Nuit et jour*) or established international stars (Juliette Binoche and William Hurt in *Un divan à New York*) make these works more accessible to a wider audience, even though, as we shall see, their style remains what Hamid Naficy calls 'accented' (Naficy 2001).

Like the documentaries that were the subject of the previous chapter, the five fictional works that will be discussed here share thematic and formal characteristics that give them unity beyond their

---

1 'have a success at the box office.'
2 'I think of the box office, not because my films do well, but it's never completely out of my mind. I never manage to have a success at the box office. It's painful ... I'd like, and be it only once, to have a box office success with one of my films. Only once. For my father, my producer and myself.'

mere chronological positioning in the director's oeuvre. The first
three form what Ginette Vincendeau has called Akerman's 'lovers in
the city' trilogy (Vincendeau 2001: 45). *Portrait d'une jeune fille de la fin
des années 60 à Bruxelles*, in a shorter sixty-minute format, continues
the director's exploration of the vicissitudes of adolescence first
developed in works such as *Saute ma ville* and *Je tu il elle*. *Demain on
déménage*, finally, in its blending of autobiography and fiction and its
strategy of rendering present the horrors of the past constitutes some
kind of *summa* of Akerman's work to date and thus offers an excellent
platform from which to revisit a career of more than forty years of
film-making. In their exploration of domestic and city spaces, their
espousal of wandering and nomadism as forms of personal freedom,
and their denunciation of the strictures of repressive social mores
and bourgeois, male-dominated structures, the five films continue to
inflect themes that are central to Akerman's oeuvre, albeit in a style
that is accessible to larger audiences.

Paradise lost: *Nuit et jour*

In *Autoportrait*, Akerman distances herself from the binary oppositions that govern Western thought and, in Derridean fashion,
expresses her desire for cumulative, non-exclusive ways of thinking:
'Dans ce monde binaire. C'est toujours ou ça, ou ça. J'aimerais tant
parfois que cela soit, et ça, et ça, et ça'[3] (Akerman 2004a: 29). *Nuit et
jour*, as suggested by the co-ordinating structure of its title, puts into
filmic practice the idea that it is possible to think the world in terms
of accretion rather than of selection, that what is traditionally thought
of in terms of opposites can be combined without the necessity of
exclusion. Julie (Guilaine Londez) lives a love idyll with Jack (Thomas
Langmann), a taxi driver by night, until she encounters his professional counterpart and physical double, Joseph (François Negret),
who drives the same cab by day. Drawn to the young man as well, she
begins an affair, loving one man by night, the other by day, unencum-
bered by a guilty conscience or a need to choose between them.
    Nuit et jour is, arguably, Akerman's most poetic film, a painterly
homage to youth, the innocence of a love uncorrupted by jealousy and

---

3 'In this binary world, it's always either this or that. Sometimes, I'd like if it were
    this, and this, and this.'

possessiveness, and the pleasures of a Parisian summer that, like in a modern-day fairy tale, will never end. The film opens with a short prologue in the form of two overhead medium close-up shots of first Jack, then Julie, lying on their bed, talking of their lover in a direct address to the spectator. After the intercut title, the next shots show the naked couple embracing, once again in medium close-up, but this time united in the same frame, engaging in pillow talk punctuated by harmonious 'moi aussi's.[4] The sky blue sheets of the bed – the centre of their domestic universe and the altar of their love – shroud the young lovers, whose heads tenderly rest against one another, in a heavenly aureole.

The warm, hyper-real colours (a predominance of blues, saturated browns and reds in the interior shots of the couple's apartment, a rich orange glow as they step out into the world), soft lighting, the strongly haptic quality of the shots (in the scenes of love-making the camera tenderly caresses the bodies of the lovers and sensually traverses their bodies in horizontal pans), the nostalgic soundtrack (Gabriel Fauré's *Après un rêve*) and the tableau quality of the scenes, from the outset, imbue the film with a dream-like, enchanted atmosphere borne out in the dialogues and pro-filmic events. Before the arrival of Joseph into their relationship, Jack and Julie, both ('probably', according to the voice-over) freshly arrived from the provinces – their non-Parisian status, in the stereotypical French division between the capital and *la province*, connotes their innocence –, live a life of perfect happiness, oblivious to the outside world, united in a blissful symbiosis. The first part of the diptych, shot in opulent, sensual photography, shows the two young people's carefree existence in a prelapsarian world of pure desire where reason, ambition and duty have been displaced in favour of touch, caress and embrace. Julie and Jack neither eat nor sleep. They make love when Jack is off duty. When he is out driving, Julie, a modern-day version of the nineteenth-century *flâneur* so beloved of French poetry and film, strolls around the streets of the nocturnal city, happily singing to herself. Showing little eagerness to make friends, the lovers carefully keep the outside world at bay, fending off intrusive neighbours who comically invade their intimacy with all sorts of domestic problems and refusing to rent a telephone line. Socialising, communicating beyond their couple and having a child are all

4 'me too.'

postponed until a hypothetical 'next year', a temporal marker of little significance in their suspended, timeless universe.

The Paris the two lovers inhabit, in Akerman's stylised *mise en scène*, becomes the magical space that tales are made of. The proverbial city of love and lights, at least in the film's first part, is a place where no-one can be hurt. Julie can stride along night-time boulevards and pause to read on the Île Saint-Louis in the early morning hours without ever being subjected to harassment or violence. 'Rien ne peut m'arriver',[5] she can reassure Jack, who reminds her to be careful. The city, with its meandering streets, open squares, inviting café terraces and idyllic river banks is an urban space of quasi-infinite possibilities and unrestrained freedom, its magic enhanced by the musical-type moments when Julie, in a style once again reminiscent of Jacques Demy, sings the praises of her excursions. 'Sometimes we see her singing while she walks and sometimes we merely hear her off-screen, but the movement of her walk and the movement of the melodic line both proceed continuously in a stream of unbroken poetry' (Rosenbaum 1997: 42).

Abstaining from the clichéd portraits of a Paris replete with iconic monuments (the Eiffel Tower, the Arc de Triomphe, Notre-Dame) offered by commercial cinema, Akerman chooses as the film's location the lesser known, socially and ethnically diverse east of the city, a still predominantly working-class area with a significant proportion of mainly Northern African and Jewish immigrants at the time when the film was made. The filmic epicentre is the Place de la République whose imposing statue of France's national symbol, the Marianne, serves both as a meeting point for Julie and Joseph and as an allegory for liberty and female agency. The habitual homage to a capital famous for its history, cultural heritage and glamour is eschewed in favour of a more integrative celebration of Paris as a space of social and ethnic diversity. Joseph's recitation of the pleasures of the everyday uttered on his first nightly walk with Julie constitutes the verbal high point in Akerman's filmic tribute to *le Paris populaire*. Belleville's Asian restaurants are placed side by side with more traditional French brasseries and cafés as the manifold spaces the cosmopolitan city offers the modern *flâneur* in a poetic incantation that evokes both the poet and scriptwriter Jacques Prévert (Vincendeau 2003: 126) and fellow writer

5 'Nothing will happen to me.'

and director Georges Perec, whose family history and literary writings are intimately bound up with the east of Paris. The long back-tracking shot that accompanies Joseph's monologue, and which gradually moves away from the two young people to reveal first the statue and then the square circled by traffic, in a visual strategy reminiscent of *News from Home*, mimics the individual's absorption in the city space, whilst a henceforth disembodied voice continues to celebrate the pleasures of the quotidian it offers the curious newcomer.

Unlike many contemporary art films shot in Paris, such as Leos Carax's *Les Amants du Pont Neuf* (1991) or Cédric Klapisch's *Chacun cherche son chat* (1996), which 'make the living city a "real" character, *Night and Day* proposes a self-consciously distanced city, one that is turned into a set' (Vincendeau 2003: 126). Not only do the anti-naturalist views from Julie and Jack's apartment and the idiosyncratic organisation of their domestic space – a sinuous succession of rooms complete with a vertiginous outdoor plank that links bathroom and kitchen – self-consciously foreground the fact that the interiors were shot in a studio but the streets of the capital also, frequently devoid of other inhabitants, are made to resemble an empty set: the magic décor of a modern-day fairy tale (ibid.).

Labelled as 'irréalisme poétique' by the French press, the film's depiction of youthful innocence and irresponsibility, as Ginette Vincendeau explains, inscribes the work in a long tradition of French film-making, from the Golden Age of the 1930s, alluded to in the interiors and in the homage to *le Paris populaire*, via the New Wave, up to the 'neo-romantic' streak of the late 1980s and 1990s, whilst, at the same time, twisting and challenging the representational codes of its predecessors (Vincendeau 2003: 117–18). The theme of the young lovers as symbolic lost children can be traced back to René Clair and Marcel Carné, but it comes to particular prominence in the cinema of the New Wave which characteristically sets off the playful, adven-turous spirit of the young generation against the moral, emotional and artistic staleness of their parents. Likewise, after the realist experiments of the 1970s and 1980s, directors like Carax returned to the theme of youthful romance, but signalled the impossibility of a realistic depiction of idealistic young love through a highly stylised, theatrical *mise en scène*; others like Eric Rochant and Laetitia Masson acknowledged the changing gender relations of the period in their filmic output. *Nuit et jour* 'combin[es] the latter two tendencies' but 'also subtly challenges the neo-romantic model through its concern with gender' (Vincendeau 2003: 122).

The opposition between the young lovers and the parental genera-tion is brought to light, above all, in the sequence when Jack's parents make an unannounced visit on Sunday, the only day the two lovers have entirely to themselves and which they routinely spend in bed. Julie and Jack bid the parents in, yet their body language betrays their yearning for an undisturbed tête-à-tête. Filmed in shot/counter-shot to accentuate their difference, the two couples, sitting on the most barren of chairs, form a comically antonymic pair: the parents' conven-tional clothing and stiff, visibly ill-at-ease posture stand in caricatured contrast with the semi-nakedness and relaxed charm of the children's generation. The parents' worries about careers, health and parent-hood ('vous n'êtes pas enceinte au moins?'[6]), that is, their concern with bourgeois respectability and projection into the future, are the exact opposite of Julie and Jack's insouciance and firm grounding in the present moment (Julie has no intention of finding herself a job, Jack is contented with being a taxi driver). Under the embar-rassed eyes of the parents, who avert their gaze so as not to witness the young people's intimacy, Jack's hand sensually caresses Julie's leg whilst his foot, shot in close-up, tenderly interlocks with hers. In New Wave style, the parental generation is portrayed as dried up, stifled by convention and social aspiration and incapable of spontaneity and authenticity, though Akerman presents them more as victims of a normative society than as its perpetrators (Julie's meditation about parental anxiety after they have bid them farewell touchingly acknowl-edges the torments of parental love).

In the wider context of Akerman's critique of bourgeois, repressive ideology, the two lovers' refusal to sleep, one of the filmic leitmotifs, serves as a metaphor for the younger generations' vigilance against the amnesia that has befallen the older generation, who have wilfully assimilated into the daily routine of *métro, boulot, dodo*[7] and abdicated any desire for self-realisation. In the first shot after the title, Jack reminisces that, as a child, sleeping constituted his real life, for it offered an escape from reason into the world of dreams. Now that the lovers have found their own personal utopia, sleep, symbolic of

6 'you aren't pregnant, are you?'
7 'Metro, work, sleep', a popular saying in French to describe the routine of urban working life.

the internalisation of societal demand – the 'somnambulism' that modernist writer Hermann Broch so forcefully identified as the plight of Western citizens, robotised by habit and by the uncritical reproduction of common belief systems and values – becomes the enemy. As in Akerman's earlier works, most importantly *Jeanne Dielman* and *Les Rendez-vous d'Anna*, this critique of received ideas is pursued on the level of the film's discourse as well as of its diegesis. Reflecting on the 'on dit' and 'les gens disent' of public opinion, Julie concludes 'Il faut pas toujours croire ce que disent les gens',[8] and firmly rejects *doxa* and reason in favour of instinct, spontaneity and personal freedom.

Significantly, it is the female character in the film who goes furthest in her quest for self-realisation and in her exploration of new forms of relationships outside the confined paths of bourgeois morality and conjugal fidelity. In Julie's free interpretation of love, jealousy, possessiveness and guilt are concepts without meaning. Binary opposition (the either-or paradigm which deconstructivist philosophy holds responsible for hierarchical, centre-based thinking) is relinquished in favour of a non-hierarchical co-presence: Julie can in all innocence answer Joseph's question 'Tu l'aimes [Jack]?' with 'Oui', but, by the same token, reply to the young man's anguished, 'Et moi?', 'Toi aussi'.[9] The physical resemblance between the two actors and the diametrically opposed personalities of the characters (Jack is cheerful, Joseph is melancholic and tormented) underlines their complementarity in Julie's love life. The trio, as Amina Danton and Ginette Vincendeau have pointed out, form different vectors in a complex identity map that echoes Akerman's own multi-layered existence: with his anglicised name, 'Jack is the American pole and Joseph the biblical pole between which Chantal Akerman's identity and culture exist' (Danton 1991: 62). Julie, on the other hand, represents the French pole (Vincendeau 2003: 129), but Guilaine Londez's Belgian nationality equally alludes to Akerman's own origins and her interstitial position between the two countries. On an intertextual level, moreover, the lovers' alliterative names, the anglicised pronunciation of 'Jack', use of a voice-over narrator and, above all, the bohemian male–female–male love triangle also evoke Truffaut's classic New Wave piece *Jules et Jim* (1962) which Akerman uses as the blueprint for her filmic *Paradise Lost*.

8 'They say', 'people say'; 'One shouldn't always believe what people say'.
9 'Do you love him?' 'Yes.' 'And me?' 'You too.'

Problems in the love trio start when Julie begins to confuse her lovers' utterances in a comic flow of *déjà entendus* and when Joseph's awakening jealousy and increasing demands on the young woman jeopardise the utopia of a free, unpossessive love. Symbolically, disharmony sets in when Julie has drifted off to sleep for a moment after making love with Joseph, an unforeseen (taboo) event which, as in *Jeanne Dielman*, deregulates the female protagonist's life, thus creating a teleological momentum that inexorably leads to the dissolution of both relationships. Back home seconds before Jack's return, she confesses to him, 'Il nous est presque arrivé quelque chose. Quelque chose comme un mensonge'.[10] Henceforth, both lovers anxiously cling on to the young woman: Joseph wants her to stay longer every night; Jack asks her to join him on his nightly taxi ride, disturbing even further the fragile night-and-day balance (and thus the strict symmetry on which the film was based up till then). Chance and control metaphorically clash in Jack and Julie's inverse reactions to her taking the pill one morning: for the first time, she is conscious about taking contraception whilst he would prefer her to take the chance of getting pregnant. Linguistically, the increasing distance between the lovers is reflected in their use of intermediaries, such as dreams and invented siblings, to communicate their feelings and in the verbosity that has replaced their calm, bodily fusion.

A powerful visual metaphor, the destruction of the partition wall that separated the lovers' bedroom from their living room, translates the end of utopia and the process of wounding that has replaced idyllic unison. For Jack, knocking down walls is a desperate (symbolic) attempt to see clearer in a relationship that increasingly escapes him, yet, ultimately, this act will strike the last blow to an already ailing love. With the partition wall, the barrier the lovers had carefully upheld against the outside world finally collapses: neighbours, and with them the dreaded reality of 'normal' social existence and its temporalities, are allowed into their sheltered world, turning the constantly deferred hypothetical 'next year' into an immediate threat. A noisy television set and the more 'reasonable' colours with which they have repainted their 1960s-style flat that was covered in flowery wallpaper bring home their abdication to the normalising

10 'Something almost happened to us, something like a lie.'

instances of societal pressure. After a flat-warming party where they dance with separate partners to the schmaltzy sounds of Jean-Louis Aubert's ominous *Si d'aventure* (a song about a broken relationship), Julie finally tells Jack about her affair with Joseph and leaves. The last scene, a playful subversion of the Cinderella myth, shows her dumping two pairs of shoes (associated with each of her lovers) in the municipal waste bin and self-assuredly walking down the street whilst the voice-over soberly comments, 'Et c'est ainsi que Julie quitta Jack et Joseph'.[11]

A post-feminist modern fairy tale, *Nuit et jour* thus, rather than ending in the 'princess marries prince' mode of mainstream fiction, has the female protagonist reaffirm her freedom and autonomy after having lived her desire and affection for two men to the full. Though met with relative indifference from feminist critics, as most of Akerman's work from the 1980s onwards, the film, as shown by Vincendeau, begs interesting questions as to the portrayal of masculinity and femininity, the differences between female and male authorship, and gender stereotyping (Vincendeau 2003: 122–5). Unlike many contemporary directors, who privilege more evanescent, conventionally feminine actresses in their casting (Juliette Binoche is a classic example of the ideal of feminine fragility in French cinema), Akerman has chosen an actress with generous curves to be framed by men with a slighter, almost feminine build. The unusual choice of a female voice-over further foregrounds the materiality of the female body. In the film, Julie, in an intertextual citation from Truffaut's *Baisers volés* (1968), which itself references Flaubert's *L'Education sentimentale* (1869), rejects any idealised image of femininity: 'Je ne suis pas une apparition, je suis une femme, c'est tout le contraire'.[12] The young woman is resolutely in command of her own story: she is the unquestioned centre of the narrative, the focal point of the camera, which follows her every move, and even, it has been argued, she provides the voice-over comment of the pro-filmic events, that is, she retrospectively recounts her own story (Rosenbaum 1997: 46). Unlike the female protagonist in *Jules et Jim,* Julie does not need to exert pressure on her lovers, nor does she lose her self-determination in the heterosexual triangle. Where Truffaut's male-authored love story tragically ends with the death of Jules and Catherine in a car accident

11 'And that's how Julie left Jack and Joseph.'
12 'I am not an apparition. I am a woman, which is the complete opposite.'

provoked by the latter, Akerman's heroine can self-confidently walk out of both relationships without looking back (her independence is in stark contrast to Joseph who, by breaking the taboo of looking at her when she leaves in the morning – a play on the Orpheus and Eurydice myth which forms a leitmotif in the film –, loses her forever). With her depiction of a strong female character and her emphasis on the actress's physicality and voice, Akerman, then, challenges the stereo-typed representations of a more ethereal and elusive femininity of many male-authored films. Julie knows when to move on. As she leaves, walking towards the camera at an assertive pace, a bright new day has begun in Paris.

Mimetic desire: *Portrait d'une jeune fille de la fin des années 60 à Bruxelles*

Akerman's 1993 film *Portrait d'une jeune fille de la fin des années 60 à Bruxelles* (hereafter *Portrait d'une jeune fille*) is part of a television series entitled *Tous les garçons et les filles de leur âge* (*All the boys and girls of their age*) commissioned for the French national arts channel La Sept/ARTE. Nine directors of different age groups, including, amongst others, Claire Denis, André Téchiné and Olivier Assayas, were invited to film an autobiographically inspired tale of adolescence set against the backdrop of their own teens. Based on personal memories, the series was thus designed to reflect the spirit, atmosphere and socio-political make-up of the recent French past stretching from, roughly, the early 1960s to the early 1990s. Beyond the focus on adolescence, the film-makers were required to use music from the period in question, to include a party scene, to respect the medium format of a sixty-minute film and to work within a limited budget (5.4 million francs per film). The opening credits of Akerman's film posit its temporal frame as April 1968, that is, just one month before the student revolts in Paris which 'function as a mythical origin story in narratives of the new Left, poststructuralist theory and film culture' (White 2008: 417). By virtue of 'being not quite Paris, not yet May' (ibid.), the film's setting decentralises the revolutionary spirit from the capital to a periphery, thus fitting the autobiographical remit required by the series whilst at the same time extending its scope from a strictly metropolitan French to a European Francophone context.

The film chronicles one day in the life of Michèle (Circé Lethem, the daughter of Belgian experimental director Roland Lethem, acknowledged as 'Circé' in the credits), a teenager ill at ease with herself and the world who has decided to quit school as her first act of revolt against the parental generation (her first spoken words are an ominous 'Au revoir, papa'[13]), the strictures of repressive morality and traditional gender roles and the boredom of social conformism. At the movies, she meets Paul (Julien Rassam), a young deserter with whom she strolls along the city's boulevards, talking, shoplifting, kissing and eventually making love for the first time (or, at least, so it is suggested, even if the sexual act is not shown). After a party at a friend's, she 'offers' Paul to her best friend Danielle (Joëlle Marlier), visibly unsure of the nature of her own sexual desire in relation to them both. The last scene, set in an idyllic rural setting, shows her walking away with her back turned to the camera, her juvenile body growing more and more distant as a pale morning sun rises over open fields and the chant of birds mingles with the noise of cars and aeroplanes.

Coming of age and youthful rebellion are, of course, favourite themes of French cinema – one may think of Truffaut's classic *Les 400 coups* (1959) or, more recently, Claude Miller's *L'Effrontée* (1985) and Catherine Breillat's *36 fillette* (1988) and *A ma sœur* (2001) – and, as such, they were not altogether new to Akerman, who had offered original studies of adolescence in works such as *Saute ma ville, Je tu il elle* and her 1984 *J'ai faim, j'ai froid*, a twelve-minute contribution to the omnibus film *Paris vu par… vingt ans après* that follows the journey of two teenage girls who run away from Brussels to Paris. The vicissitudes of love and friendship and the quest for sexual initiation, both important themes of *Portrait d'une jeune fille*, are among the standard topoï of this popular sub-genre and thus rather predictable in terms of genre convention. Where Akerman can be seen to innovate on the coming-of-age narrative is in grafting upon the more conventional heterosexual encounter that is the staple diet of this type of film the tale of one girl's attraction for another, and in showing the complex ways in which the relations with the female love-object are fashioned by the heterosexual norm. As Judith Mayne explains,

> this film explores how lesbian desire is both shaped and repressed by
> the codes and conventions of heterosexual romance. On the surface,

13 'Goodbye, dad.'

the film could be described as a somewhat conventional girl-meets-boy tale. But what shapes the girl-meets-boy story is the simultaneous desire, for the girl, to connect to another girl and to tell stories. In other words, this is a lesbian narrative with a difference; girl still meets boy, but that classical and timeworn plot is the pretext for the connection between the two girls. (Mayne 2003: 150)

Like *Nuit et jour,* the film examines the dynamics of triangular love and desire, with the difference that here Akerman is no longer interested in deconstructing binary opposites but rather, in what literary critic René Girard has termed the phenomenon of 'mimetic desire', that is, an erotic attraction mediated and shaped by a third Other (Girard 1961). In a revealing scene towards the beginning of the film, we see Michèle and Danielle kissing two young men in a café. Michèle pauses in her kiss to cast a long and insistent gaze at her friend, who is locked in a passionate embrace. When Danielle looks up, the two girls exchange a complicit smile. It soon becomes clear that their erotic adventures with the opposite sex are not so much driven by pleasure (they disparagingly comment on their experience with the young men) than by a desire to discuss and share them with one another. In other words, it is not so much the heterosexual experience as such that is of interest to them, but its abstraction into a mutually owned tale and the complicity and bond gained from such a sharing of experiences. Michèle later confesses to Paul that she has allowed him to kiss her in the cinema 'pour faire souffrir quelqu'un, pour le raconter aussi',[14] and insistently evokes the absent Danielle in her conversations with the young man, establishing her as an object of desire and a substitute of herself. Inversely, when Michèle meets Danielle in front of the school gate, Paul stays behind, but is positioned in the reverse field of Michèle's sightline, 'hovering offscreen' (Mayne 2003: 152). The very same technique where the Other is implied offscreen instead of being shown directly, and thus where he or she is spatially set up as a mediator of desire, is used in the penultimate scene where Danielle exits the frame, in all likelihood to join Paul, whom we suspect, once again, to be located on the periphery of the frame.

Commentators of the film have tended to read *Portrait d'une jeune fille* as a lesbian coming-out story (Mayne 2003: 150), 'a lesbian coming-of-age' story (Taubin 1995: 65) or as an example of lesbian minor cinema (White 2008). Whilst homoerotic desire is indeed

14 'to make somebody suffer and also to talk about it.'

central to the filmic narrative, given the intersection between the two relationships, it may be more accurate to describe the film as a meditation on the fluidity of sexual desire and, like the earlier *Je tu il elle*, as a study of an adolescent's experiment with different – hetero- and homosexual – sexual identities. Though generally subsumed into a canon of lesbian film-making, Akerman's filmic oeuvre, as is evidenced in a work like this, is in fact more often preoccupied with mobile, nomadic sexual identities rather than with an exclu- sively homosexual desire, eschewing, like the director herself, any ready assimilation into a specific sexual or identity politics. Rather than tracing a coming-out, that is, a teleological narrative that presup- poses some kind of resolution in the form of a confession, a love declaration or, at least, a clear sign of self-awareness or acceptance, the pro-filmic events remain ambiguous and open-ended, the lack of closure 'inviting a spectatorial participation that is not reducible to identification or catharsis' (White 2008: 422).

At the party, Danielle chooses Michèle as her partner in a popular ring dance where a group of interlocked dancers circle around an alternating couple in the middle. Surrounded by the circle, the two girls, forming a joyful couple, dance to the upbeat rhythm of Trini Lopez's interpretation of the song *La Bamba*. When it is Michèle's turn to choose a new partner, she first hesitates, moving around the circle a number of times, but then once again picks Danielle, thus publicly asserting her affection. Yet, as soon as the music changes to a slower tempo, her friend is snatched up by a dark-haired young man and Michèle is left standing alone gazing at the couple dancing in a close embrace. The refusal of a point-of-view shot (Michèle is framed in close-up looking at the couple, but Danielle and her partner remain offscreen) and the lyrics of James Brown's *It's a Man's Man's Man's World* to which the couple dance symbolise Michèle's exclu- sion in a heterosexually dominated world (inversely, Leonard Cohen's *Suzanne* which accompanies the scene where she supposedly makes love with Paul serves as a musical metaphor for the heterosexual couple's intellectual and sensual fusion). When, after a tender walk hand in hand with her friend across the open countryside, Michèle finally pushes Danielle into Paul's arms, it is difficult not to see her sacrifice as some form of self-conscious exorcism, for she explains, 'Après, je serai tranquille. Tu ne devras plus me raconter. Je ne devrai plus observer ta recherche. Je pourrai de nouveau vivre comme avant,

après.'15 Between 'avant' and 'après', two markers which remain fluid
in the film's temporal frame, lies the abyss of the 'love that dare not
speak its name', a love that Michèle hardly seems ready to confess
to herself, let alone to her friend, a love that has no right of place
and possibility of expression in the conservative social space of 1960s
Belgium, where young women, as the protagonist complains, are still
bound by traditional models of femininity and female conduct and
destined and educated above all for marriage and motherhood.

Set on the threshold between adolescence and womanhood,
where personalities are formed and role models adopted or rejected,
the film traces the protagonist's struggle at liberating herself from
the shackles of her (petit) bourgeois upbringing and the strictures
of repressive social norms and institutions. As already seen in *Je tu
il elle*, the emancipation of the female character takes the symbolic
form of a stripping process: after having bid her father farewell,
Michèle writes a series of increasingly macabre sick notes which, one
by one, in a succession of burlesque causalities, kill off her whole
family, including, at the end, herself – 'Veuillez excuser Michèle:
elle est morte'.16 'The fantasy of her own death is also a fantasy of
rebirth, of shedding the various institutional identities she possesses,
those associated with the family and school' (Mayne 2003: 151). In
celebration of her newly gained freedom, she tears up a class book
and elatedly throws the pieces up in the air. In the deserter Paul she
finds a fellow outsider and rebel, who has shed off his comfortable
existence as moneyed young man and, who, like her, henceforth, lives
a nomadic life of wandering and chance encounters.

In a move away from Akerman's corporeal cinema, more than by
their gestures or acts, the two young people are defined by their talk
– compulsive self-revelation in the case of Michèle, a more restrained
probing and acquiescing in that of Paul. 'Michèle-Circé parle, n'arrête
pas de parler, non pour s'étourdir, mais pour se découvrir. Pour que
ses paroles soient plus fortes qu'une réalité qu'elle refuse, pour que
le verbe devienne chair'17 (Aubenas 1995: 45). Unlike in *Je tu il elle*,

15 'Afterwards, I'll be easy in my mind. You won't have to tell me anymore. I won't
have to watch you searching anymore. I'll be able to live again like before, afterwards.'
16 'Please excuse Michèle, she died.'
17 'Michèle-Circé talks, doesn't stop talking, not to stun, but to discover herself. So
that her words are stronger than a reality she refuses, so that the word becomes
flesh.'

which forms a filmic counterpoint to *Portrait d'une jeune fille*, here self-expression and agency are no longer the privilege solely of the male character. On the contrary, in a subversion of traditional gender stereotypes, it is Michèle who asks Paul to kiss her and to undress, she who breaks into the cousin's flat which will become the deserter's hiding place, she who cites by heart long passages from Kierkegaard and analyses the current state of the world and, finally, she who gives him away to a third party as if he were a precious gift or an object. The filmic frame is almost without exception dominated by Michèle, shown in close-up (often frontal shots) or followed by long tracking shots as she wanders around town, boyish in her dress and demeanour and clumsily assertive in her adolescent rebellion. The intensity of her presence is enhanced by the little depth of field in the majority of shots except the last one, where we see her walk away from the camera across a hazy meadow bordered by trees whose vanishing lines mark a symbolic new trajectory in her life.

True to her modernist agenda and her distrust of verisimilitude, Akerman makes no effort to reconstruct the Brussels of the late 1960s that is the film's temporal frame. The urban space, interiors and costumes all have a distinct 1990s feel and anachronisms like the presence of DVDs in a record shop and contemporary cars in the streets blatantly evince the director's disinterest in the accuracies demanded by a period-style historical reconstruction. The spirit of the age is situated outside the filmic image; it is made palpable in the profound malaise of the two protagonists, their contestation of conservative gender roles, social injustice and repressive sexual mores as well as in the interspersed references to the social and political struggles that announced, and the philosophies that shaped, the events of May 1968: the Vietnam War, women's liberation, the sexual revolution, Sartre's existentialism, the critique of consumer society, all give the film a distinct *air du temps*. The impending revolution, prophesied by the two protagonists – 'Tu ne sens pas que quelque chose va arriver? Ça ne peut pas rester comme ça',[18] Paul says to Michèle during one of their urban peregrinations – imbues the pro-filmic events with a heavy emotive charge and creates a spectatorial expectation that propels the narrative forward, yet ultimately remains suspended just like the two youngsters' personal utopia of a future where there will be no more

18 'Don't you feel that something will happen? It can't stay like this.'

poverty, no more war, no more Nazis.

Like *Nuit et jour*, *Portrait d'une jeune fille* self-consciously evokes the tradition of 1960s French film-making that shaped Akerman's own film style. The film 'takes place in an imaginary landscape of the New Wave of French cinema, a cinemascape revisioned, adapted and paid homage to throughout the film' in the guise of manifold intertextual resonances, from Agnès Varda's *Cléo de 5 à 7* (1961) to Godard's *Vivre sa vie* (1962) and his *Deux ou trois choses que je sais d'elle* (1966) (Mayne 2003: 158–9). Yet, far from being simply a nostalgic evocation of a period that redefined cinematic forms of expression and provoked a radical rethinking of social and political structures and of interpersonal relations, the film asks fundamental questions as to the legacy of 1968 for our present generation. At a time when this legacy is perhaps more contested than ever, when the idea that May 1968 heralded an era of greater social justice tends to be superseded by claims that, on the contrary, it furthered the dominance of global capitalism and opened the doors to a ruthless individualism, the film invites us to meditate on the relevance of the events for our own time and to compare Michèle and Paul's idealistic expectations with the current state of the world. Akerman's (auto)portrait of a young girl at the end of the 1960s thus becomes a filter through which we can examine our own relations to one of the defining social events of the second half of the twentieth century.

Transatlantic banter: *Un divan à New York*

Golden Eighties, which received mixed reviews from critics and failed to charm larger audiences, left a question mark over Akerman's talent for light-hearted entertainment. With *Un divan à New York* (1996), the second part of her 'lovers in the city' trilogy, the director made a further attempt at moving into the mainstream, this time by revisiting the genre of romantic comedy, an all-time favourite amongst audiences and a genre which, like the musical, is closely associated with the Hollywood dream machine. Akerman, for the first time, unites a truly international cast led by highly acclaimed French actress Juliette Binoche, who came to prominence through her work with independent directors such as Godard, Téchiné, Carax and Kieslowski, but became known to a wider audience through her role in the heritage production *Le Hussard sur le toit* (1995), and William Hurt, a popular American actor of both commercial and independent films whose fluency in French and residency in France made him an ideal choice for her film on a transatlantic love affair. The high-budget film, which oscillates between the two adoptive poles of Akerman's life – New York and Paris – was co-produced by Belgian, German and French production companies.

A man and a woman in their thirties, of different nationalities, social class and diametrically opposed personalities, swap apartments during the summer holidays: Henry Harriston, a successful, psycho-rigid Manhattan psychoanalyst beleaguered by narcissistic patients, escapes to Paris, whilst Béatrice Saulnier, an attractive young dancer harassed by countless admirers, seeks peace and quiet on the other side of the Atlantic. Systematic (and rather tedious) cross-cuttings between the two locations trace each character's adaptation to the other's idiosyncratic domestic space – while Béatrice thrives in Henry's minimalist loft on Fifth Avenue complete with a depressive dog and harassing clients, he despairs in her bohemian top-floor flat in multi-ethnic Belleville, plagued by deficient plumbing and neurotic former lovers. The twist comes when orderly Henry, unable to cope any longer with the cheerful chaos of Beatrice's garret, precipitously returns to New York, finds that the young woman has taken over his practice and, immediately attracted to her, poses as one of his own patients. The symmetrical cross-cultural exploration gives way to a theatrical game of mistaken identities and missed confessions (standard ingredients of romantic comedy and its sub-genre, screwball comedy, which Akerman uses as her generic models) and, after a series of burlesque twists and turns, ends in the unlikely couple's happy union.

The cross-cultural setting in principle would have offered ample opportunities for a playful examination of cultural stereotypes, yet, unlike her earlier work which foregrounds *idées reçues* with a view to denouncing their gross distortions, *Un divan à New York* endorses much of what it posits as simplistic commonplace. 'Il paraît que les ascenseurs sont très rares en France, comme les salles de bain',[19] muses the liftman upon Béatrice's arrival in the chic Manhattan apartment block, a prejudice confirmed by Henry's arrival in the Belleville garret where an old-fashioned bathtub sits in the open-plan

---

19 'It seems that lifts and bathrooms are very rare in France.'

living room. A lot of the film's comic effect, again rather too systematically, revolves around Americans' alleged inability to express their feelings as opposed to the proverbial French passion, exuberance and penchant for drama: whereas the timid Henry struggles to confess his love to Béatrice, her French lovers voice their passion in unrestrained hyperbole ('je suis un violent, un taré ... je te tue, je me tue'[20]).

True to the conventions of romantic comedy, the film operates through a series of reversals, which efface difference and render the union of two individuals of disparate social and cultural backgrounds possible. Subjecting himself to Béatrice's amateurish analysis, Henry loosens up, reconciles himself to his underprivileged background (on the couch, he confesses his guilt at having distanced himself from his working-class mother), and throws overboard the restrictive social conventions of a class he has conquered through education, but into which he has never fully assimilated. Béatrice, on the other hand, a *femme fatale* who, according to one of her lovers, 'n'aime personne',[21] falls for the awkward charm of her supposed patient. Psychoanalysis, though it creates the conditions for the two characters' rapprochement, is satirised as a frivolous pastime for rich New Yorkers (a familiar topos of Woody Allen's comedies) that ultimately does more harm than good, and whose intricacies, in the naive understanding of Béatrice and her friend Anne (Stephanie Buttle), boil down to oedipal complexes, sibling rivalry and a caricatured syntax of 'mhms' and 'yeses'. It was not least this clumsy parody of the talking cure that discredited the film in the eyes of many of its critics: 'Le discours sur la psychanalyse est d'une niaiserie absolue ... à l'image d'une grande partie des dialogues'[22] (Ardan: 1996).

In spite of its various shortcomings, *Un divan à New York* is arguably Akerman's most colourful homage to her former adoptive home. From the film's first shots taken across Central Park which frame the glistening skyscrapers of Manhattan to Paolo Conte's upbeat 'It's Wonderful', New York is celebrated as a fairytale land of quasi-infinite possibilities and a traditional haven for European and other immigrants. Yet, behind its glossy images, the film implicitly laments the disappearance of the run-down, anarchic metropolis of the 1970s in the wake of major gentrification projects and the yuppification of

20 'I'm violent and crazy ... I'll kill you and myself.'
21 'loves no-one.'
22 'The discourse on psychoanalysis is totally silly like most of the dialogues.'

its middle classes. Multi-ethnic Belleville and Brooklyn, depicted as last bastions of communitarian, authentic living not yet overtaken by corporate culture and global capitalism, serve as visual counterpoints to the streamlined Manhattan skyline and as reminders of the vitality and artistic creativity born out of neighbourhood spirit, cheap housing and cultural diversity. The clashing anti-naturalism of Béatrice's apartment, whose sinuous layout and sloping walls recall the French poetic realism of the 1930s and the heyday of German expressionism (the interiors were shot in the famous Babelberg studios in Berlin which produced some of the masterpieces of expressionist cinema such as *The Cabinet of Dr Caligari* and *Metropolis*), undercuts the deceptive fiction faked in the opening sequence.

With its star cast, sparkling subject matter and glamorous locations, Akerman's pastiche of 1940s and 1950s Lubitsch-style romantic comedy promised to be a popular success, yet 'Divan le Terrible', as the film has been dubbed by Gérard Lefort (Lefort 1996), became the greatest flop in the director's career, both in financial and in critical terms. With hindsight, its failure to seduce mainstream audiences seems predictable: far from severing its avant-garde origins, the film retains a sufficient dose of signature Akerman style – long takes, flattened dialogues, comparatively sparse musical accompaniment, privileging of open over closed form, anti-naturalist acting and sets – to bewilder the average movie-goer. One need only look at the anticlimactic ending to see the gap between Akerman's de-dramatised syntax and conventional Hollywood style: in a scene replete with Shakespearean overtones, the two lovers, invisible to one another, at last confess their love across adjacent balconies. When Béatrice realises that her patient John Wire is none other than Dr Henry Harriston, she climbs over the cast-iron grid, the two embrace stiffly and disappear inside the flat, mumbling barely audible platitudes about domestic problems ('j'ai réparé la fuite d'eau; les pompiers sont venus'[23]). The grand scene of the lovers uniting, the undisputed high point of classic romantic comedy, traditionally shot in close-up and accompanied by a sentimental soundtrack, falls flat and simply fizzles out as the couple withdraws from sight. As often with Akerman, narrative pleasure and drama are not situated where the viewer expects them to be and spectatorial identification is hampered by distancing effects.

---

23 'I've repaired the leak; the fire brigade came.'

Unpopular with mainstream audiences, the film fared little better among professional critics who were scathing about its platitudinous dialogues, predictable turn of events, lack of rhythm and heavy-handed approach to comedy. Jean-Michel Frodon, one of the most staunch and long-standing promoters of Akerman's work, sums up what is wrong with the film: 'Le film, sympathique, agréable même, manque par trop de tonus, ou d'enjeu ... on retrouve la patte d'une grande réalisatrice, mais les règles du jeu qu'elle s'est elle-même imposées paraissent lui peser'[24] (Frodon 1996). In more recent years, academic criticism has seen a tendency to rehabilitate the film as an underrated and misunderstood example of Akerman's avant-garde practice and of her revision of Hollywood style (White 2005, Capp 2001). Whilst such readings are not altogether unjustified, they change little in the fact that, despite its undeniable charm and idiosyncrasies, *Un divan à New York* rates amongst the director's weakest works. Akerman herself has long distanced herself from the film, which she describes as an infelicitous departure from her minority position: 'Ce n'était pas pour ça que j'avais voulu faire du cinéma après avoir vu *Pierrot le fou* ... J'avais quitté le mineur dont parle Deleuze. Et j'étais tombée dans le bruit'[25] (Akerman 2004a: 123). In fact, so great was her disappointment after the film's release that she briefly contemplated abandoning film-making altogether and effectively did not make another feature for the next three years. It was with *La Captive*, her ingenious adaptation of Proust, that she was to make her return to the cinema, offering one of its most beautiful examples of the creative interplay between literature and film and a masterpiece in the exploration of human subjectivity.

The Proustian web of jealousy: *La Captive*

Literary adaptation, for reasons that are easily understandable, is not a genre readily associated with experimental or *auteurist* practices of film-making (despite the fact that *auteurs* like Truffaut or Godard

24 'The film, though pleasant and even amusing, far too much lacks muscle and drive ... one recognises the style of a great director, but the rules she has imposed upon herself seem to weigh heavily on her.'
25 'It is not for this type of film that I wanted to become a film-maker after having seen *Pierrot le fou* ... I had left the minority position Deleuze is talking about. I had merely produced noise.'

made several films based on literary sources). Whereas commercial cinema, mainly under the guise of the heritage genre, capitalises on the classics of world literature which it exploits as a lucrative foil for popular productions, the *auteur* tradition, as suggested by its name, has developed largely in rivalry with the literary medium, privileging its own scripts over a pre-existing source text which would impose on the director a preordained plot and aesthetic vision. Like many directors of the post-New Wave generation, Akerman, though an avid reader, was initially sceptical about the practice of literary adaptation, which she considered irreconcilable with her more purist conception of film-making and adverse to the development of her own personal film style:

> I thought that literary works should not be adapted to film, that music should not be used, that cuts and shots/counter-shots should not be used – these kinds of prohibitions. I was very radical, undoubtedly too much so, but I needed to be in order to define myself, form myself as a film-maker. (Akerman 2001: 15)

As she reveals in an interview, she began to toy with the idea of adapting Proust's *A la recherche du temps perdu* (1913–1927) back in the 1970s, more precisely after she finished *Jeanne Dielman*, yet what she herself calls her 'too dogmatic' conception of the cinema prevented her from taking the project any further at the time. It was only some twenty-five years later, having experimented with a wide range of genres, production modes and film styles, that she felt she had the sufficient openness and versatility required to tackle a text as complex as Proust's seven-volume modernist masterpiece. Rather than taking on the whole of the *Recherche* – a project attempted by Luchino Visconti and Joseph Losey in the 1970s, but unfortunately never brought to fruition (cf. Beugnet and Schmid 2005) –, she eventually decided to make a film loosely inspired by the fifth volume, *La Prisonnière*.

Whereas Proust's modernist style, exceptional narrative complexity and radically new conception of the self, time and space have deterred commercial directors and given his work the unjustified reputation of being unadaptable, it is precisely these aspects that were of interest to a director like Akerman, who comes from the experimental tradition.[26] *La Prisonnière* in particular, with its focus on interiority, its

26 Before Akerman, Volker Schlöndorff and Raoul Ruiz directed part adaptations of *Un amour de Swann* and *Le Temps retrouvé* retrospectively. For a discussion of

iterative and circular narrative structure, blurred temporality, setting in an enclosed space, and plot revolving around confinement and obsession, shares great affinities with the director's avant-garde film language and allowed her to revisit the themes of mental and spatial imprisonment that were central to films like *Jeanne Dielman, Je tu il elle* and *L'Homme à la valise*. The book's exploration of sexual fluidity, homosexual desire and the torments of a heterosexual relationship gave her the opportunity to continue her study of love, intimacy and desire developed in such diverse works as *Les Rendez-vous d'Anna, Toute une nuit, Les Années 80* and *Golden Eighties* as well as in her more recent lovers' trilogy of which *La Captive* forms the last part. More than just a venture into yet another filmic genre hitherto unexplored in her oeuvre, *La Captive* allowed Akerman to form an alliance between her own cinema of modernity and Proust's modernist writing which, far from reducing film to a subsidiary and derivative product as is often unjustly claimed of literary adaptation (cf. Hutcheon 2006: 2–4), allowed her, on the contrary, to demonstrate the medium's capacity to chart human consciousness and subjectivity to no lesser a degree than the most acclaimed literary works.

One of the least-known volumes of the *Recherche, La Prisonnière* tells of the Narrator's tormented relations with his lover Albertine, whom he suspects of infidelities with other women. Life in the parental flat where he holds her captive soon turns into mutual torture for the two lovers. The Narrator obsessively watches Albertine's every move and interrogates her over her daily activities and encounters, yet, despite his cunning strategies to extract confessions from her, he never obtains clear evidence of her suspected lesbianism. An allegory of the impossibility of fully knowing another person, *La Prisonnière* is also a powerful meditation on human subjectivity and delusion. The genius of Proust in this volume, the most introspective of the *Recherche*, is to exhibit the destructive mechanisms of a jealousy that has become pathological and which, like an illness, gradually invades the lover's entire physical and mental being.

An *auteur* even within the confines of the adaptation genre, Akerman is outspoken about the liberties she has taken with the Proustian source text. Her film, she states in an interview, makes no

---

these various projects and of the relationship between Proust and the cinema more widely, see Beugnet and Schmid 2005. The book also contains a detailed chapter on Akerman's adaptation elements of which have been reused here.

claims to 'faithfulness', a principle she considers as restrictive and unproductive (and which, indeed, has for a long time hampered both the practice and the study of literary adaptation). Rather than strictly adhering to detail, her approach, based (like Proust's novel) on memory, privileges proximity of vision and a dialogical relation with the source text:

> Je n'ai pas essayé de coller au texte. L'unique question que je me suis posée fut la suivante: que reste-t-il en mémoire? Adapter un monument comme Proust revient tout simplement à filmer l'affection, l'émotion, la tristesse. Ensuite nous sommes revenus au livre pour quelques détails. Il y a eu comme cela des va-et-vient littéraires et concrets. La lettre au cinéma n'est pas une excellente solution surtout lorsqu'il y a une adaptation littéraire en jeu. On ne peut pas s'inspirer du livre sinon cela devient une sorte de bataille – perdue d'avance – contre la littérature.[27] (Le Corre and Ardjoum 2009)

The filmic title, *La Captive*, and names of the protagonists, Ariane and Simon, rather than Albertine and Marcel, signal the inherent affinities between source text and adaptation, whilst at the same time positing the film's status as an autonomous art work which transcends the literary universe that inspired it (the assonance Ariane/Albertine and the similarities between the name of the male protagonist, Simon, and Albertine's surname in the novel, Simonet, resonate with the source text). The film's plot and spatio-temporal organisation evince a similarly free, but no less symbiotic approach to the source. Akerman and her co-scriptwriter Eric de Kuyper have preserved most of the key scenes that relate to the Narrator's tormented relations with Albertine, but have cut all sub-plots, most importantly the story of Charlus and his lover Morel that echoes the demise of the hetero-sexual couple. Several scenes, including Simon's interrogation of two young lesbian actresses, are borrowed from the subsequent volume, *Albertine disparue*, whilst others, such as Ariane's visit to the Rodin Museum and Simon's venture into the Bois de Boulogne red-light

---

27 'I didn't try to stick to the text. The only question I asked myself is the following: what remains in memory? To adapt a monument like Proust simply amounts to filming affection, emotion, sadness. Afterwards we got back to the book for some details. We thus went forwards and backwards between the text and the film. Literality in the cinema is not the best solution, especially when a literary adaptation is at stake. One cannot draw one's inspiration from the book other-wise one gets caught in a battle – lost from the outset – against literature.'

district, are invented. The director's most far-reaching departure from the original is in the film's ending, that is, Ariane's supposed death at sea, which, whilst once again borrowing material from the sixth volume, also radically changes the circumstances under which this death occurs and the connotations it carries. In the *Recherche*, Albertine is killed in a riding accident after having fled from the Narrator's flat; in Akerman's rewriting of the scene, she drowns in the sea, in all likelihood driven to suicide by her lover's obsessive need for control and knowledge. Evoking the tragic fate of Alfred Agostinelli, Proust's secretary and lover who crashed into the Mediterranean during a flying lesson in 1914, this death by drowning endows the film with an autobiographical dimension that the original carefully dissimulates (Raoul Ruiz, in his 1999 adaptation of Proust's *Le Temps retrouvé*, similarly, in contrast to the source text, stresses the autobiographical).

Akerman and de Kuyper have modernised the source, but nonetheless preserve a temporal fluidity that, mimicking Proust's involuntary memory, permits the spectator to navigate forwards and backwards in time and acts as a bridge between the early twentieth-century source text and its twenty-first century adaptation: the marine-style outfits of Ariane's friend Andrée evoke the 1920s, the décor of the flat where Simon holds Ariane captive is reminiscent of the period between the wars when Proust finished writing his novel, and the convertible Peugeot driven by Simon evokes the 1960s, heyday of the French New Wave and time of Akerman's own youth. The cordless phones with which the lovers communicate, on the other hand, anchor the pro-filmic events in our own present.

Even in terms of a free adaptation, *La Prisonnière* presents multiple difficulties. The privileging of reflection over action, setting in a restricted space, the iterative nature of the plot, and, above all, the focus on interiority and subjectivity, all raise questions of their own: how can a film give visual form to mental obsession? How can it capture the claustrophobic atmosphere of the text, the increasing anxiety and torment of the jealous lover, the web of lies that imprisons the two protagonists? In other words, how can complex psychological states and thought be translated into visual images? Akerman renounces what would have been the easiest (but least cinematic) equivalent of the first-person narrator's extensive descriptions of his state of mind, that is, the use of voice-over. Instead, *La Captive* seeks to recreate the pathological universe of the focal character by means of a serial structural pattern which subjects the entire film narrative to the laws of obsession (Benoliel 2000: 15). The film compulsively repeats figures, postures and motifs that visually evoke the jealous lover's mind: car chases around Paris's fashionable districts, interrogations of the young woman and her acquaintances, trickeries and intrigues aimed at penetrating her suspected secret life permeate the film narrative, giving it a distinctly circular feel. Rather than building into a teleological, resolution-driven narrative, the film's scenes are but multiple variations of the same unresolved predicament: Simon (Stanislas Merhar), a young man of leisure unable to cope with uncertainty, ambivalence and sexual fluidity, seeks to control every aspect of his mistress's (Sylvie Testud) life by submitting her to a tight regime of surveillance, yet the more he spies on her, the more the truth and, ultimately, the young woman herself, escape him. The circle and the spiral, two leitmotifs in the film's narrative organisation, are emblematic of the workings of a mind that cannot tolerate difference and ambiguity and thus remains inexorably caught in the prison of an obsessive jealousy (for it is the male rather than the female protagonist who is the real captive of text and film). By giving the film itself the structure of obsession, Akerman charts a complex 'atlas of emotions' (cf. Bruno: 2002), a metonymical visual map that allows the spectator to travel freely through the lover's tormented mind.

The *mise en scène* of the apartment which, as in *Jeanne Dielman*, is the locus of most interior shots, serves a similar purpose. The old-fashioned décor of Simon's vast, but claustrophobic flat, with its winding corridors, imposing antique furniture, heavy draperies, and wealth of doors that suggest spaces invisible to the camera, more than just a historical set designed to evoke the temporal setting of the novel and the stifling mores of the upper classes, is, to use another term coined by Giuliana Bruno, an 'emotional architecture' which subtly evokes the protagonist's mental state. Like in Alain Resnais's classic *L'Année dernière à Marienbad* (1961), which famously explored the complex workings of memory by means of an extended architectural metaphor, the labyrinthine narrative space in *La Captive* comes to represent an internal, mental landscape, that of Simon's fixation (Beugnet and Schmid 2005: 181).

Anchoring her film in its own medium-specific history, Akerman adapts Proust's modernist novel of consciousness to the cinema of obsession, in particular the thriller and the *film noir*, which offers a visual corollary to Proust's exploration of extreme mental states (cf. Delorme 2000; Beugnet and Schmid 2005). Where Proust's sickly Narrator keeps to his room, Akerman releases Simon onto the street in a playful translation of Douglas Sirk's famous dictum on cinema's power to render affect kinetically ('motion is emotion'). Through a dense game of citations, Simon is set up as a double of that most famous of twentieth-century film characters keeping watch over and chasing after a mysterious beautiful woman: private detective Scottie in Hitchcock's *Vertigo* (1958). The Hitchcockian thriller, revered for its suspense, hypnotic camerawork and astute character psychology, meets Akerman's more static film syntax in a bold synthesis of paralysis and movement, Akermanian duration and Hitchcockian tension.

Beyond the references to *Vertigo* in the extended car chases and the rear projection effects in the scene where Simon is chauffeured to the Odéon theatre from where he will abduct Ariane (who is attending an after-show party with her female friends), the most obvious citation of Hitchcock comes in the museum sequence when Simon, hidden from view in an adjacent room, watches Ariane contemplating a symbolic double of herself. The young woman has paused in front of the Rodin bust of a modern-day Aphrodite, creature of the sea and object of desire like herself – this pause before the sculpture, as Benoliel comments, symbolises an encounter between the real and the mythical woman (Benoliel 2000: 17) –, just like Madeleine, who falls into contemplation in front of the portrait of her alleged ancestor Carlotta Valdes whilst being closely observed by Scottie. The bust's artfully tied chignon, starkly evocative of Carlotta's conspicuous hairdo as well as that of her imitator, the aptly named Madeleine, establishes an explicit link between the two scenes. The thematic resonances between *Vertigo* and *La Captive* are of course obvious – in both an obsessive male character projects onto, fashions and ultimately destroys a young woman –, yet Akerman's citation of Hitchcock is more than just a playful pastiche used to signal affinities (and possibly influences) between the two works. Stepping out of the immediate fictional universe of the two films to evoke film history more widely, the Hitchcockian intertext pays homage to European art cinema's fascination with the American modern masters, Hitchcock in particular, who was revered by the New Wave and the *Cahiers du cinéma*, and to the fruitful fusion of European and American traditions that not only characterises Akerman's own approach but has inspired such masterpieces as Godard's *A bout de souffle* (1960) and *Alphaville* (1965) in the generation before her. A transnational director who has consistently worked between America and Europe, Akerman here celebrates the rich intersection between two fundamentally different filmic traditions (independent film and Hollywood) and production modes (the artisanal versus the studio system), demonstrating that, across the boundaries of national film styles and traditions, a powerful new film language can be forged.

In one of the film's most beautiful scenes, situated directly after the title credits, we see Simon projecting an 8mm film of Ariane and her female friends frolicking on the beach in the privacy of his house. A microcosm of the 35mm film that will follow, this homemade production (in all likelihood shot by Simon himself), with its far grainier and jumpier images, acts as a *mise en abîme* of both the pro-filmic events and the director's interstitial position at a crossroads between an artisan, experimental film style and the more polished images of commercial film-making. The soft lighting, translucent colours and scratched film surface give a tenderly tactile quality to these first filmic images (Beugnet 2007: 134) suffusing them with the nostalgic charm of *Belle Epoque* leisure so unforgettably described by Proust in his second volume, *A l'ombre des jeunes filles en fleurs*. At first, none of the young women is singled out in the idyllic gynoecia devoid of men until the camera focuses on two girls and, then, in a close-up, on one: Ariane. Drawn by the filmic image, Simon abandons his position next to the projector and sits down in front of the screen, his dark silhouette engulfing the figure of his lover, who, at this precise moment, turns her back to the camera and disappears into the waves. Benoliel comments, 'La position dit aussi son fantasme: le fondu, la fusion, faire corps avec elle(s), non pas traverser l'écran ... mais entrer dans l'image, rejoindre l'objet rêvé dans son espace, ne faire plus qu'un avec la femme-océan'[28] (Benoliel 2000: 16). Voyeurism and the need for control, unbridgeable separation and a desire for total fusion, nature and domesticity, memory's power to resuscitate the past (the subsequent film narrative suggests that the introductory 8mm sequence is situated *after* the film's diegetic ending, its images thus conjuring up the memory of the deceased Albertine) – many of the film's central concerns are already present in this filmic prologue whose Impres-

---

28 'His position also reveals his fantasy: blending, fusion, becoming one with her/
them, not to traverse the screen ... but to go into the image, to join the object of
his dreams in her space, to be one with the ocean-woman.'

sionist colours and scenery evoke the *Recherche*'s indebtedness to late nineteenth-century painting and inscribe each of the protagonists in their natural habitat: Ariane/Aphrodite, the mythological creature of the sea, Simon, the morbid city dweller.

La Captive's art, as Raymond Bellour explains in a masterful study, 'consists in endlessly varying and reinventing' this same figuration of the 'gaping rift specific to desire between men and women' (Bellour 2002: 34–5). Be it in the scene where the two lovers take a bath in adjacent bathrooms, their bodies separated by a frosted glass wall which distorts Ariane's graceful silhouette into an elusive figure of absence, or in their idiosyncratic love-making which essentially consists of Simon rubbing his body against the young woman who feigns to be asleep, or in his interrogation of the two lesbian lovers who are visually set apart from the heterosexual male through shot/counter-shot, Akerman inflects, through multiple permutations of the same pattern, Proust's pessimistic vision of the impossibility of a shared love between the sexes. In this obsessive reiteration of the same, the question of whether or not Ariane is betraying Simon, and thus of whether his jealousy is grounded in an objective reality, is deliberately left open. *La Captive*, like the source text from which it is adapted, in an exercise close to hypnotism, straddles the permeable frontier between reality and delusion, paranoia and deception, challenging one of the main prejudices that surrounds literary adaptation: that cinema is less able to render ambiguity and subjectivity than literature.

Akerman's characterisation of the two protagonists, though refraining from any overt psychology, elicits a deep concern with questions of class and gender, issues that are equally important to Proust's fictional universe. Born into wealth and privilege, Simon leads the leisurely life of a nineteenth-century gentleman of private means, a double of the Proustian Narrator and his alter ego Swann, but also of Marcel Proust himself, who was never forced to take a profession and thus was free to dedicate himself entirely to his literary oeuvre. A sickly character allergic to pollen, noise and light, Simon feigns working on a study of Racine, but remains a 'bachelor of art', one of the many sterile figures in the *Recherche* who contemplate art but are unable to find transcendence in creation. With his old-fashioned grey suits, chauffeured Rolls and the polite distance he keeps from his friends and mistress, Simon cuts a distinctly outmoded figure, closer to the time of Proust's youth than the late twentieth century. 'Though pictured in a cinematic universe – a universe of movement and constant change – Simon, associated with stasis, is a character out of sync, and, as such, an essentially anachronistic figure' (Beugnet and Schmid 2005: 182). Visibly unquestioning of his privileged social position, the young man is free to command at whim both his servants and the submissive Ariane, whom he summons and dismisses as he pleases, shields from society, and even abducts brutally under the startled eyes of her friends.

Ariane, on the other hand, in tune with Proust's Albertine, is presented as the elusive social and sexual Other whose inscrutability fuels the protagonist's fetishist fascination. An orphan with no family ties save an aunt who lives in the country (and who, as we know from the text, seeks to marry her impoverished niece off to a wealthy husband), she has found an adoptive family in the artistic circles of the theatre and the opera, yet also rubs shoulders with the upper classes into which she is gradually assimilated. As an interloper between two worlds, she keeps the freshness and spontaneity of her more bohemian milieu, but is increasingly stifled by the manners of the *haute bourgeoisie* and by her lover's obsessive keeping watch over her every move. Contrary to the source text, in which she gradually emancipates herself and grows in self-assurance, wit, and literary creativity – as evidenced by her bravura monologue on the pleasures of ice cream, a stylistic masterpiece full of sexual innuendo –, in the adaptation, she is crushed by Simon's anguished and morbid passion, which reduces her to muteness and, as the last scenes seem to suggest, drives her to suicide.

The non-diegetic music, as analysed in more detail by Beugnet and Schmid (Beugnet and Schmid 2005: 195–8), dramatises the struggle between life-affirming and life-denying forces, *libido* and *destrudo*, through the association of a specific musical theme with each of the two protagonists: Rachmaninov's symphonic poem *Isle of the Dead* with Simon, Mozart's popular opera *Così fan tutte* with Ariane. Whilst Rachmaninov's dark and brooding romantic score underpins the male protagonist's morbid fascination with his lover and orchestrates scenes where he seeks to bring her under his domination, Mozart's more light-hearted *Così*, on the contrary, asserts Ariane's quest for autonomy and freedom, but also her potential for betrayal (Mozart's *opera buffa* does, after all, revolve around the themes of male suspi-

cion and female infidelity). Music lessons are introduced early on in
the film as a means by which the young woman withdraws from her
obsessive lover and joins in the company of female friends. In one of
the most symbolically charged scenes of the film, Ariane stands on
the balcony of their shared flat singing a love duet from *Così* together
with an older woman at the window opposite (Aurore Clément) whom
we assume to be the singer Léa. Ariane's amateur voice mingles with
the rich sounds of the professionally trained singer in a perfectly
co-ordinated duet that alludes to some greater intimacy in their lives,
whilst her lover powerlessly watches the scene, unable to break the
closeness between the two women.

In Akerman's creative rewriting of the source, the Freudian struggle
between *libido* and *destrudo* can be resolved only through the death of
the person that fuels the anguish. When, in one of the last scenes,
Simon forces the driving Ariane to kiss him, sending their Peugeot
dangerously off-road, the spectator is made to anticipate the film's
melodramatic ending: Ariane's flight and death in the night-time sea.
Accompanied by the crescendo and amplified sound of Rachmaninov's *Isle of the Dead*, the young woman and Simon, who seeks to
rescue her from the waves, are engulfed by darkness. Their struggling
bodies fleetingly revealed by the camera leave the question of whether
we are witnessing a suicide or an accident open. Ultimately, in the
film's logic of a destructive passion, they amount to one and the same.
The last shot of a dazed and trembling Simon slowly approaching
the camera in a boat, heavily charged with artistic and mythological
resonances, confirms him as a figure of death: his dark silhouette
evokes Charon traversing the Styx, but also brings to mind Arnold
Böcklin's eponymous symbolist painting *The Isle of the Dead,* which
provided the inspiration behind Rachmaninov's symphonic poem,
as well as F. W. Murnau's melodramatic silent masterpiece *Sunrise*
(1927) where a repentant husband believes his wife has drowned
after a storm. This last image, Benoliel explains, in returning to the
opening sequence, powerfully visualises the male character's imprisonment in a circular desire:

> Sa position redouble son impuissance: quand il a filmé ces images [la
> séquence du début], il n'était déjà pas du côté des femmes mais du
> côté de la caméra et, cette fois encore, il ne peut franchir la frontière,
> obligé de rester là, tout près mais à distance. Obligé en quelque sorte
> de mesurer, à son corps défendant, l'écart définitif entre les sexes [...]

Alors quand Simon, au dernier plan du film, sur l'eau, vient vers nous en barque depuis le fond de l'image, du plus loin au plus près, jusqu'à passer sous le cadre et, en somme, entrer dans la salle de cinéma, on se dit qu'il rejoint sa place initiale.[29] (Benoliel 2000: 16)

In its emotive re-figuration of the source text, *La Captive* succeeds in that demanding, but unjustly underrated, artistic challenge – to adapt from one medium to another in a complex exercise of translation and negotiation. A visual masterpiece and one of Akerman's most mature films, it subtly evokes Proust's lost time neither by freezing it in the past nor imprisoning it in the present, but, on the contrary, by forging what Deleuze calls a 'crystal image', that is, a vision which 'constantly exchanges the two distinct images which constitute it, the actual image of the present which passes and the virtual image of the past which is preserved' (Deleuze 1989: 81).

Sex and survival: *Demain on déménage*

A grand piano attached to two ropes dangles in mid-air accompanied by the sound of anxious whispers and the cracking noise of a hydraulic device. The dangerously exposed and vulnerable instrument spirals around on its own axis, its shiny black frame silhouetted against a clear blue sky. The camera, in reverse shot, cuts to a multi-ethnic crowd of spectators, in their midst an attractive middle-aged woman with delicate features (Aurore Clément) who is gradually singled out by a zoom-in. The group comically mimics the instrument's moves whilst the woman, an outmoded suitcase firmly pressed against her chest, mumbles directions. Her worried, tense face eventually relaxes into a smile as she heaves sighs of relief, her whole body invested in an exercise of stylised expressiveness.

---

29 'His position doubles his impotency: when he filmed these images [the opening sequence], he already wasn't on the side of the women but on the side of the camera, and, here again, he cannot cross the boundary, he has to stay put, very close, but nonetheless distant. In a sense, he has to measure, unwillingly, the definitive distance between the sexes [...] Thus, when, in the film's last shot, at sea, Simon, moves towards us from the depth of the image in a small boat, from a point in the far distance to one which is very close, until he passes under the frame, and, in short, enters the cinema, we sense that he is coming back to his original place.'

From its opening sequence, *Demain on déménage* situates itself in the realm of the spectacle, the dangling instrument, as commentators have pointed out, serving as an easily decipherable metaphor for the cinema, a spectator art par excellence whose poetry and magic, inherently dependent on technology, appear fragile and permanently threatened to the captivated viewer (Lefort 2004). After a series of experimental documentaries (*Avec Sonia Wieder-Atherton, De l'autre côté*) made in the wake of *La Captive*, Akerman returns to fiction in sparkling form with this delightfully burlesque and energetic comedy whose choreographed *mise en scène*, song and dance numbers and upbeat, absurdist humour celebrate cinema's power to entertain, but also, as we shall see, on a deeply personal and ethical level, to pay homage to humanity's resilience and capacity for laughter in the wake of unspeakable horror. Working once again within the parameters of a more commercially oriented production, the director gathers a prestigious cast, uniting for the first time before the camera her fetish actress Aurore Clément and her female lead from *La Captive*, the wonderfully versatile Sylvie Testud, as an endearingly dysfunctional mother–daughter couple. Jean-Pierre Marielle, one of France's most popular actors known above all for his work on stage, and young talents Natacha Régnier and Elsa Zylberstein are enlisted in supporting roles as a melancholic estate agent haunted by the Holocaust, a heavily pregnant woman who doesn't want a child and a glamorous, upper-class wife and mother who seeks refuge from family life in a shared rented studio. Where *La Captive* had exceptionally led her to the chic west side of Paris, here the director returns to more familiar territory, multi-ethnic and socially mixed Ménilmontant, an area to the north-east of the capital where she herself has lived for several decades and which served as first abode for many Ashkenazi Jews emigrating to France in the 1920s and 1930s.

As in *Toute une nuit*, albeit in a less radical form here, classical linear narrative is eschewed in favour of a looser organisation reliant on rhythm, music and choreography rather than on the more conventional model of conflict, suspense and resolution. The script, which, like *La Captive*, was co-written by Eric de Kuyper, incorporates disparate fragments and stories that Akerman was jotting down, without any specific project in mind, on a daily basis after the hostile reception of *Un divan à New York* – a writing exercise she likens to self-preservation in an interview with *Le Monde* (Akerman 2004b). With the help of de Kuyper, the fragments were woven into a multi-layered narrative without, however, seeking to impose any kind of rigid teleology, for, as Akerman comments, 'je n'avais pas envie qu'on sache exactement où on allait et que le film à ce titre devienne classique. La ligne droite n'est pas mon fort'[30] (Azoury and Lefont 2004).

Catherine Wienstein (Aurore Clément), a deliciously lively, extro-vert piano teacher and recent widow, moves in with her daughter Charlotte (Sylvie Testud), a comically nerdish writer struggling to finish a commission for a pornographic novel, in the latter's cluttered, bohemian loft, which was formerly the workshop of her Jewish grandfather. When the two women decide to sell the flat, a stream of visitors – mainly middle-aged couples in different states of marital agony and dissolution – invades their home in an increasingly burlesque ballet of arrivals and exits, punctuated by snappy and often absurdist dialogues which debunk the stereotypes of romantic love ('On fait l'amour tous les jours! – Vous aimez cela, alors? – Non, on s'y fait'[31]) and satirise the codified, bedazzling language of the real-estate business ('les nuisances', 'le tout électricité', 'aucun mur porteur'[32]).

The film unravels to the rhythm of the characters' encounters in an atmosphere of joyful delirium – 'déménager' in colloquial French also means 'to lose the plot' – enhanced by Akerman's habitual princi-ples of serialisation, accumulation and escalation. No longer bound by the strictures of realism and traditional character psychology, the narrative, flowing like an orchestral piece, develops its many narra-tive strands and voices, as marital and familial tensions mount and dissolve, middle-class prospective buyers tune in to the contagious gaiety and chaos of the two women's bohemian existence, disaffected couples split up and new ones form in a constant coming and going across the two levels of the flat – a spatial metaphor for the Freudian unconscious according to Serge Kaganski (Kaganski 2004). Though not a musical in any conventional sense, *Demain on déménage* insis-tently flirts with the genre through its intermittent song-and-dance numbers, interspersed piano recitals, and the lively choreography of the actors who whirl around the cinematic space, dancing even when they are performing banal tasks like cleaning the oven or washing the sink.

30 'I didn't want the audience to know exactly where the film was going and, thus, to make it conventional. I'm not good at straight lines.'
31 'We make love every day! – You must like it, then? – No, you get used to it.'
32 'noise pollution', 'all-electric', 'no load-bearing wall'.

Close to the work of Jacques Demy and Alain Resnais, who similarly
lend enchantment to the quotidian through song and dance in their
musical comedies, and to the popular operas of German composer
Kurt Weill, the film also, once again, reveals Akerman's predilection
for Lubitsch-style comedy and her deep affinity with Yiddish theatre
and the music-hall, the two birthplaces of the burlesque.

Though she often evokes her tragic family history in interviews,
Akerman had never addressed it in any direct way in her filmic oeuvre.
Here, for the first time, she places at the centre of her film the difference between first and second generation Holocaust survivors (that
is, the constellation of her own family) with regard to their attitude
to memory and their passing down of stories as well as their more
general existential condition. Catherine, who is born in the camps and
has lost her mother in the Holocaust, lives 'dans la force de la vie'.[33]
A whirlwind of energy and unbridled emotion, she loves music and
dance, company and spontaneous parties, making love and making
friends. Her irresistible charm and vitality, contagious humour and
artistic exuberance seduce all who come into her orbit, from the
melancholic Monsieur Popernik, a fellow Holocaust survivor, to the
mummified prospective buyers who, unlike her, are straight-jacketed
by social convention and aspiration, patriarchal gender roles and
stifling conformism.

Her daughter Charlotte, on the other hand, visibly out of sync with
herself and the world, comically unable to access her imagination and
adamant in her refusal to confront her family's traumatic past ('je
déteste la nature, les grand-mères et les armoires bretonnes',[34] she
declares in one of the film's many funny lines), leads a reclusive life,
apparently without friends or lovers. In Akerman's playful reversal
of traditional mother and daughter roles, the mother is given the
frivolity and vulnerability of a teenage girl (it is she who, plagued by
insomnia, comes to sleep in her daughter's bed), whilst the daughter
confronts the world with the seriousness of an old child, a condition
which Akerman, with reference to her own childhood, identifies as
the lot of second-generation Holocaust survivors – faced with the
sufferings of the parental generation, she explains, the children of the
Holocaust are 'privé[s] d'adolescence, donc de révolte'[35] (Azoury and

33 'infused with vital energy.'
34 'I hate nature, grandmothers and Breton wardrobes.'
35 'deprived of adolescence and, thus, of revolt.'

Lefort 2004). By thus subverting the stereotypes traditionally associated with youth and old age, especially with regard to the New Wave
celebration of youth which we have already mentioned in the context
of *Nuit et jour*, Akerman establishes the parental generation as the
bearers of hope, happiness and romantic love in a moving cinematic
homage to her own parents and to the lost generation that suffered
the horrors of World War II and the camps.

Sylvie Testud, in a bravura performance, slips into the burlesque
persona of Charlotte, a would-be writer in quest of an artistic, sexual
and cultural identity. Dressed in baggy trousers and hiding behind
heavily rimmed glasses, chain-smoking and hacking away on her
computer, she brings to her commission for a pornographic novel
the seriousness of a diligent schoolgirl – she comically eavesdrops
on love-making couples and watches porn movies in search of
inspiration –, and the nerdish energy of the caricatured scientist.
Half Buster Keaton, half Charlie Chaplin, to whom the name of her
screen persona playfully alludes (Chaplin is lovingly called 'Charlot'
in France), her acting style evokes the heyday of slapstick comedy,
whilst at the same time mimicking Akerman's own burlesque performances in films such as *Saute ma ville* and *L'Homme à la valise*.
Indeed, through Testud, who bears a strong physical resemblance to
Akerman – 'Sylvie Testud [...] c'est un peu mon Antoine Doinel',[36] the
director reveals in an interview with *Libération*, alluding to the famous
resemblance between Truffaut and his fetish actor Jean-Pierre Léaud
(Azoury and Lefort 2004) –, she not only revisits the silent era and the
burlesque which, as we have seen, inform a great many of her works,
but also seems to pay homage to her own multifaceted career in the
cinema. A double return to origins – the early days of the cinema
and the beginnings of her own work –, *Demain on déménage* contains
various autotextual citations from *Saute ma ville*, most notably when
Charlotte, in a scene where she is looking for coffee, carelessly flings
pots and pans out of the cupboard. As in a palimpsest, an artistic
form that befits Akerman's aesthetic of traces (which was discussed
in detail in Chapter 3), the earlier work remains tangible under the
surface of the new.

Akerman, as we have seen throughout this book, is ethically
opposed to any direct representation of the Holocaust and prefers
instead an oblique evocation, either by means of metonymy – most

36 'Sylvie Testud is a bit my Antoine Doinel'.

notably through the recurrent figures of imprisonment and displacement in her work – or through the dialectical image which we
have discussed in the context of her documentary work. *Demain on
déménage* is no exception, despite the fact that it refracts the tragedy
of the camps in a burlesque mode.

> C'est un sujet [l'Holocauste] qu'on ne peut aborder de face de toute
> façon. La fiction, le jeu, sont nécessaires. D'une certaine manière,
> cette histoire, je la récris depuis toujours, à chaque fois de manière
> différente.[37]

Akerman comments in an interview for *Le Monde* coinciding with
the film's release (Akerman 2004b: 27). Whilst in *Golden Eighties* and
Histoires d'Amérique the horrors of the extermination system were
evoked largely in the form of testimonials, here, by contrast, traces
of the Holocaust come to haunt the quotidian in a collision between
past and present similar to the inscription process we have already
identified in her documentary tetralogy and in *Les Rendez-vous d'Anna*.
Though apparently unconsciously, as she insists in interviews,
Akerman once again operates what one could call a poetics of substitu-
tion applied to the pro-filmic events. The family flat, with its prolifera-
tion of armchairs, rattan stools, lampshades and flowerpots, broken
chandeliers and dusty bookcases, piled up, staggered and stapled
over two floors, in the director's baroque *mise en scène*, is connoted
as a place of transit and thus, together with the mother's suitcase,
becomes a visual reminder of deportation, of the Jewish Diaspora and
the malediction attached to the 'wandering Jew' (Kaganski 2004).
The string of visitors, on the other hand, who all have conspicuously
French names and who rapaciously examine and measure every inch
of the family flat, including the paintings on the wall, more than
just a satire of bourgeois materialism, bring to mind the French
citizens who profiteered from the misfortune of their Jewish neighbours, a painful aspect of French history which is at the centre of
another Holocaust fiction, Joseph Losey's *Monsieur Klein* (1976), the
disturbing story of an art dealer who takes advantage of the situation
of the Jews in occupied France until he gets himself embroiled in the
horrors of deportation.

---

37 '[The Holocaust] is a subject that cannot be tackled directly anyway. Fiction and
play are necessary. In a way, I've been rewriting this story for ever, but each time
differently.'

More pervasively, the concentrationary universe, with its crema-toria, gas chambers, and industrial-style annihilation, infiltrates the filmic fiction by literally spilling over into the characters' quotidian. Whether it be the ubiquitous smell of disinfectant – 'ça sent la Pologne'[38] – that haunts Monsieur Popernik, the dense black smoke billowing from the family oven and Hoover or the dark fumes that emanate from Popernik's car, the object world is contaminated by traces of the past that, at any given moment, risk invading the benign surface reality. Even apparently anodyne dialogues are invested with double meanings: 'Voici la salle de bains', Charlotte explains to a prospective buyer, to which he replies ominously, 'Très bien, comme ça il n'y a pas de souci avec le gaz'.[39] Earlier in the narrative, Catherine explains her sudden tearfulness by a somewhat surreal, but no less charged, 'c'est ce poulet, il est si jeune, ils meurent si jeunes les poulets'.[40] In a similar vein, the empty fridges that are extensively inspected and commented upon by prospective buyers and tenants and the insistent talk about food (another Akerman classic with which we are already familiar from *Histoires d'Amérique*) recreate the concen-trationary universe amidst a deceptively banal domestic context. As already seen in her documentary series, but in a burlesque register – 'la comédie y naît des flancs de la tragédie, le désir y prend essor depuis l'anéantissement',[41] observes Jacques Mandelbaum (Mandel-baum 2004: 214) –, Akerman infuses the everyday with a powerful affective charge that unsettles the present and convokes the horrors of the past behind a seemingly banal surface reality.

In a compelling study on the interplay between everyday life and horror in concentrationary art, Max Silverman draws on the writings of the poet and concentration camp survivor Jean Cayrol, who provided the text for Alain Resnais's acclaimed Holocaust documentary, *Nuit et brouillard* (1955). 'Cayrol's vision of an "art concentrationnaire", in which the image of humanity can no longer ignore the experience of the concentration camp', he argues, 'reflects critically on the role of the image in creating what we might call a "concentrationary imagi-nary". The dehumanising nature of its mode of representation ("the

---

38 'it smells of Poland.'
39 'Here's the bathroom', 'Great, so we needn't worry about the gas.'
40 'it's this chicken, it's so young, they die so young, these chickens.'
41 '[in *Demain on déménage*] comedy is born out of the womb of tragedy, desire emerges from annihilation'.

Nazi gaze") is interrupted through the creation of an anxious tension between the concentrationary universe and everyday life' (Silverman 2006: 13). In *Demain on déménage*, we encounter a comparable representational strategy which similarly consists of breaking down the boundaries between trauma and ordinary existence, past and present, the visible and the invisible. By means of a persistent exercise of defamiliarisation, Akerman's film transforms the banal object world of the everyday into a reminder of the horrors of the camps. More importantly, perhaps, the film's organic, meandering form, with its numerous subplots and digressions, clownish effects of accumulation and *coups de théâtre*, is posited as an anti-system which, in setting up chaos and improvisation in opposition to the deathly rigidity and control that characterises the concentrationary universe, serves to shield cinema from the 'Nazi gaze' and, with it, from the clutches of rationalisation, objectification and, ultimately, dehumanisation.

Far from making light of the Holocaust, as is done to alarming and tasteless effect by Roberto Benigni in *La Vita è bella*, released in 1997, *Demain on déménage* catapults the horrors of the past into our own present, thus inviting spectators to confront the traumatic legacy of twentieth-century atrocities and to remain vigilant against the conditioning, amnesia and indifference that rendered them possible in the first place. Humour, in this context, not only serves as a powerful weapon against oblivion, it also, as already seen in *Histoires d'Amérique*, celebrates the (quintessentially Jewish) capacity of stepping back and laughing in the face of adversity and of re-appropriating one's history and destiny, however painful and traumatic. Ernst Lubitsch gave a classic example of such an attitude of defiance in his Nazi comedy *To be or not to be* (1942), 'a particularly audacious attempt to sabotage the presumptions not only of Nazi rule, but of all tyrannical holds on the real' (Elsaesser 1997: 185). With *Demain on déménage*, Akerman once more reveals herself as one of Lubitsch's worthy heirs, a fellow expert in the art of using laughter to revisit some of humanity's darkest hours.

Arguably (together with *Histoires d'Amérique*) Akerman's most Jewish film, *Demain on déménage* is also one of her most explicitly autofictional works. A 'Portrait of the artist as a young woman', like *Les Rendez-vous d'Anna* almost thirty years earlier, it reconfigures personal experience in a fictional mode, accumulating autobiographical references, whilst, at the same time, consistently blurring the boundaries between autobiography and fiction. We have already seen that the director establishes her main actress, Sylvie Testud, as her alter ego, that she has chosen Ménilmontant, her own district in Paris, as the film's location, and that the constellation of characters revolving around the opposition between first and second generation Holocaust survivors mimics that of her own family. Beyond these evident parallels between real life and fiction, Akerman's family history is more directly incorporated into the film in the form of a diary, belonging to Charlotte's grandmother who has perished in the camps and which mother and daughter rediscover together in a deeply moving scene that constitutes the filmic epicentre. As the director reveals in *Autoportrait*, the diary in question is modelled on that of her own maternal grandmother, Sidonie Ehrenberg, who died in Auschwitz in 1942, and of whom this text, written when she was an adolescent, constitutes the sole remaining vestige. The words from the diary which Catherine in the film deciphers from Polish for the benefit of her daughter echo those of the original even if they have been modified, for, as Akerman explains, 'il fallait bien en passer par la fiction'[42] – a phrase which, a few pages later, is qualified as 'Enfin presque'.[43] As she explains, this almost literal transposition from real life to fiction constitutes a novelty in her filmic oeuvre: 'Jamais, je n'ai fait ça, prendre ses paroles [les paroles de la mère], les lui prendre et les mettre immédiatement, et à peine transformées, dans une comédie comme seuls les pessimistes peuvent en faire'[44] (Akerman 2004a: 71 and 74–5).

First shown in *Demain on déménage*, the diary has since been incorporated into an installation work entitled *Marcher à côté de ses lacets dans un frigidaire vide* (To Walk Next to One's Shoe Laces in an Empty Fridge) which has toured galleries and museums around the globe, most recently, the Camden Art Gallery in London (2008). The installation consists of, in the first room, a diaphanous tulle spiral upon which is projected a text with Akerman's thoughts about the cinema and a text about her family biography and her growing-up in the shadow of the Holocaust; in the second, the grandmother's diary is projected on a tulle screen and there is a short documentary in which Natalia Akerman deciphers her mother's diary for her daughter

42 'I had to fictionalise.'
43 'Well, almost.'
44 'I've never done this before: take her [my mother's] words, take them from her and insert them immediately and barely altered into a comedy like only pessimists can make.'

and, for the first time, shares her experience of the camps with her. As Edna Moshenson explains, 'Taken together, the two parts of the installation ... summarize years of creative work in which Akerman searched for a way to replace an invented memory and autobiography with a reconstruction of her family biography through a process of opening up and talking, acceptance and reconciliation with the past' (Moshenson 2006: 19).

In *Demain on déménage*, we discover that the grandmother was a gifted painter (the diary is adorned with a charming watercolour of a young woman, possibly a self-portrait), but that, as so many women of her generation, she struggled against the social constraints that burdened women's professional and individual self-realisation in the first half of the twentieth century. The diary's incipit, 'Je suis une femme. Il ne faut donc pas dire mes pensées à voix haute. Je ne peux donc croire qu'aux choses cachées',[45] lucidly expresses the limitations of the female condition filtered through the mind of an adolescent. The diary, then, as the only remaining trace of a life brutally cut short in the flower of youth and as a feminist reminder of women's limited agency in male-dominated societies, leaves a void, an artistic destiny that needs to be filled by future generations of women: the writer Charlotte Wienstein in the film, the author-director Chantal Akerman in real life.

The film's autofictional markers invite us to read Charlotte's discovery of her artistic voice and creative talent at the end of the film as a *mise en abîme* of Akerman's own career. The young woman's comic struggle with her pornographic commission (that is, with a particularly exploitative type of fiction) and her emergence as a prose writer concerned with the condition of women trapped in the banality of provincial life and motherhood, in other words, as a modern-day female Flaubert, evoke the director's own rebellion against the strictures of the entertainment industry and her persistent interest in the multifaceted forms (social, mental, domestic) of female imprisonment. The linguistic parody of pornographic fiction, whose trite mechanisms of sexual arousal Akerman deflates comically, throws into relief the codified, nauseatingly predictable style of commercial mass production against which it posits forms of art that unsettle spectator expectation and, in so doing, challenge received ideas and

---

45 'I am a woman. I therefore can't speak my thoughts out loud. I can only believe in what is hidden.'

conservative world views (with its concentrationary subtext, the film, moreover, could also be seen as denouncing the lucrative Holocaust industry which turns suffering into spectacle).

In one of the film's last scenes, the piano is seen spinning in mid-air whilst another crowd, gathered around Catherine, watches anxiously in a variation of the opening sequence. With *Demain on déménage*, Akerman herself has performed a vast loop which sums up and sheds light on her entire oeuvre. In this tragi-comic work, informed by a diasporic and post-Holocaust consciousness, her last full-length feature film to date, the director revisits many of her most cherished themes, developed in a plethora of registers and genres, over a career that spans more than forty years: wandering and uprooting, the precariousness of Jewish memory and transmission, the female condition in male-dominated societies, the mummification of language and thought, the privileged relations between mothers and daughters, the fragility of heterosexual love and the alternative of same-sex partnerships (the film ends on Charlotte and the pregnant woman who didn't want a child jointly raising the latter's baby). As Jacques Mandelbaum explains, the film's burlesque saturation retrospectively sheds light on what was evoked more obliquely in her minimalist work of the 1970s – the trauma of the Holocaust – whilst at the same time postulating art's privileged role as a mediator between individual and collective spheres, between past and present:

> Ce petit monde à l'envers que dépeint le film révèle rien moins que l'envers du monde, ce lieu destiné à ne jamais être ni vu, ni représenté. Jadis figuré, dans le cinéma de Chantal Akerman, à travers le dénuement de l'espace et l'évidement des personnages, c'est ce même lieu qui ne cesse de la hanter aujourd'hui, en disant son nom, qui est celui de la promiscuité, du chaos et de la mort. Ce trop-plein semble rétrospectivement nous éclairer sur la nature du vide qui a longtemps hanté son oeuvre. Tels les meubles dont se débarrassent sur le trottoir, nuitamment, les protagonistes du film à mesure que l'appartement et la mémoire s'encombrent, Chantal Akerman pose donc, plus que jamais, avec *Demain on déménage* la question de la possible transposition, et plus encore du possible partage, d'une expérience infiniment intime, singulière et douloureuse dans l'espace public par une opération de l'art.[46] (Mandelbaum 2004: 214)

46 'This little upside-down world that the film depicts reveals no less than the reverse side of the world, a place destined to be neither seen, nor shown. Formerly evoked in Chantal Akerman's cinema through bare spaces and

References

Akerman, Chantal (2004a), *Chantal Akerman: Autoportrait en cinéaste*, Editions du Centre Pompidou/Editions Cahiers du cinéma.

Akerman, Chantal (2004b), '"Je croyais vraiment que j'avais écrit une comédie toute simple"', *Le Monde*, 3 March, p. 27.

Akerman, Chantal (2001), '*The Captive*: Frédéric Bonnaud talks to Chantal Akerman', *Enthusiasm*, 4, pp. 12–17.

Ardan, Michel (1996), 'Duo sur canapé', *Les Echos*, 10 April.

Aubenas, Jacqueline (1995), *Hommage à Chantal Akerman*, Brussels, Commissariat général aux relations internationales de la communauté française de Belgique.

Azoury, Philippe and Gérard Lefort (2004), 'La Ligne droite n'est pas mon fort', *Libération*, 3 March.

Bellour, Raymond (2002), 'Images of an Indivisible Order', *Afterall*, 6, pp. 30–51.

Benoliel, Bernard (2000), '*La Captive*: Le temps retrouvé de Chantal Akerman', *Cahiers du cinéma*, 550, pp. 14–19.

Beugnet, Martine (2007), *Cinema and Sensation: French Film and the Art of Transgression*, Edinburgh, Edinburgh University Press.

Beugnet, Martine and Marion Schmid (2005), *Proust at the Movies*, Aldershot, Ashgate.

Bonnaud, Frédéric (2000), 'Librement inspiré', *Les Inrockuptibles*, 26 September, pp. 46–7.

Bruno, Giuliana (2002), *Atlas of Emotion: Journeys in Art, Architecture, and Film*, London, Verso.

Capp, Rose (2001), 'A Couch in New York: Chantal Akerman and Sex in the City', *Screening the Past*, 13.

Danton, Amina (1991), 'Tout ou rien', *Cahiers du cinéma*, 447, pp. 62–3.

Deleuze, Gilles (1989), *Cinema 2: The Time-Image*, trans. Hugh Tomlinson and Robert Galeta. Minneapolis, University of Minnesota Press.

Delorme, Stéphane (2000), 'L'Œuvre au noir', *Cahiers du cinéma*, 550, pp. 20–1.

Elsaesser, Thomas (1997), 'Ernst Lubitsch', in Geoffrey Nowell-Smith (ed.), *The Oxford History of World Cinema*, Oxford, Oxford University Press, pp. 184–5.

Frodon, Jean-Michel (1996), 'Les Quiproquos transatlantiques de Chantal Akerman', *Le Monde*, 11 April.

Girard, René (1961), *Mensonge romantique et vérité romanesque*, Paris, Grasset.

Hutcheon, Linda (2006), *A Theory of Adaptation*, London, Routledge.

hollowed-out characters, it is this same place which keeps haunting her today, and which finally speaks its name: over-crowding, chaos and death. Retrospectively, this excess seems to shed light on the emptiness that has long haunted her work. Like the furniture which, by night, the protagonists jettison on the pavement as their flat and their memory get cluttered, Chantal Akerman, thus, more than ever, with *Demain on déménage*, asks the question whether art can transpose and, more importantly, make us share an infinitely private, singular and painful experience in the public space.'

Kaganski, Serge (2004), 'ça déménage!', *Les Inrockuptibles*, 3 March.
Le Corre, Yves and Samir Ardjoum (2009), 'Entretien avec Chantal Akerman, http://www.fluctuat.net/cinema/interview/akerman2.htm.
Lefort, Gérard (2004), 'On déménage, emballant', *Libération*, 3 March.
Lefort, Gérard (1996), 'Chantal Akerman, Divan le Terrible', *Libération*, 11 April.
Mandelbaum, Jacques (2004), 'Demain on déménage', in *Chantal Akerman: Autoportrait*, p. 214.
Mayne, Judith (2003), 'Girl Talk: *Portrait of a Young Girl at the End of the 1960s in Brussels*', in Foster (ed.), *Identity and Memory*, pp. 150–61.
Moshenson, Edna (2006), 'Chantal Akerman: A Spiral Autobiography', in Moshenson (ed.), *Chantal Akerman: A Spiral Autobiography*, Tel Aviv Museum of Art, pp. 13–36.
Naficy, Hamid (2001), *An Accented Cinema: Exilic and Diasporic Filmmaking*, Princeton, Princeton University Press.
Rosenbaum, Jonathan (1997), *Movies as Politics*, Berkeley and Los Angeles, University of California Press.
Silverman, Max (2006), 'Horror and the Everyday in Post-Holocaust France: *Nuit et brouillard* and Concentrationary Art', *French Cultural Studies*, 17, pp. 5–18.
Taubin, Amy (1995), 'The Nouvelle Femme', *The Village Voice*, 7 March, p. 65.
Vincendeau, Ginette (2003), 'Night and Day: a Parisian Fairy Tale', in Foster (ed.), *Identity and Memory*, pp. 117–31.
Vincendeau, Ginette (2001), 'The Captive', *Sight and Sound*, 11, p. 45.
White, Jerry (2005), 'Chantal Akerman's Revisionist Aesthetics', in Jean Petrolle and Virginia Wright Wexman (eds.), *Women and Experimental Filmmaking*, Urbana and Chicago, University of Illinois Press, pp. 47–68.
White, Patricia (2008), 'Lesbian Minor Cinema', *Screen*, 49, pp. 410–25.

Conclusion

Chantal Akerman's last short film to date, a contribution to the omnibus *L'État du monde* (2007), a thoughtful meditation on the state of our world signed by six cutting-edge directors from around the globe, ends on a typically Akermanian long-take. As night falls, the mighty glass towers of Shanghai, like so many giant screens, reflect a maelstrom of images, from a multicoloured Mona Lisa to Walt Disney cartoons, whilst the cacophonic sounds of commercial clips saturate the aural space. The urban skyline morphs into an outdoor cinema where the signs and signifiers of a global world project the dazzling spectacle of simulacra. Over a career of more than forty years, Akerman, in the many guises of her highly diverse film language, has interrogated the images of this world, both in the tangible surfaces that they offer to our eye and in what they tell us about the manifold ways in which individuals behold and apprehend reality. From the interior of the home which has been the privileged territory of her early work to the open spaces of the international metropolis, from Eastern Europe to the heart of the Americas and Asia, her camera captures a world caught between stasis and movement, suspended in a transitional space between past, present and future. At once a phenomenologist and a radiographer, a traveller between inside and outside, she seeks to render visible the invisible, to uncover personal and historical inscriptions behind the habitats, landscapes and material objects that constitute our world. Whether in fictional or in documentary mode, in the kitchen of a Belgian housewife, the waiting room of a Moscow train station or the streets of China's largest city, her cinema draws a complex map of human experience. It constitutes what Giuliana Bruno calls an 'atlas of life' (Bruno 2002: 102).

What emerges perhaps most forcefully in the rich and multifaceted body of work that is Akerman's cinema, and across the many tones and registers of her cinematic language, is this persistent engagement with the forms and conditions of human existence, and, more specifically, with the threat of dehumanisation that faces the individual in the private and the collective sphere. From a 'cinema of the body' (Deleuze 1989: 190) in the tradition of the post-New Wave, Akerman has gradually moved to a wider exploration of the relation between the self and the other (be it sexual, social or racial), and to a greater engagement with history and memory. Her own position as a transnational director between cultures and countries has profoundly shaped and lends a personal dimension to her exploration of nomadic and diasporic identities and to her sustained meditation on questions of belonging, uprootedness and marginality. The rigour and aesthetic demands of her visual style, thrown into relief once more by an experimental work like *Tombée de nuit sur Shanghai*, should not blind us to the profound humanity that emanates from all her films, be they in a light-hearted or a more serious mood, and to the social and ethical commitment of her documentary work in particular. Klaus Ottmann pays tribute to this little acknowledged but essential aspect of her cinema, when he writes with regard to *De l'autre côté*, 'We are summoned by the work to responsibility, not by "propagandist slogans", but by an extreme existentialist-humanist formalism' (Ottmann 2008: 37).

Though a tireless experimenter with cinematic form and genre, Akerman never pursues formal experimentation for its own sake, but always puts her film style in the service of a uniquely personal and empathetic vision of humanity. The demands she makes on her spectators, her insistence on the viewing process as an active and embodied act and the various anti-naturalist strategies at work in her cinema are instrumental in her quest for authenticity in a world increasingly prey to cliché, disinformation and manipulation. In their resistance to easy readability and appropriation and their stark sculptural beauty, her multilayered images, which resonate between past and present and are imbued with a deep ambiguity and indeterminacy, posit an alternative vision to the flatness and uniformity of commercial media and the entertainment industry in general. Refusing to offer any ready answers and dwelling instead on the subjectivity and fluidity of human experience, Akerman forces upon her spectators a new regime of vision, a critical and independent gaze. Radically modern, yet haunted by the memories of a past that is no more, her cinema, with its hypnotic rhythms, chant-like dialogues and raw intensity, is animated above all by a desire for understanding and truth, or, as Akerman herself, ever cautious of absolutes, would say, 'un peu de vérité'[1] (Akerman 2004: 32).

References

Akerman, Chantal (2004), *Chantal Akerman: Autoportrait en cinéaste*, Editions du Centre Pompidou/Editions Cahiers du cinéma.

Bruno, Giuliana (2002), *Atlas of Emotion: Journeys in Art, Architecture, and Film*, London, Verso.

Deleuze, Gilles (1989), *Cinema 2: The Time Image*, trans. Hugh Tomlinson and Robert Galeta, Minneapolis, University of Minnesota Press.

Ottmann, Klaus (2008), '*From the Other Side (De l'autre côté)*', in Sultan (ed.), *Chantal Akerman*, pp. 28–39.

1 'a bit of truth.'

Filmography

Saute ma ville (Blow up My Town) (1968) 13 min., b/w

Screenplay: Chantal Akerman
Camera: René Fruchter
Editing: Geneviève Luciani
Sound: Patrice
Cast: Chantal Akerman

L'Enfant aimé ou je joue à être une femme mariée (The Beloved Child, or I Play at Being a Married Woman) (1971) 35 min., b/w

Cast: Claire Wauthion, Chantal Akerman, Daphna Merzer

Hotel Monterey (1972) 63 min., col. (silent)

Production: Chantal Akerman
Screenplay: Chantal Akerman
Camera: Babette Mangolte
Editing: Geneviève Luciani

La Chambre 1 (The Room 1) (1972) 11 min., col.

Camera: Babette Mangolte
Editing: Geneviève Luciani
Cast: Chantal Akerman

La Chambre 2 (The Room 2) (1972) 11 min., col. (silent)

Camera: Babette Mangolte
Editing: Geneviève Luciani
Cast: Chantal Akerman

Le 15/08 (1973) 42 min., b/w (co-directed with Samy Szlingerbaum)

Screenplay: Chantal Akerman and Samy Szlingerbaum
Camera: Chantal Akerman and Samy Szlingerbaum
Editing: Chantal Akerman and Samy Szlingerbaum
Cast: Chris Myllykoski

Hanging out Yonkers (1973) approx. 40 min., col. (unfinished)

Production: Chantal Akerman
Camera: Babette Mangolte

Je tu il elle (I... You... He... She...) (1974) 90 min., b/w

Camera: Bénédicte Delesalle
Editing: Luc Freché
Sound: Alain Pierre, Samy Szlingerbaum
Cast: Chantal Akerman, Niels Arestrup, Claire Wauthion

Jeanne Dielman, 23, quai du Commerce, 1080 Bruxelles (1975)
200 min., col.

Production: Paradise Films (Brussels), Unité Trois (Paris)
Camera: Babette Mangolte, Dominique Delesalle
Editing: Patricia Canino
Sound: Benie Deswarte, Françoise Van Thienen
Cast: Delphine Seyrig, Jan Decorte, Henri Storck, Jacques Doniol-
    Valcroze, Yves Bical

News from Home (1976) 89 min., col.

Production: Paradise Films, Unité Trois (Paris), INA (Paris), ZDF
    (Mainz)
Screenplay: Chantal Akerman
Camera: Babette Mangolte
Editing: Francine Sandberg
Sound: Dominique Dalmasso, Larry Haas

Les Rendez-vous d'Anna (Meetings with Anna) (1978) 127 min., col.

Production: Hélène Films-Unité Trois (Paris), Paradise Films (Brussels),
    ZDF (Mainz)
Camera: Jean Penzer, Michel Houssiau
Editing: Francine Sandberg
Sound: Henri Morelle
Cast: Aurore Clément, Helmut Griem, Magali Noël, Lea Massari,

Hans Zischler, Jean-Pierre Cassel

Aujourd'hui, dis-moi/Dis-moi (Tell Me) (1982) 45 min., col.

Made for the French television series *Grand-mères*
Production: Institut National de l'Audiovisuel
Camera: Maurice Perrimond, Michel Davaud, Francis Lapeyre
Editing: Francine Sandberg
Sound: Xavier Vauthrin, André Siekierski
Cast: Chantal Akerman

Toute une nuit (All Night Long) (1982) 90 min., col.

Production: Paradise Films, Avidia Films
Camera: Caroline Champetier, François Hernandez, Mathieu Schiffman
Editing: Luc Barnier, Véronique Auricoste
Sound: Ricardo Castro, Miguel Rejas, Henri Morelle, Daniel Deshays
Cast: Aurore Clément, Tchéky Karyo, Jan Decorte, Natalia Akerman,
     Véronique Silver, Samy Szlingerbaum

Les Années 80 (The Eighties) (1983) 79 min., col.

Production: Paradise Films, Abilène (Paris)
Camera: Michel Houssiau
Editing: Nadine Keseman, Francine Sandberg
Sound: Marc Mallinus, Daniel Deshays, Henri Morelle
Music: Marc Hérouet
Cast: Aurore Clément, Magali Noël, Lio, Pascale Salkin

L'Homme à la valise (The Man with the Suitcase) (1983) 60 min., col.

Made for the French television series *Télévision de chambre*
Camera: Maurice Perrimont
Editing: Frédéric Sandberg
Sound: Jean-Claude Brisson
Cast: Chantal Akerman, Jeffrey Kime

« *Un jour Pina a demandé…* » (One Day Pina Asked Me) (1983)
57 min., col.

Made for the French television series *Repères sur la modern danse*
Production: A2, RM arts, INA, RTBF, BRT
Camera: Babette Mangolte, Luc Benhamou
Editing: Dominique Forgue, Patrick Mimouni
Sound: Jean Minondo

Family Business (1984) 18 min., col.

Made for Channel 4
Production: Large Door LDT (London)
Camera: Luc Benhamou
Editing: Patrick Mimouni
Music: Marc Hérouet
Cast: Aurore Clément, Colleen Camp, Chantal Akerman, Marilyn Watelet, Lloyd Cohn, Leslie Vandermeulen

J'ai faim, j'ai froid (I'm Hungry, I'm Cold) (1984) 12 min., b/w

Segment for the omnibus film *Paris vu par... vingt ans après*
Production: JM Productions, Films A2
Camera: Luc Benhamou, Gilles Arnaud, Luis Peracta
Editing: Francine Sandberg
Cast: Maria de Medeiros, Pascale Salkin, Esmoris Hannibal

Lettre d'une cinéaste: Chantal Akerman (Letter from a Filmmaker) (1984) 8 min., col.

Made for the French television programme *Cinéma, cinéma*
Camera: Luc Benhamou
Music: Marc Hérouet
Cast: Aurore Clément, Chantal Akerman, Colleen Camp, Marilyn Watelet, Leslie Vandermeulen, Lloyd Cohn

Golden Eighties (aka Window Shopping) (1986) 96 min., col.

Production: La Cecilia (Paris), Paradise Films (Brussels), Limbo Films (Zurich), Le ministère de la culture (France), Le ministère de la communauté française (Belgique)
Screenplay: Chantal Akerman, Jean Gruault, Léora Barish, Henry Bean, Pascal Bonitzer
Camera: Gilberto Azevedo, Luc Benhamou
Editing: Francine Sandberg
Sound: Henri Morelle, Miguel Rejas
Music: Marc Herouet, lyrics Chantal Akerman
Cast: Myriam Boyer, John Berry, Delphine Seyrig, Nicolas Tronc, Lio, Pascale Salkin, Fanny Cottençon, Charles Denner, Jean-François Balmer

Letters Home (1986) 104 min., col.

Live filming of a stage production directed by Françoise Merle

Production: Jacor Productions Théâtrales-Centre Simone de Beauvoir
 with the participation of the Ministry of Culture
Camera: Luc Benhamou
Editing: Claire Atherton
Sound: Alix Comte
Cast: Delphine Seyrig, Coralie Seyrig

Le Marteau (The Hammer) (1986) 4 min., col.

Camera and Editing: Claire Atherton

Portrait d'une paresseuse/Le Journal d'une paresseuse/La Paresse
(Sloth) (1986) 14 min., col.

Made for German television ZDF for a project entitled *Seven women,
 seven sins*
Camera: Luc Benhamou
Cast: Chantal Akerman, Sonia Wieder-Atherton

Rue Mallet-Stevens (1986) 7 min., col.

Camera: Luc Benhamou
Sound: Alix Comte
Cast: Sonia Wieder-Atherton, Coralie Seyrig, Chantal Akerman

Histoires d'Amérique: Food, Family and Philosophy (American
Stories: Food, Family and Philosophy) (1988) 92 min., col.

Production: Mallia Films, Paradise Films, La Sept, La Bibliothèque
 publique d'information, Le Centre Pompidou, La RTBF
Camera: Luc Benhamou
Editing: Patrick Mimouni
Sound: Alix Comte
Cast: Maurice Brenner, Carl Don, David Buntzman, Judith Malina,
 Eszter Balint, Dean Jackson, Roy Nathanson

Les Trois dernières sonates de Franz Schubert (Franz Schubert's
Last Three Sonatas) (1989) 49 min., col.

Production: La Sept, Unité de programmes spectacle Guillaume
 Gronier, INA
Camera: Jean Monsigny
Editing: Francine Sandberg
Sound: Xavier Vauthrin
Cast: Alfred Brendel

Trois strophes sur le nom de Sacher ('Three Stanzas on the Name Sacher', by Henri Dutilleux) (1989) 12 min., col.

Production: Mallia Films, La Sept, ARCanal, Centre Pompidou
Camera: Raymond Fromont
Music: Henri Dutilleux

Pour Febe Elisabeth Velasquez, El Salvador (1991) 3 min., col.

Segment for the omnibus film *Contre l'oubli*
Production: PRV for Amnesty International
Camera: Joan Monsigny
Music: Mino Cinelu interpreted by Sonia Wieder-Atherton
Cast: Catherine Deneuve and Sonia Wieder-Atherton

Nuit et jour (Night and Day) (1991) 90 min., col.

Production: Pierre Grise Productions (Paris), Centre national de la
   cinématographie (Paris), Canal+, Sofinergie 2, Paradise Films,
   Ministère de la communauté française de Belgique, La RTBF,
   George Reinhart Productions (Zurich)
Camera: Jean-Claude Neckelbrouck, Pierre Gordower, Bernard Del-
   ville, Olivier Dessalles
Editing: Francine Sandberg, Camille Bordes-Resnais
Sound: Alix Comte, Pierre Tucat
Music: Marc Hérouet
Cast: Guilaine Londez, Thomas Langmann, François Négret

Le Déménagement (Moving In) (1992) 42 min., col.

Production: Le Poisson volant, La Sept
Camera: Raymond Fromont, Piotr Stadnicki
Editing: Rudi Maerten
Sound: Alix Comte, Pierre Tucat
Cast: Sami Frey

D'Est (From the East) (1993) 110 min., col.

Production: Centre de l'audio-visuel à Bruxelles (CBA), La RTBF (Carré
   Noir)
Camera: Raymond Fromont, Bernard Delville
Editing: Claire Atherton, Agnès Bruckert
Sound: Pierre Mertens, Thomas Gauder, Didier Pécheur

Portrait d'une jeune fille de la fin des années 60 à Bruxelles
(Portrait of a Young Girl from the Late Sixties in Brussels) (1993)
60 min., col.

Made for the French television series *Tous les garçons et les filles de leur âge*
Production: IMA, La Sept/Arte, SFP
Camera: Raymond Fromont
Editing: Martine Lebon
Sound: Pierre Mertens
Cast: Circé, Julien Rassam

Chantal Akerman par Chantal Akerman (1996) 63 min., col.

Made for the French television series *Cinéma, de notre temps*
Production: AMIP/Producteur délégué Xavier Carniaux-La Sept Arte/Unité de programme Thierry Garrel-INA/Claude Guisard – Chemah I.S.
Camera: Raymond Fromont
Editing: Claire Atherton
Sound: Xavier Vauthrin

Un divan à New York (A Couch in New York) (1996) 105 min., col.

Production: Les Films Balenciaga, France 2 Cinéma, M6 Films, Babelsberg Film Production, Paradise Films, RTBF
Screenplay: Chantal Akerman, Jean-Louis Benoît
Camera: Raymond Fromont
Editing: Claire Atherton
Sound: Pierre Mertens, Gérard Lamps
Cast: Juliette Binoche, William Hurt, Stéphanie Buttle, Barbara Garrick

Le Jour où (1997) 7 min., col.

Production: Silvia Voser, Waka Films AG, TSI – Televisione Svizzera, Arte GEIE
Camera: Raymond Fromont
Editing: Claire Atherton
Sound: Nicolas Lefebvre

Sud (South) (1999) 70 min., col.

Production: AMIP, Paradise Films, Chemah I.S., Carré Noir-RTBF Liège, INA

Camera: Raymond Fromont
Editing: Claire Atherton
Sound: Thierry de Halleux

La Captive (The Captive) (2000) 107 min., col.

Production: Gemini Films, Arte France Cinema, Paradise Films
Camera: Sabine Lancelin
Editing: Claire Atherton
Sound: Thierry de Halleux
Cast: Stanislas Merhar, Sylvie Testud, Olivia Bonamy, Aurore Clé-
    ment, Liliane Rovere, Françoise Bertin

Avec Sonia Wieder-Atherton (2002) 52 min., col.

Camera: Sabine Lancelin
Editing: Claire Atherton
Sound: Pierre-Antoine Signoret
Cast: Sonia Wieder-Atherton, Imogen Cooper, Sarah Iancu, Matthieu
    Lejeune

De l'autre côté (From the Other Side) (2002) 102 min., col.

Production : AMIP, Arte France, Paradise Films, Chemah-I.S.
Camera: Raymond Fromont, Robert Fenz, Chantal Akerman
Editing: Claire Atherton
Sound: Pierre Mertens

Demain on déménage (Tomorrow We Move) (2004) 110 min., col.

Production: Paradise Films, Gemini Films, Arte France Cinéma, La
    RTBF
Camera: Sabine Lancelin
Editing: Claire Atherton
Sound: Pierre Mertens
Cast: Sylvie Testud, Aurore Clément, Jean-Pierre Marielle, Lucas Bel-
    vaux, Dominique Reymond, Natacha Régnier, Elsa Zylberstein,
    Gilles Privat

Là-bas (Over There) (2006) 78 min., col.

Production: AMIP
Camera: Chantal Akerman, Robert Fenz
Editing: Claire Atherton

Tombée de nuit sur Shanghai (Nightfall over Shanghai) (2007)
15 min., col.

Segment for the omnibus film *O Estado do Mundo*
Production: Lx Filmes
Camera: Chantal Akerman
Editing: Claire Atherton
Sound: David Lassale

A l'Est avec Sonia Wieder-Atherton (2009) 43 min, col.

Producer: AMIP, Arte, Chemah I.S., Cléa Productions
Cast: Sonia Wieder-Atherton

Select bibliography

For critical works and interviews on individual films, see the References sections at the end of each chapter.

Books on Chantal Akerman

Akerman, Chantal (2004), *Chantal Akerman: Autoportrait en cinéaste*, Paris, Editions du Centre Pompidou/Editions Cahiers du cinéma. Chantal Akerman by Chantal Akerman. A fascinating, lavishly illustrated self-portrait and an invaluable source for understanding the ideas and aesthetic principles that have shaped her films.

Akerman, Chantal, Catherine David, Michael Tarantino, intro. by Kathy Halbreich and Bruce Jenkins (1995), *Bordering on Fiction: Chantal Akerman's D'Est*, Minneapolis, Walker Art Centre.
A fine collection of essays and a text by Akerman herself on her documentary *D'Est*.

Aubenas, Jacqueline (1995), *Hommage à Chantal Akerman*, Brussels, Commissariat général aux relations internationales de la communauté française de Belgique.
A brief overview of Akerman's films and a 'dictionary' of major concepts in her work. Contains interesting comments by Akerman herself on her film-making.

Foster, Gwendolyn Audrey (ed.) (2003), *Identity and Memory: The Films of Chantal Akerman*, Carbondale and Edwardsville, Southern Illinois University Press.

An excellent collection of essays written by leading scholars in the field. Explores major themes in Akerman's work from sexuality to Jewish diasporic identity.

Margulies, Ivone (1996), *Nothing Happens: Chantal Akerman's Hyperrealist Everyday*, London, Duke University Press.
A groundbreaking and indispensable book on Akerman's film aesthetics and evolution as a director. Absolutely central for understanding this complex director.

Moshenson, Edna (ed.) (2006), *Chantal Akerman: A Spiral Autobiography*, Tel Aviv Museum of Art.
Catalogue accompanying an exhibition of Akerman's video installations at the Tel Aviv Museum of Art. Particularly enlightening on the blending of autobiography and fiction and on the importance of borders and memory in her work.

Sultan, Terrie (ed.), *Chantal Akerman: Moving Through Time and Space*, Blaffer Gallery, the Art Museum of the University of Houston.
An excellent collection of essays on her documentaries *D'Est*, *Sud*, *De l'autre côté*, and *Là-bas* and on her recent video installation *Femmes d'Anvers en novembre*.

Overviews of her work

Bergstrom, Janet (1999), 'Chantal Akerman: Splitting', in Janet Bergstrom (ed.), *Endless Night: Cinema and Psychonalysis, Parallel Histories*, Berkeley, University of California Press, pp. 273–90.
Bergstrom, Janet (1999), 'The Innovators 1970–1980: Keeping a Distance', *Sight and Sound*, November.
Fowler, Cathy (1998), 'Chantal Akerman', in John Hill and Pamela Church Gibson (eds.), *The Oxford Guide to Film Studies*, Oxford, Oxford University Press, pp. 489–91.
McRobbie, Angela (1992), 'Passionate Uncertainty', *Sight and Sound*, 2, pp. 28–9.

General reference works

Deleuze, Gilles (1989), *Cinema 2: The Time-Image*, trans. Hugh Tomlinson and Robert Galeta, Minneapolis, University of Minnesota Press.

Kuhn, Annette (1982), *Women's Pictures*, London, Routledge.

Mayne, Judith (1990), *The Woman at the Keyhole: Feminism and Women's Cinema*, Bloomington, Indiana University Press.

Petrolle, Jean and Virginia Wright Wexman (eds.) (2005), *Women and Experimental Filmmaking*, Urbana and Chicago, University of Illinois Press.

Index

CPSIA information can be obtained
at www.ICGtesting.com
Printed in the USA
JSHW061512050822
28968JS00006B/95